ACCEPTING POPULATION CONTROL

NORDIC INSTITUTE OF ASIAN STUDIES

Recent Monographs

ACCEPTING POPULATION CONTROL

Urban Chinese Women
and the One-Child Family Policy

Cecilia Nathansen Milwertz

CURZON

Nordic Institute of Asian Studies
Monograph Series, No. 74

First published in 1997 by Curzon Press
St John's Studios, Church Road, Richmond
Surrey, TW9 2QA

Printed in Great Britain by
TJ Press (Padstow) Ltd, Padstow, Cornwall

British Library Cataloguing in Publication Data
A catalogue record for this book is available from the British Library
ISBN 0-7007-0437-X (Hbk)
ISBN 0-7007-0457-4 (Pbk)

Publication of this work was assisted by a grant from
the *Danish Council for Development Research*.

To my parents
Ilse Nathansen Milwertz and Jørgen Guldbrandt Milwertz

Contents

Figures and Tables

Figures

Tables

Acknowledgements

The process of planning and implementing data collection in China is comparable to the process of attempting by bicycle to cross a rush-hour intersection in downtown Beijing, one supposedly regulated by traffic lights. It is a nerve-racking experience. In principle everyone is well aware of the basic rule that the green light means that you are allowed to proceed , while the red light indicates that you should stay where you are. In practice, almost no one follows the rules. Because the whole situation is totally chaotic, at least from a non-local's perspective, you will be unlikely to succeed if you politely wait your turn. In order to get through to the proposed target, both cyclist and scholar alike must swerve flexibly between various obstacles – be they motor vehicles or authorities of various types and sizes, and regardless of whether the lights are red or green. The tricky part is not to harm anyone in the process.

With the support of many people in both China and Denmark I managed to get through not only the process of data collection, but also of writing the Ph.D. dissertation, which was the beginning of this book, and finally of transforming this into its current form.

I thank friends at the Haoyuan Binguan, where I lived for three years from 1984 to 1987. Many talks and discussions with them sowed the seeds for this research enterprise. Axel Lunddahl, my professor at the Department of Cultural Sociology, Copenhagen University, encouraged me to begin the project. Then Erik Baark, Jørgen Delman and Ole Odgaard helped me to do so. My friends He Youxiang, Wen Hao, Tao Guojian and Wu Ji together with Chen Shengchao and Gong Hui offered their advice during the initial stages of the project in Denmark. Without the quick-witted assistance of He Youxiang in China at a later stage not only this, but several of my other endeavours in China, would never have been realized. I am thankful for the accomodation I received during the research period at Copenhagen University's Centre for East and Southeast Asian Studies and the Danish Council for

Development Research for funding this research. My thanks, too, go to Thommy Svensson and the Nordic Institute of Asian Studies for providing office space and a friendly and inspiring working environment during the phase of transforming the dissertation into a book.

I am grateful to Shen Chonglin, Zhao Kebin, Dai Kejing, Yang Yabin and other colleagues at the Sociological Institute at the Chinese Academy of Social Sciences who facilitated my participation in the International Conference on Sociological Research in China in 1991. At the conference several scholars shared their experience of doing social science research in China and thereby greatly aided the design of the present study. Wu Xin, Wang Fenyu and Li Lulu at the National Research Centre for Science and Technology for Development were my collaborators in Beijing. Li Lulu and his students provided assistance in designing and carrying out the questionnaire survey. In Shenyang, Zhao Zixiang and his staff at the Institute of Sociology, Liaoning Academy of Social Sciences, facilitated official arrangements for data collection. Mao Jiashu and her colleagues transcribed hours of taped interviews. I wish to thank them for their formal assistance and hospitality as well as their informal aid to me personally. None of them bears any responsibility for the analysis or conclusions in this book.

I thank Zhou Xiaozheng for many long talks that provided much inspiration and food for thought. Hatla Thelle and Bente Rosenbeck provided me with suggestions and helpful comments from the perspectives of sinology and women's studies. Geir Helgesen shared his experience of cross-cultural research and commented extensively on several drafts of many chapters. Qi Wang and Liu Li shared their insights about Chinese women and culture. Torsten Foersum gave statistical assistance. And Susan Young made a critical reading of the dissertation, weeding out as well the worst language errors. I also want to thank the working group on women and population at the NGO, K.U.L.U. – Women and Development, for keeping me focused to the global issue of population control. I am profoundly grateful to Tabita and Tais and Kresten Thor Nielsen. The latter was a 'model husband' (*mofan zhangfu*), even when he was seriously ill, and they all coped with long stretches of my absence and absentmindedness.

Without the participation of the 857 women who patiently filled in questionnaires and sat through hours of interviews there would have been no book. I am grateful to every one of these women for sharing their experiences with me. As far as possible my aim has been to set aside my image of their reality in order to grasp their image. However, I have conducted the final analysis in which the experiences of women become data. Data is conceptualized and concepts are related to each other so as to form a theoretical rendition of reality. Although the aim of the theoretical formulation is that it can explain reality, the women involved will not necessarily recognize nor agree with my interpretation. The interpretation goes beyond the self-understanding of the informant and is not only a presentation of the how urban city district women manage the one-child policy but also a representation based on my interpretation.

In my attempt to represent the experience of another culture, not only the people mentioned here but also many others whom I am unable to mention by name have offered their support, encouragement and advice. Their insights have helped to eliminate many errors and misinterpretations.

Finally, I would also like to thank the members of my Ph.D. evaluation committee as well as the two anonymous reviewers whose lengthy comments helped me to transform my dissertation into the present study. My thanks, too, to Kirstine Theilgaard for permission to use one of her photographs for the cover illustration. And last but not least, my gratitude goes to Gerald Jackson for careful editing of the manuscript and transforming it into book form, and to Leena Höskuldsson and Liz Bramsen for all their labours ensuring both the quality of the finished work and that it saw the light of day.

In the end, of course, I alone bear responsibility for the result.

About the Illustrations

The vignettes at the beginning of each chapter are used in China as part of the ideological education work to communicate the population policy to the populace. It is common for birth planning workers to use drawings like these on blackboards at workplaces or in residential areas together with various texts on the population policy. Such vignettes are obtained from sources such as birth planning newspapers and are then copied and used by the birth planning workers.

It was not possible to locate the copyright holders of the two cartoons reproduced in Chapter 6 before this book went to print. The author and publisher would be pleased to hear from any such copyright holders and to print due acknowledgements in the next edition of the book.

Introductory Notes

> China should be proud and happy with her achieve-
> ments in family planning and population control
> within a short period of merely some ten years.
>
> *Nafis Sadik, April 1991*
>
> But behind the numbers being manipulated are real
> women with human rights and health needs.
>
> *Vandana Shiva 1992*

In 1978–79 the one-child family policy was formulated in China.
The policy permits one child per married couple only. By the
late 1970s China had reached near replacement level fertility i.e.
an average of just over two births per women. None the less,
population control came to be viewed by the post-Mao leadership
as a prerequisite for economic development and thereby for the
success of the Four Modernizations programme to industrialize
and modernize China. Chinese interpretation of population
increase thus developed in the direction of the internationally
dominant reading of the 'population problem'.

Evolving International Responses to the 'Population Problem'

Internationally, attention became seriously focused on the so-
called 'population problem' in the 1960s. Since then the definition
and identification of the elements included in the problem, as
well as of core factors causing the problem, have been a con-

troversial issue. This theoretical and ideological interpretation of the causes of the 'population problem' has serious implications for the remedial measures adopted to solve the problem. A fundamental relationship between overall socio-economic development and population development has been acknowledged internationally since at least the 1974 World Population Conference in Bucharest. Here it was established that policies aiming at fertility decline should take place within the framework of general socio-economic development. In other words, the 'population problem' was recognized as a population *and* development problem that should therefore also be solved as such (Jackson 1977, Epstein 1977). Resulting from an intense political debate, the Bucharest Conference's key document – the World Plan for Population Action – was widely revised to include the acknowledgement of family planning as an integral element of development at large. Through these revisions, social and economic concerns came to prevail over quantitative demographic targets (Correa 1993: 2). One incisive conference slogan urged: 'Take care of the world's people and population will take care of itself.' The slogan was symbolic of the final conference document which amounted to a refutation of the Malthusian contention that population numbers and growth rates are the root cause of social and economic problems.[1]

A basic relationship between the overall economic, social, political and cultural environment and fertility has been recognized. In this interpretation high fertility rates are treated as a symptom of broader developmental problems rather than as a problem in itself. None the less, the dominant readings of the 'population problem' as well as the remedial measures applied by the international population establishment have mainly dealt with population as an isolated phenomenon. In this interpretation the 'population problem' means something quite specific, 'namely the rapid population growth of the developing countries and the necessity to take action in order to limit this growth through birth

1. For a brief review of main perspectives on and interpretations of the 'population problem', see Lappé and Schurman 1990. For accounts of the history and ideology of population control and the population establishment see Greer 1984, Hartmann 1987 and Dixon-Mueller 1993. For a Foucauldian interpretation of the 'power–knowledge' discourse of population control, see DuBois 1991. For a concise and relatively recent version of the debate on the question of whether family planning programmes and/or economic and social development will solve the 'population problem', and on the contribution of academic research to these issues, see Jejeebhoy 1990, Kelley 1990 and McNicoll 1990. They update the situation described in Berelson 1975.

control' (Hofsten 1980: 213). Based on this interpretation the population establishment, shaped and led by United States funding and research, has favoured and pushed for *population control* as opposed to *family planning* as the main solution to the 'population problem' (Dixon-Mueller 1993). Family planning – meaning the right to plan the size of a family – was accorded international recognition as a human right at the International Conference on Human Rights in Tehran in 1968. The conference was held to mark the twentieth anniversary of the Universal Declaration on Human Rights. The Proclamation of Teheran on Human Rights stated that 'Parents have a basic human right to determine freely and responsibly the number and the spacing of their children' (paragraph 16). Subsequently the words 'individuals and couples' were included in the statement instead of 'parents' and the important phrase 'and to the information and the means to do so' was added. The statement was then reaffirmed by, among others, the World Population Conference in 1974, the International Conference on Population in 1984 and the Conference on the Decade for Women in 1985 (UNFPA 1991: 10). The 1974 World Population Plan of Action states that governments should 'respect and ensure, regardless of their overall demographic goals, the right of persons to determine in a free and informed and responsible manner, the number and spacing of their children.' Thereby it was affirmed that there is a basic distinction between *family planning* and *population control*. The problems associated with rapid population growth were recognized, but at the same time coercion was official y condemned. Education, information and the freedom of individi als to decide upon the size of their family was in principle emphasized.

In practice, twenty years later, adherence to human rights in population policies has not yet been achieved globally. On the one hand United Nations documents endorse human rights in population policies. On the other hand they affirm the right of individual nations to sovereignty in population policies. Problems, therefore, emerge when national policies do not respect human rights and fundamental freedoms (Tomaševski 1994). The distinction between family planning as a human right and population control is a very important one.

> Population control is a philosophy and practice which identifies rapid population growth as a – if not the – principal cause of poverty, underdevelopment, and now environmental degradation.

> Population control agencies have a long history of targeting
> women's fertility in their drive to reduce birth rates as fast and
> cheaply as possible, in the absence of fundamental improvements
> in people's lives. Contraception and sterilization are wielded more
> as weapons than as tools of reproductive choice. (Hartmann
> 1994: 1)[2]

Reacting to this reality, alternative understandings and solutions
to the 'population problem' have developed the concept of family
planning as a human right further to concepts of reproductive
health and reproductive rights (Dixon-Mueller 1993, Sai and
Nassim 1989, Sen *et al.* 1994).

The initiative behind the Bucharest conference came from the
countries of the North, while those of the South were reluctant to
address population as a developmental issue. Strongly pressed by
the North, governments of the South have gradually changed
their attitude and have come to view their population growth
rates as an obstacle to economic development. Following a similar
logic, the leadership of China has set a limit to the fertility of her
citizens. The importance attached by the Chinese leadership to the
population policy is indicated by the drafting of a law on the one-
child family policy[3] intended for submission to the Fifth National
People's Congress in August–September 1980.[4] Following the
aborted attempt at legislation, the State Council issued a request
for the implementation of the one-child family policy. On 25
September 1980, the Central Committee of the Chinese Communist Party (CCP) issued an *Open Letter to All Party and Youth
League Members*, calling on them, and especially on cadres at all
levels, to play a leading role in carrying out the request issued by
the State Council.

---

2. For an elaboration on the meanings and application of population control,
see Bergström 1994.
3. The term 'one-child family policy' is used as a shorthand reference even
though the policy more precisely has the form of what Susan Greenhalgh has
termed a *one-child-with-exceptions-policy* (Greenhalgh 1993: 249). However,
though the phrase one-child family policy oversimplifies the nature of the
policy nationwide, in urban China (and especially in the city districts of urban areas which this study focuses on), the phase is appropriate.
4. In 1984 work on the law was still underway (see White 1992: 39). To date
a law has still not been passed. Commenting on the drafting of a one-child
law in 1980 both those in favour of and those against legislation in the field
of population policy referred to the prevailing fear of the use of coercion in
their arguments. Those in favour of legislation maintained that a law would
prevent the use of coercion, while those against maintained that a law would
legalize coercion (Wang *et al.* 1980).

While a national population law has as yet not been passed, the one-child family policy has been included in other forms of legislation. As early as 1978 birth planning was included in the Constitution of China with the wording 'the state advocates and encourages birth planning' (Article 5).[5] In the revised 1982 Constitution the wording on population policy is stronger. Birth planning is included as a responsibility of the State Council (Article 89), while the general section on the role of the state stipulates that: 'The state promotes birth planning in order to achieve compatibility between population and socio-economic development' (Chapter I, Article 25). Article 49 when addressing the basic rights and duties of citizens states that: 'both husband and wife have the duty to practise birth planning.' Following the unsuccessful attempt to enact a law on birth planning, several of the articles of the draft law were instead included in the 1980 revision of the Marriage Law. This now stated that: 'Husband and wife are in duty bound to practise birth planning' (Chapter II, Article 12). Still lacking national legislation specifically on the population policy, the 1992 Law of the People's Republic of China on the Protection of Rights and Interests of Women states that: 'Women have the right to childbearing in accordance with *relevant regulations of the state* as well as the freedom not to bear any child' (Chapter VII, Article 47, emphasis added). By the late 1980s the 'relevant regulations of the state' were the local laws and regulations on birth planning which had been promulgated and implemented by provinces, autonomous regions and municipalities (Han 1990: 51).[6] In practice the birth planning articles of the Constitution and the Marriage Law as well as local birth planning regulations have been seen to amount to the fact that 'Not practising planned births is illegal,' as admonished in a book published by the State Family Planning Commission (Cao 1990: 214).

---

5. The term *birth planning* is translated from the Chinese *jihua shengyu*, literally 'planned birth giving, fertility or procreation'. In China the term is usually translated as family planning. However, as the term is mainly used to designate state intervention into the fertility decisions of the family, I prefer the translation 'birth planning' to 'family planning' to avoid confusing the international definition of family planning as a human right with the Chinese definition that does not distinguish between population control and family planning.
6. For a summary of the common points of the regulations that vary in detail, see Davin 1987: 113–115.

Economic reforms in rural China have both strengthened the desire and ability of peasants to contravene birth planning regulations and weakened enforcement mechanisms. This has led to the relaxation of the one-child requirement in rural China since 1984. Meanwhile, control in urban China has on the contrary been strengthened. One major birth control document issued in 1984 by the Central Committee of the Communist Party specifically states that the Central Committee and the State Council stipulate that, 'Except for those who have received permission for special circumstances, among state-employed cadres and workers and urban residents, each couple may only give birth to one child' (Document No. 7 in White 1992: 33). In 1988 Zeng Yi, Deputy Director of the Institute of Population Research at Beijing University in an interview in the English language periodical *People*, expressed views in favour of a two-child policy. He is quoted to have said: 'It would seem necessary gradually to introduce a universal two-child policy for urban as well as rural areas not later than the end of the century' (Rowley 1989: 22). As we approach the end of the century it would seem more likely that the statement was merely an expression of the official Chinese practice of speaking with two tongues. As several scholars have pointed out, official comments on the enforcement of one-child family policy tend to differ according to whether they are made in a national (Chinese language) context or in an international (English language) context (Davin 1990: 82, Greenhalgh 1989: 4). Urban policy has to date adhered strictly to the principle of 'one couple one child' and has been enforced by severe control. In the city districts of urban China the state has thoroughly succeeded in assuming authority over the family in fertility decisions.[7] As such, the probability that urban city district residents employed in state and collective units will have more than one child is extremely small. The popular saying, 'the sky is high and the emperor far away' (*tian gao huangdi yuan*) – meaning that whatever measures are imposed from on high, there is ample room for manoeuvring and applying countermeasures from below – does not apply to the urban city district populace as far as the one-child family policy is concerned.

---

7. China's municipalities (Beijing, Shanghai and Tianjin), as well as other urban areas such as provincial capitals, include substantial rural populations (see Chapter 2 for fuller details). The use of the term 'urban city district' throughout this study has been adopted to indicate the purely urban nature of the research areas.

The official Chinese view has emphasized that under socialism population growth and population control will not be subject to disadvantageous laws governing the people, as is said to occur under capitalism. Control will instead be subject to plans formulated by the people and implemented by the people (Xu 1981). However, the current population policy in China, when viewed from a human rights perspective, is diametrically opposed to these principles. If family planning is an individual right, then the direct intervention of the Chinese leadership into the fertility decisions of the individual and family amounts to a violation of basic human rights. The Chinese leadership has recognized that some violations of human rights do take place periodically and locally during implementation of the policy. And the leadership has assumed responsibility for local level coercion in implementing the policy (White 1992: 36). However, violation of human rights does not, as the leadership would have it, take place only at the implementation level of the policy. On the contrary, violation of human rights is implicit in the policy itself. Viewed from a human rights perspective, violation of individual rights takes place at the level of the policy because here the leadership intervened in the right of individuals to decide on their number of children by setting a limit of one child per couple.

The issue of human rights in population policies is not confined to China alone. Women's groups and organizations in the countries of the South have been prominent in drawing attention to this issue when scrutinizing how many 'family planning' programmes – essentially these have often been population control programmes – have been implemented in the last twenty to thirty years (see for instance Akhter 1990, 1991, Berer 1990a, 1990b and 1993 and Estrada-Claudio 1991). Supported by like-minded organizations in the countries of the North, they have called attention to the violation of human rights resulting from targeting women and the wombs of women.[8]

Ultimately, the feminist critique of the demographic imperative rests on a conviction that women have a right to make their own

---

8. Among these organizations are the South-based Development Alternatives with Women for a New Era (DAWN); Ubinig, Bangladesh; Asian Women's Human Rights Council, the Philippines; Gabriella, the Philippines; and the North-based International Women's Health Coalition, USA; Women's Global Network for Reproductive Rights, the Netherlands; Women in Development Europe (WIDE), the Netherlands; and KULU – Women and Development, Denmark.

decisions and to 'own and control' their own bodies without governmental intervention (Dixon-Mueller 1993: 53).

In the context of reproductive rights, the voice of women in China is not heard. Chinese women were not, for instance, represented at the first organizational meeting for a Women's Health Network in the East and Southeast Asia Region held in December 1993 (see A. Johansson 1993). Nor were they represented at major meetings in Dhaka in December 1993 or in Rio de Janeiro in January 1994, held by women's organizations in preparation for the 1994 International Population and Development Conference. Among Euro-American scholars of China the issue of violation of human rights in relation to the population policy is a sensitive field. Most seem to prefer to remain silent. Very few China scholars have directly criticized or condemned the Chinese population policy for violation of basic human rights. Prominent among those who have are Judith Banister and John S. Aird (see Banister 1987: 194–195, Aird 1990: chapter 1). Until the student and worker protests in 1989, China was the 'human rights exception' in the sense that, although violations of human rights were known to take place, practically no one was willing to expose or oppose these (Cohen 1987, Svensson 1993: 110). The field of population policies, not only in China but in general, is still the human rights exception. Monitoring governmental compliance with population-related human rights has yet to be introduced. One reason for the paucity of international attention to violations in the area of population policies may be that victims are women and protection of human rights of women lags far behind that of men (Tomaševski 1994: 7–8).

Others hold positions contrary to the human rights position, maintaining that in the case of China, 'however we look at it, there is absolutely no way of evading the population pressure and the planners have no choice but to reduce it *whatever the cost*' (Bianco and Hua 1988: 148, emphasis added). Although not willing to justify the Chinese policy, Lucien Bianco and Chang-ming Hua state that:

> The methods to which communist China has recently resorted, to enforce the single-child policy on a recalcitrant population, have been more brutal than is generally recognized. Without wishing to justify them, we can agree that the dictatorial nature of the regime is, in this area, neither the sole nor even the main reason for recourse to coercion; after much wasted time (in Mao's lifetime and by Mao's doing), China had no choice but to accelerate the demographic transition artificially, without waiting for the socio-economic conditions to mature. (Bianco and Hua 1988: 162)

The latter 'whatever the cost' view has in recent years been gaining momentum not only with regard to population policy in China but globally. This trend is linked to the increasing visibility and credibility being given to contentions that population growth is a major cause of environmental problems. Previously, large numbers of poor people were feared due to their potential support of communist regimes (DuBois 1991: 13). In the post-Cold War period the threat is seen in terms of poor people from the countries of the South migrating to the countries of the North. Often this fear is disguised in claims that population numbers and growth rates in the South are the major threat to the global environment. The environment has been on the agenda of international concern at least since the Stockholm Environment Conference in 1972 (V. Shiva 1992: 3). However, the close linking of environmental degradation and unsustainability to population growth is more recent.

In 1981 one of the rationales for family planning that was merely touched upon at 'The International Conference on Family Planning in the 1980s' was that which linked population growth and environmental degradation (*Family Planning in the 1980s* 1981: 7). Some ten years later at the United Nations Conference on Environment and Development (UNCED) held in Rio de Janeiro in June 1992, the link between environment and population was the source of much controversy (Cohen 1993), there being a tendency to identify the South as the main source of environmental problems and the North with its technology and capital as the main source of environmental solutions. The tendency was also to reduce the problem of the reproduction of society, in the face of declining resources and declining access to resources, to the status of a 'population problem'. This is, as Vandana Shiva has pointed out, symptomatic of the tendency to treat people of other cultures, races and places not as human beings but as numbers to be manipulated (V. Shiva 1992: 5). Tragically, the issue could not be constructively addressed as the North was not willing to widen the discussion to include examination of its own consumption and production patterns with that of high population growth rates in the South as sources of environmental degradation. It is most likely that the more focus is placed on the population aspect of the environmental issue, the more the family planning and human rights perspective in relation to solving the global 'population problem' will be overshadowed by a 'whatever the cost' mentality. This will lead to population control being advocated once again and more forcefully as the necessary solution.[9] It is therefore necessary to separate an acceptance of the need to acknowledge that there are serious crises associated with population growth, poverty and economic development from an acceptance of the dominant readings of such crises. This is necessary not least because the factors that do cause fertility reduction are little known (Egerö 1992: 52), and many years of experience with instrumental population control have proved that the solutions following the dominant readings of the crisis do not work (Bose 1993, M. Shiva 1992).

The 'Success' of China's Population Policy

Given this renewed and more forceful focus on the 'population problem', coupled with an awareness that most population policies have failed and indeed that what determines fertility levels is not yet fully understood, much international attention has been directed towards the Chinese population policy – for this has seemed to work, at least demographically. Not only were the achievements of China's one-child family policy commended in 1991 by Nafis Sadik, Executive Director of UNFPA, but also some years earlier (in 1983) Qian Xinzhong, head of China's State Family Planning Commission, received the first United Nations Population Award. The Chinese one-child family policy is referred to as 'a unique accomplishment' (Kaufmann *et al.* 1992: 18) and is advanced as a model for other countries to emulate. For instance:

> The difficulties of one-child families, even in China, must not how-ever be underestimated. The point is that for many communities they are the *only* alternative to starvation, and communities must be made to see this. (King 1992: 44)

> China makes family planning possible for everyone in the enormous country in a way that can be a model for many countries. (S. Johansson 1993: 71)

Paul and Ann Erhlich answer the question of what is 'the best strategy for achieving population control in poor nations' by suggesting an examination of 'the most successful population-control program in the world – that in the People's Republic of

---

9. Birth planning, environmental protection and land resources protection have been classified as the three 'basic national policies' (*jiben guoce*) in China.

China' (Erhlich and Erhlich 1991: 205).[10] Some proponents of Chinese population control do have reservations about the coercive elements of the policy (King 1992: 44, S. Johansson 1993: 71), even though coercion is at the very core of the policy's demographic success. A key point to be made in this study is the ability of the state to coerce or convince its citizens to accept its population policy. Here, the continuing urban–rural divide in Chinese society is quite apparent.

Quantitatively, the policy has been a success in urban China where a majority of women give birth to only one child. In rural China most women give birth to at least two children, while some give birth to three or more. However, although varying levels of enforcement have been reflected in different success rates for urban and rural China, indications are that in both areas there is a common preference to have more than one child. Although traditional norms of having many children (especially many sons) have become less strong, there remains a discrepancy between the two-child norm that has gradually been established for large parts of the population and the population policy requirement of only one child. Surveys carried out in both rural and urban areas confirm that the number of children desired continues to exceed policy requirements. In a 1983 rural survey, 99 per cent of respondents said they wanted at least two children; 84 per cent of women below 30 years and 90 per cent of women aged 30–44 said they wanted at least three children (Freedmann and Guo 1988). Another early 1980s study found that more than three-quarters of urban women said that the ideal number of children would be two or more (Wolf 1985: 254). Data from the 1987 In-Depth Fertility Survey (IDFS) indicate that there is a big gap between the one-child ideal being advocated and actual fertility preferences, both in urban and rural areas. IDFS results from Beijing and Liaoning, the two areas of this study, indicate that in Beijing 67 per cent of women with one child stated that their preferred number was two children. In Liaoning 70 per cent of one-child mothers preferred two children (Xu and Yu 1991: 180–181). One 1990 study concludes that 75 per cent of the one-child parents studied would prefer two children, while only a minority of 2.4 per cent would prefer more than two children (Feng 1990). Based on a compilation of data from a number of surveys conducted in

10. See also Johnson 1987: 310–312.

both rural and urban areas in the first half of the 1980s Martin King Whyte and S.Z. Gu conclude that only very few respondents either preferred three or more children or one child. With few exceptions it appeared from these surveys that in both rural and urban areas two children was the preferred number (Whyte and Gu 1987). A 1990 survey by the All-China Women's Federation confirms that a minimum of two children is the preferred number of children in both rural and urban China (Sun Rong 1993). These results clearly indicate a discrepancy between the policy fertility limits and the fertility preferences of respondents. Verbal compliance to the state policy must furthermore be taken into account with the possibility that the discrepancy between the policy and fertility preferences is even larger. The few surveys of fertility desire that have included indications of the preferred sex of children suggest the preferred combination of two children to be one girl and one boy. Therefore, Whyte and Gu assume that a considerable number of couples with either two girls or two boys could be expected to prefer more than two children (Whyte and Gu 1987).

Several studies have demonstrated that the one most important fertility determinant in China in families that have only one child is the fertility limit set by the population policy *and* its strict implementation. A 1985 study of rural areas of Jilin province concluded that women were having fewer children than the ideal of two children owing to strong enforcement of the population policy (Choe and Tsuya 1991). Based on data from the 1987 In-Depth Fertility Survey, Guo Fei and Minja Kim Choe conclude that, while urbanization, parental education level, filial survival rate, living standards and population composition have an influence on the level of fertility, the population policy has the greatest influence (Guo and Choe 1991). Another study concludes that, although education, profession, geographical differences and urban-rural differences strongly influence contraceptive use, the most important social factor is the state policy and its population control programme (Cai, Zhou and Li 1991). One study found that 74.8 per cent of one-child families said the reason they had only one child was that the government policy does not allow for more children. Only 13.5 per cent stated not wanting more than one child as the reason they had only one child (Feng 1990: 101). Griffith Feeney and Wang Feng conclude that it is likely that about half of the fertility decline from about six children per woman prior to 1970 to near replacement level in 1990 may be attributed to government intervention specifically aimed at reducing fertility (Feeney and Wang 1993: 95).

Several studies have thus shown that there is a disparity between fertility preferences and the one-child limit mandated by the population policy. However, knowledge is limited of the non-demographic consequences of imposing a fertility limit by way of population control contrary to family size preferences. Based on a study of the consequences of a disparity between the actual one child and the preferred number of children, Feng Xiaotian concludes that there has not been sufficient study of this phenomenon in China. Such research is important for an understanding of issues in relation to the psychology and behaviour of the only child, and the behaviour and perception of happiness of the family as such. It is also important for understanding social problems that might evolve in connection with policy implementation (Feng 1990: 95–96). Studies of the consequences of the policy have mainly focused on consequences in the policy implementation phase. Based on reports from the PRC press and interviews in Hong Kong, the following consequences of one-child family policy implementation in the early 1980s have been documented: abuses and violence in the form of forced abortion and sterilization, economic penalties for unplanned births, destruction of housing as a penalty, maltreatment of women giving birth to daughters, female infanticide carried out by parents, and children of second- and third-parity births being killed by hospital personnel (Bianco and Hua 1988).[11]

About This Study

The objective of this study is to contribute to the knowledge of consequences of applying population control as a means to limiting population growth rates. The concern is with a context where the major fertility determinant is population control in the form of a strictly implemented fertility limit. The study focuses on how urban city district one-child mothers experience policy implementation and on their cultural and individual management of consequences of the policy. Furthermore, the objective is to make visible a level of population control that otherwise

---

11. For a detailed description of coercive elements of policy implementation, see Banister 1987: 192–215.

receives little attention in the population policy studies – most oriented to socio-economic and demographic issues – which dominate the field.[12] This is the level at which the people behind the statistics lead their everyday lives.

The studies of everyday life[13] have inspired this study as an overall point of departure. The essence of the theories of everyday life comprises a combined analysis of that everyday life studied and the structures of the society in which it occurs. These theories were developed as a reaction to theories that emphasized the determining forces of the structures of society and understood the actions of people as determined by these. In theories of everyday life the three levels of the individual, of interpersonal relations and of the structures of society are included with a view to understanding not only the structures of society, but also the everyday lives of the people who create, maintain and change these structures. Moreover, studies of this kind offer a holistic understanding of society in an attempt at combining the local, national and international perspectives of society, while ensuring that the analysis of society remains grounded in the everyday world (see Bloch and Højgaard 1986, Bloch *et al.* 1988, Stepputat 1987). This study has applied the everyday life understanding of society as a point of departure, but has concentrated on the local level. At this level the study has adopted the everyday life study mode of understanding culture as a social process. Culture is created not only for people but also by people. Thus everyday life is seen as a cultural manifestation, not merely as social reproduction. Culture is human praxis. Culture is the meanings that are inherent in praxis as illustrated by James Spradley with the example of culture as a map of shared meaning systems that people use to regulate their behaviour, customs and emotions.

---

12.   John S. Aird, Ansley Coale, Leo A. Orleans and H. Yuan Tien have written extensively on socio-economic, political and demographic aspects of the population of China over the past twenty to thirty years. For English language studies of this type see for instance John. S. Aird (1963, 1973, 1978), Leo A. Orleans (1960, 1962, 1969, 1979), H. Yuan Tien (1973, 1980a, 1980b, 1983, 1991) and Ansley Coale (1981a, 1981b, 1991). More recent studies of various aspects of population change include, among others, Peng Xizhe 1991 and Wang and Hull 1991. Susan Greenhalgh has written extensively on local level implementation on population control: Greenhalgh 1988, 1989, 1990, 1993.

13.   Theories of everyday life, originally deriving from the Birmingham School in England, were applied and developed at the Department of Cultural Sociology, Copenhagen University (see Bloch *et al.* 1988, Bloch and Højgaard 1986 and Stepputat 1987).

Culture as praxis means that people are seen not only as map-readers, but also as map-makers. People read the map and follow the paths, the roads and structures that are delineated by former generations, but they also create new paths. Thus people create, maintain and change social reality. The study has adopted Spradley's definition that 'Culture refers to the acquired knowledge that people use to interpret experience and generate social behavior' (Spradley 1979).

Implicit in the aim of understanding women's management of the consequences of the population control policy is the objective of making visible the lives of women. In this respect the study is a continuation of the Euro-American women's studies project of making visible and understanding an aspect of human life that is otherwise overlooked – the lives of women, seen from their own perspective. However, in terms of women's studies, the study has not followed the general trend that in recent years has shifted the main focus from making women visible and entering women into the existing theories, to confronting the theories with the dimension of gender with a view to transforming the theories (Flax 1989, Harding 1989 and Hawkesworth 1989). The main aim of the present study is to make visible the everyday life of women in managing the one-child policy. The rationale underlying the focus on women is that, although all family members are affected by the one-child family policy, women bear the main brunt of the policy. The policy runs contrary to traditional family norms, thereby disrupting family structures and affecting not only women but all family members – children, women and men; young as well as old. However, physically as well as socially, women are the first to be confronted with the one-child family policy. Not only are the bodies of women as childbearers immediately implicated by the fact of pregnancy or abortion; it is also commonly assumed that women bear the primary responsibility for contraceptive practice (Davin 1990, Honig and Hershatter 1988: 187). The majority of contraceptives available are for female use, the most frequently used one being the IUD. Socially the role and status of a woman are closely linked to the number and sex of her children. Studies have documented that China's population policy therefore meant new pressures being placed on women to give birth to a son (Davin 1987: 119, Honig and Hershatter 1988: 189). There is no doubt that women bear the brunt of psychological as well as physical and social costs, not least when women, regardless of their own desire, are caught between the policy requirement of one child and family demands for a son. This is especially the case in rural China, where the consequences of population control are more physical and therefore also more visible than in urban China (Wolf 1985: 250).

In rural China women are held responsible for the sex of their children. Ill-treatment as well as actual physical assault of women who give birth to girls – in the form of persistent abuse, violent beatings and even murder – has been widely documented (Davin 1990: 85, Honig and Hershatter 1988: 189–190). Provincial regulations prohibiting the divorce of women who are sterile or have given birth to a female child indicate that the problem is recognized as serious. The 1983 Sichuan regulations state that the fact that a woman has given birth to a girl or that a woman is sterile is not a valid reason for obtaining divorce (Sichuan 1983: 504, paragraph 5). Guizhou and Ningxia regulations state that, if a husband wants to divorce his wife because she has given birth to a girl, he must be seriously criticized and his request for divorce should be rejected (Guizhou 1984: 513, part 5; Ningxia 1985: 553, paragraph 10). Some cases of divorce must, however, be allowed in order to protect the interests of the woman. Divorce documents should clearly indicate that the husband has required divorce due to the sex of his child, in order to limit his access to a birth permit upon remarriage (Guizhou 1984: 513, part 5).

Maltreatment of women as well as infanticide of female children is also mentioned in the provincial regulations. The Sichuan regulations state that family members' physical, mental or economic maltreatment of the mother of a girl child or the girl child herself is considered a criminal offence to be punished according to the Criminal Law (Sichuan 1983: 505, paragraph 15), and that instigating or coercing someone else to maltreat a woman who has given birth to a girl, to infanticide or to abandonment of a girl child is also considered a criminal offence (Sichuan 1983: 505, paragraph 16). Rural women are moreover subject to physical as well as mental assault from birth planning workers, who are held responsible for keeping birth rates low through a system of penalties and incentives (Banister 1987: 198–199). Women may have to undergo abortions in the second or third trimester of their pregnancy, and women trying to hide from birth planning officials to carry through an unauthorized pregnancy, if caught by birth planning workers, may be treated almost as if they were criminals (Davin 1990: 85–86). As a long-term consequence, the one-child family policy will create two major groupings of peasant families: those with a single child and those with two children. Delia Davin predicts that the first group will be privileged boys on whom family resources are concentrated. Almost all girls will belong to the second group, whose children will have to share family resources for education, health and food. In the long run the majority of girls will grow up in families which will have fewer resources to divide between more children (Davin 1990: 89).

There are other consequences of the one-child family policy for women than the more obvious ones (health hazards related to contraception and abortion, physical violence and psychological pressure induced by families and birth planning workers) mentioned above. As pointed out by Delia Davin, the one-child family policy threatens the very self-image of women whose sense of worth is linked to the familial roles of mother, daughter-in-law and wife (Davin 1987: 126). While the former consequences apply primarily to rural women, this study is concerned with the latter consequence for urban city district women who due to population control have only one child regardless of their own or their family's preferences. Of all the consequences of the one-child family policy for the women involved, this study describes and interprets their cultural dimensions focusing on the social context of the changes that are taking place as a result of that policy.

The present study draws extensively on studies on women in China by Phyllis Andors (1983), Elisabeth Croll (1983, 1987), Delia Davin (1987, 1990), Emily Honig and Gail Hershatter (1988), Kay Ann Johnson (1993), Judith Stacey (1983) and Margery Wolf (1985). Moreover, the study is a continuation of these studies in so far as it is an empirically based examination of some of the consequences of the one-child family policy to which these, based primarily on documentary studies, have pointed.

One point of departure is that the one-child family policy represents a break with tradition. The question being posed is: What are the cultural values and norms related to the fertility of women and what are the consequences for the life quality of women if fulfilment of these values and norms is threatened by the policy? Such a break induced by population control cannot be without consequences, which in turn require adjustments on the part of women. The following three areas of enquiry are therefore investigated.

First, the study examines how the policy requirement of only one child runs counter to traditional norms and values related to the role and status of women and to family structure, and thereby whether the policy is perceived by women as a negative break and interference in their lives. Traditionally in China a woman's first obligation is to bear children, especially sons, for her husband's family. In so doing, she continues his family line. And she supplies the family with labour and security for the preceding generation in old age. Although urban women now work outside the home, women's role as defined by society is still primarily the domestic role of wife and mother. In the 1980s the majority of women – rural as well as urban – were still being judged within the context of the family and their performance of familial roles (Wolf 1985: 182).

Second, in relation to studying the effects of the break with tradition, the study addresses the issue of a break with repro-ductive self-determination. Western critiques of the Chinese popu-lation policy have been based on the view that implementation of the one-child family policy implies a violation of the reproductive self-determination of the Chinese population (Hartmann 1987: 148). In view of Chinese women never having controlled their own fertility (Davin 1987: 126), the question being posed is whether the view of family planning as a basic human right is shared by Chinese women. How do Chinese women perceive reproductive self-determination, if at all?

Third, the study examines how women perceive the possibility of a positive change in the break with tradition. The policy might act as an instigator of what Judith Stacey has suggested as a form of 'feminism from above'. Because a con-striction of private patriarchal control over women's productive and reproductive activities has taken place, women might be supported in a movement away from traditional roles. Stacey does, however, stress that the policy element of 'above' rather than that of 'feminism' is likely to be dominant (Stacey 1983: 276). The proposition here is that the way in which the one-child family policy is experienced might be linked to the degree to which the woman identifies with either her public job role or her domestic role as wife and mother; hence women who identify primarily with their job role might experience the policy as a relief from traditional norms.

Related to the three areas of enquiry is an examination of the interaction between women and birthplanning institutions in implementation of the policy at the level of workplace and residential area. The context here is the official recognition that the success of the policy would depend upon an improvement in educational and job opportunities for women (Davin 1987: 124), and that policy implementation should link the concept of fewer children to the improvement of women's health and overall life situation. Two main questions are posed to this interaction. First, how and to what degree are birth planning personnel and institutions able to implement the policy based on the interests of women, if this is at all possible with a policy that is being implemented as population control? And, second, how and to what degree are birth planning personnel and institutions able to support women in making use of new possibilities that might arise as a consequence of the policy, both in relation to family and employment?

During my preliminary interviews with birth planning personnel in 1991, it became obvious that the main – and in fact sole – duty of the birth planning workers at the level where they interact directly with women is specifically and narrowly to ensure that women have only one child. It is not part of birth planning work at this level to engage more broadly in efforts to improve educational and employment opportunities for women that might facilitate acceptance of the one-child family policy. The economic reform period has, on the contrary, led to a worsening of both educational and employment opportunities for women (Jacka 1990). The birth planning institution works solely to ensure policy compliance. In this sense, birth planning personnel are in fact working against the interests and needs of many women. However, as their work also includes care for women related to their choice and use of contraceptives, the duties they perform become a combination of ensuring policy compliance and actual care for the reproductive health of women, with the distinction between the two becoming blurred. An example of birth planning personnel caring for women was expressed in one Beijing city district residential area by their resentment against the use of hormonal injectables and implants that would affect the internal balance of the body. The analysis of the interaction between women and birth planning personnel will concentrate on this combination of controlling and caring duties as well as on the ideological education work that is carried out by the birth planning institution. There is no doubt that educated women do not have any trouble understanding birth planning ideological education materials. Women in this study were well-informed regarding all aspects of the 'population problem' in China and implementation of the one-child family policy as the means to solving the problem. This study seeks to understand why a majority of urban women, contrary to their stated preferences of two children, accept population control to such a degree that 'birth planning' has become synonymous with 'one child' in the terminology of women.

Chapters 2 and 3 provide the background for the main part of the book. Chapter 2 describes the setting of the study. In Chapter 3, demographic change in China prior to and during the one-child family policy is viewed primarily in the context of the gender and population policy ideologies that have influenced birth at the micro level of the family as well as from the macro level of leadership population policies. The main aim of the chapter is to provide a historical context for this study of the impact of the one-child family policy on the lives of urban one-child women. The demographic change leading to the population size and structure that was the basis for the formulation of the one-child family policy is outlined from a gender and population policy ideology perspective.

Findings and interpretations of the study are presented in Chapters 4 through 8. In Chapter 4 the fertility preferences of the women studied are outlined and a preliminary definition of policy acceptance is introduced. In this definition a discrepancy between the ideal number of children and the mandatory one child is not viewed as analogous to non-acceptance of the policy. On the contrary, acceptance of the national policy transcends individual or family preferences when these are in conflict with the policy requirement of only one child. The following chapters focus on how urban city district women manage the consequences of the policy with respect to the norm sets of family and nation.

Chapter 5 describes and analyses the interaction between urban city district women and the birth planning institution at the local level of the workplace and residential area where birth planning cadres are responsible for policy implementation. Chapters 6 and 7 describe and analyse the management strategy employed by women towards one consequence of the policy: that their prospect of establishing an intergenerational contract as the basis of their own support in later life is weakened by the policy. I shall argue that the cultural assumptions of gender relations within which women are evaluated by others and from which women perceive of themselves are integrally linked to the concept of virtuous wife and good mother (*xianqi liangmu*); also that, together with women's dual working roles, cultural assumptions of gender relations shape a management strategy of cultivation of the perfect only child. Moreover the limited scope of expectations women have towards being able to influence their own lives based on their personal needs and interests shapes their choice of management strategy. Chapter 8 summarizes and links the main findings of the study and elaborates on the phenomenon of acceptance.

Setting

From 1980 to the late 1980s the average total fertility rate in urban China has been 1.33 versus 2.84 in rural China. These total fertility rates indicate that while a majority of urban women give birth to only one child, in rural China most women give birth to at least two children, while some give birth to three or more.

Han Changsen 1990: 52

The Areas of Study

Data for this study were collected in one city district of the municipality of Beijing and in two city districts in the city of Shenyang, the provincial capital of the northeastern Liaoning province (see Figure 1). The aim was to study the consequences of the demographically successful urban population policy. Beijing was thus selected because, as the seat of national government, the municipality has the role of setting an example for the rest of the nation to follow; it therefore has a rigorous implementation of the one-child family policy with high one-child rates. Being the largest heavy-industrial city in China, Shenyang is in many ways identical to Beijing in economic structure and educational levels. This is reflected in the fact that demographic results of the one-child family policy here are in many ways similar to those from Beijing. Therefore, Shenyang was chosen as a supplement to Beijing.

Since the introduction of economic reforms to China, the city of Beijing has undergone enormous change. In the early 1980s

Figure 1: Location and 1988 populations of Beijing and Liaoning/Shenyang

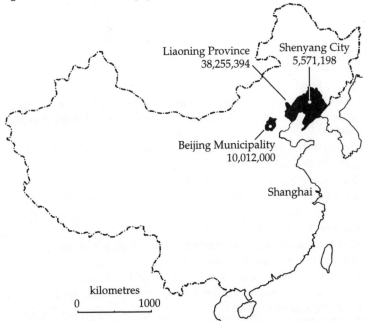

Liaoning Province
38,255,394

Shenyang City
5,571,198

Beijing Municipality
10,012,000

Shanghai

kilometres
0   1000

Beijing did not possess many of the features often associated with a national capital. There were practically no high-rise buildings, no flashing, colourful neon advertisements nor lively shopping areas full of restaurants and various amusement facilities. In fact the city seemed more like a huge village. At about nine o'clock in the evening the few state-owned restaurants and cinemas would close and the city would become quiet. It was not unusual to meet a farmer herding his flock of sheep through the dark and empty streets of night-time Beijing. In the daytime the vehicles in the streets were mostly bicycles, buses and trucks with only a few passenger cars among these. Citizens of Beijing – men and women alike – were usually dressed in blue or green cotton trousers and jackets and flat-heeled cloth shoes. A brightly clad foreigner could be detected at a great distance because of the difference in clothing and because there were so few foreigners in the city. Due to the economic reforms, production and consumption patterns have changed and foreign influences have visibly entered the city. With the opening to the outside world joint-venture hotels began to be opened in Beijing, skyscrapers rose among the traditional one-storey courtyard houses, and an increasing number of foreign airlines started operating routes to Beijing. By the mid-1980s young Chinese women in Beijing were beginning to wear high heels and silk skirts and the older women had resumed wearing the golden earrings that had been hidden in their drawers since the Cultural Revolution. Farmers from suburban Beijing began selling their vegetables in private markets. Moreover, restaurants, discotheques and karaoke bars were opened. In Beijing the streets are now crowded with Japanese cars, many of which are privately owned.

In a way, Shenyang of the early 1990s resembles Beijing of the mid-1980s. Private markets and restaurants as well as an enormous department store have also shot up here. It has become acceptable to enjoy oneself and in the evenings and weekends people dance to both traditional Chinese and Western music in the streets and parks. There are also more passenger cars in the streets of Shenyang than there were previously, but many of them are still the old and far from prestigious Shanghai model. At the centre of the city an enormous statue of Chairman Mao Zedong still looms, symbolizing the role the province holds as a Communist Party stronghold.

In 1982 Liaoning province, with a total fertility rate (TFR) of 1.7, had the fourth lowest TFR in China, following the three municipalities of Beijing, Shanghai and Tianjin. Shanghai had the lowest rate at 1.3, while Beijing's was 1.5 and Tianjin's 1.6. By 1989, Beijing had the lowest TFR nationwide at 1.3, but Liaoning still held fourth place with a TFR of 1.5 (*Zhongguo renkou nianjian* 1992: 114). Besides the low TFRs, the one-child rate – which is the percentage of all births that are first-parity births – is used as a measure of policy success. The planned birth rate is applied as another measure of policy success. This rate is calculated as the number of births conforming to birth targets during a given period divided by the total number of births during the period. Annually a population plan is drawn up for all of China with quotas for the number of births that will be permitted in each province as well as at all lower levels of the administrative system.

According to State Council Document No. 110 (1981), responsibility for population planning is divided between the State Planning Commission (SPC) and the State Family Planning Commission (SFPC). The SPC is responsible for examining, approving and issuing national and provincial population plans, supervising plan implementation, and allocating necessary funds and materials. The SFPC is responsible for working out long-term and annual population targets and implementation plans (Wang Hong 1991: 76).

In Beijing the Planning Department of the Beijing Family Planning Commission is responsible for setting the goals for each administrative level for the coming year (Croll 1985b: 198). Although the plan is drawn up following a process of negotiation between the lowest and highest levels of the administrative hierarchy, ultimately couples must comply with the plan whether or not it corresponds to their fertility preferences, and women must apply for permission to become pregnant and give birth according to the annual plan. Application procedures are elaborated on in Chapter 5. Births following granted permission are registered as planned births (*jihuanei*, literally 'within the plan'), while births that have not been permitted are registered as unplanned births (*jihuawai*, literally 'outside the plan'). The distribution of planned and unplanned births in China from 1980 to 1988 is shown in Figure 2 below.

A third measure of policy success is the one-child certificate rate. This rate is calculated as the percentage of couples with one child, where the wife is still of childbearing age, who have signed a pledge not to give birth to further children. According to statistics released by the Beijing Statistical Bureau, one-child rates have been above 80 per cent in Beijing municipality since the inception of the one-child family policy. In the city districts the rate has been higher than 99 per cent since 1982. The one-child certificate rate was 45.57 per cent in the municipality in 1979, but since then has been above 80 per cent. In the city districts the one-child certificate rate was 67.71 in 1979 and since then has been above 90 per cent (*Beijing sishi* 1990: 69–71).

Data from the (1987) second phase of the In-Depth Fertility Survey, which included both Beijing and Liaoning, indicate several similarities between the two areas with regard to population distribution and educational levels – two of many factors affecting fertility levels.[1] Both Beijing and Liaoning have

---

1. The China In-Depth Fertility Survey was carried out by the State Statistical Bureau in two phases, the first in 1985 and the second in 1987. The 1987 survey was conducted in Beijing municipality as well as in the provinces Liaoning, Shandong, Gansu, Guangdong and Guizhou. The population surveyed were married women below 50 years. In Beijing 7,622 married women and in Liaoning 6,567 married women were surveyed (*Zhongguo dierqi* 1989, vol. 1: 1–9). In this study the survey is referred to as the In-Depth Fertility Survey (IDFS).

Figure 2: Percentage distribution of planned and unplanned births in China, 1980–88

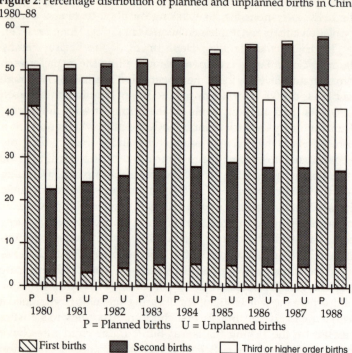

P = Planned births   U = Unplanned births

⧅ First births   ■ Second births   □ Third or higher order births

Source: *Zhongguo renkou nianjian* 1992: 574.

high percentages of non-agricultural population and the population in both Beijing and Liaoning has relatively high educational levels. Since 1982 the majority of births in both Beijing and Liaoning have been first births, and most births are planned births. Fertility preferences in urban Beijing and Liaoning are also somewhat similar, a subject I shall return to in Chapter 4. Though fertility transition has followed dissimilar patterns in Beijing and Liaoning, fertility has reached relatively similar levels during the one-child family policy period. Fertility in Beijing declined prior to the initiation of government population policy programmes in the 1960s and 1970s, with fertility declining more in urban than in rural areas and falling below replacement level – an average of just over two births per woman – in the mid-1970s. In the period 1967–71, 75.8 per cent of women in Beijing with one child gave birth to a second child within five years, whereas only 16.5 per cent of the women who had one child did so during 1982–87. In Liaoning fertility declined rapidly from 1968. In the period 1967–71, 91.6 per cent of women with one child gave birth to a second child within five years. In the period 1982–87 only 11 per cent gave birth to a second child. And in 1982–87 among women who had two children, only 13.1 per cent in Beijing and 12.1 per cent in Liaoning gave birth to a third child. Fertility in Beijing has not changed much since reaching a level well below replacement level in the mid-1970s. In Liaoning fertility reached replacement level around 1980 and continued to decline (Choe *et al.* 1992, Guo and Choe 1991: 209–210).[2]

As previously stated, this study was carried out in city districts of Beijing and Shenyang. In the city districts of urban areas the majority of the population is classified as non-agricultural. All citizens in China are classified as either agricultural (*nongye*) or non-agricultural (*feinongye*). Approximately 80 per cent of the Chinese population have since 1949 been classified as agricultural, while the remaining approximately 20 per cent are classified as non-agricultural (*Zhongguo renkou nianjian* 1992: 498).[3] Beijing municipality as the capital has a relatively high percentage of non-agricultural population. Of the 1988 permanent Beijing population, 61.3 per cent were non-agricultural and 38.7 per cent were agricultural (*Beijing sishi* 1990). In the city districts the majority of the population is non-agricultural, meaning also that they hold an urban household registration (*chengshi hukou*) which in principle entitles them to state food supplements as well as to employment in state and collective enterprises. Chapter 5 will elaborate on the significance of this dependency on the state in relation to one-child family policy implementation. Figure 3 illustrates the distribution of agricultural and non-agricultural population in Liaoning province, Shenyang city and the five city districts of Shenyang. In the whole province in 1988 41.7 per cent of the population were non-agricultural. Only a small percentage of

---

2. Following the 1982 census, the series *Zhongguo Renkou* (China Population Series) with one volume covering the demographic and population policy histories of each province, municipality and autonomous region was published by the China Financial and Economic Publishing House with Sun Jingzhi, Beijing Economics College as chief editor. For the Beijing and Liaoning volumes, see Li Muzhen 1987 and Song 1987. Publication of the series, which has been translated into English, was supported by the United Nations Population Fund (UNFPA) (see Greenhalgh 1988: 12–13).

3. For a discussion of various definitions of urban place and urban population that have confused characterization of the size of urban population since the establishment of the People's Republic, see Goldstein 1990.

Figure 3: Distribution of agricultural and non-agricultural population Liaoning province, Shenyang city and Shenyang city districts, 1988

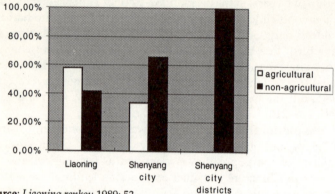

Source: *Liaoning renkou* 1989: 53.

agricultural population was registered in the city districts. The percentage of non-agricultural population in Shenyang and Beijing in 1990 ranged between 94.84 per cent in Beijing's Xicheng district and 97.53 per cent in Shenyang's Tiexi district (*Zhongguo 1990* 1993, vol. 1: 219, 227).[4]

Chinese cities are administratively divided into urban, suburban and rural areas. The municipality of Beijing (see Figure 4) thus consists of eight rural counties (*xian*), two outer suburbs (*yuan jiaoqu*), four inner suburbs (*jin jiaoqu*) and four city districts (*chengqu*). The four city districts Dongcheng, Xicheng, Chongwen and Xuanwu are located at the centre of the municipality (*Beijing sishi* 1990 and Li Muzhen 1987: 12). In 1988, permanent city district residents constituted approximately one quarter of the total number of Beijing residents.[5] The city of Shenyang is administratively divided into two rural counties, four suburban areas and five city districts (see Figure 5).

High one-child rates are mainly found in urban China and even more so in the city districts of urban areas where the population is mainly non-agricultural and registered as urban house-

4. In 1989, according to the *Beijing Socio-economic Statistical Yearbook*, there were no agricultural households in the four city districts of Beijing (*Beijingshi shehui* 1990: 192).

5. Population numbers from 1988 are used because the fullest set of statistics on one-child rates, planned birth rates and one-child certificate rates I was able to get hold of in China in 1992 for both Liaoning and Beijing were 1988 statistics.

Figure 4: Administrative division of Beijing with 1988 city district populations

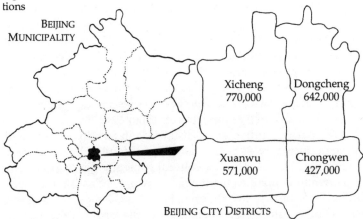

Source: *Beijing sishi (1949–89)* 1990: 55–57.

holds. Fertility rates have been higher in rural than in urban China since the 1960s. From 1980 to the late 1980s the average TFR in urban China was 1.33 versus 2.84 in rural China. These TFRs indicate that, while a majority of urban women give birth to only one child, in rural China most women give birth to at least two

Figure 5: Administrative division of Shenyang city districts with 1988 populations

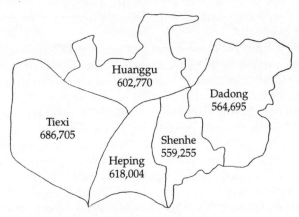

Source: *Zhongguo renkou nianjian (1992)* 1992: 267.

children, while some give birth to three or more (Han 1990: 52).In 1987 the average birth rate nationwide for inhabitants of urban residential areas (*chengshi jiedao*) was 14.30 per thousand. In rural areas the rate was 24.94 per thousand. And in the first half of 1988 the one-child rate in urban residential areas was 89.30 per cent and the percentage of second-parity births was 1.19. In comparison, in rural areas the first-parity percentage was 48.94 and the second-parity percentage was 17.63. Rural China thus accounts for 94.2 per cent of second or higher parity births (Han 1990: 52).

The national urban–rural distinction in fertility is replicated in the municipality of Beijing urban-rural fertility pattern where women classified as non-agricultural generally give birth to one child, while a significant number of women classified as agricultural give birth to two children. Hao Hongsheng, Gao Ling and Shen Qing conclude from their study of the fertility of women in Beijing that in the city districts of Beijing the one-child family policy has reached the limit of what it can achieve, and that further lowering of fertility must take place in the rural areas (Hao *et al.* 1991: 23). An urban fertility pattern similar to the national as well as the Beijing pattern is found in Liaoning province. In 1988 a majority of births in Liaoning province were first-parity births, with higher one-child rates in urban than in rural areas. The distribution of births by birth order in Liaoning province, Shenyang city and Shenyang city districts is illustrated in Figure 6. The successful implementation of the one-child family policy as measured by high one-child rates in the five city districts of Shenyang is identical with the situation in the four city districts of Beijing (see Table 1 overleaf).

The validity of both national and local-level Chinese statistics has been questioned by non-Chinese scholars. For instance, in her study of Chinese women, Margery Wolf was provided with local-level fertility statistics that did not concur with the reality she encountered during interviews (Wolf 1985: 138–139). Another example is the two sets of statistics on rural private enterprise, compiled by the State Statistical Bureau and the Ministry of Agriculture respectively, mentioned by Ole Odgaard (Odgaard 1991: 23–24). Curiously, the population numbers for 1990 for the four city districts of Beijing given in the 1992 Almanac of China's Population (*Zhongguo renkou nianjian* 1992), taken from the manual tabulations of the 1990 census, are all lower than these 1988 population numbers from the statistics in Beijing Forty Years

Figure 6: Percentage distribution of births by birth order in Liaoning province, Shenyang city and Shenyang city districts, 1988

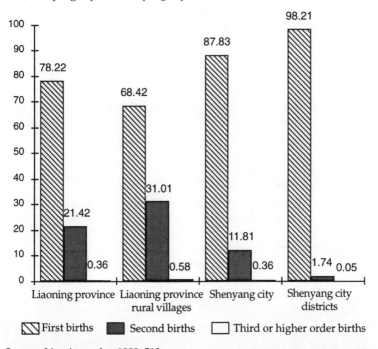

Liaoning province Liaoning province Shenyang city Shenyang city
                   rural villages   districts

➤ First births   ▤ Second births   □ Third or higher order births

Source: *Liaoning renkou* 1989: 513.

(Beijing sishi 1990).[6] There may be inaccuracies in the statistical data reproduced in this chapter, most likely in the form of under-reporting of births, with one-child rates and numbers of planned births possibly being lower than those presented in and cited from the statistical works available. However, as statistics from the In-Depth Fertility Survey (IDFS) confirm the overall picture given by other statistics, there is no reason to doubt that the one-child family policy is in fact demographically very successful both in

---

6. Dongcheng 606,203, Xicheng 755,813, Chongwen 417,651 and Xuanwu 556,877 (*Zhongguo renkou nianjian (1992)* 1992: 256 – also cited in *Zhongguo 1990 nian renkou pucha ziliao*, vol. 1, 1993: 82.). These population numbers are also lower than those given for 1989 population by the *Beijingshi shehui (1989)* 1990. These are for the four city districts: Dongcheng 645,000, Xicheng 774,000, Chongwen 430,000 and Xuanwu 578,000 (*Beijingshi shehui (1989)* 1990: 195). A possible explanation, which Thiagarajan Manoharan kindly brought to my attention, may be that in 1989 measures were taken to send large numbers of the 'floating population' out of Beijing.

Beijing and in Liaoning, which is the main point in the context of this study. The high quality of the IDFS data is acknowledged both by the International Statistical Institute in the Netherlands which assisted the project and by scholars without affiliation to the survey (Hermalin and Liu 1990: 340, Shen and Jia 1991).

Table 1: One-child rates (OCR) and one-child certificate rates (OCCR) for Beijing municipality and Beijing city districts, 1979–88

Year	Municipality OCR	Municipality OCCR	City District OCR	City District OCCR
1979	83.96	45.57	92.54	67.71
1980	90.97	83.44	97.95	94.16
1981	89.34	85.00	98.94	96.87
1982	88.92	90.67	99.49	99.35
1983	92.75	95.35	99.83	99.84
1984	93.20	–	99.89	–
1985	94.18	93.63	99.88	94.08
1986	92.72	92.22	99.88	92.76
1987	92.82	93.54	99.83	99.73
1988	95.31	92.75	99.85	99.82

Source: *Beijing cishi* 1990. 69–71.

The Four Cases

Based on the research design of studying a factory and a residential area in each of the two settings, the four cases were selected by the Chinese collaborating institutions in cooperation with local authorities. Although the women in the cases were studied following official agreements made by the Chinese collaborating institutions, neither the officials involved in the cases nor the women interviewed were necessarily able to anticipate possible negative consequences of taking part in the study. An attempt has therefore been made to protect the people involved by omitting the exact names and localities of the cases. However, as Martin Whyte has noted, even changing the names of places and people will not protect people if the authorities do decide to track them down and cause them harm, just as Chinese scholars who collaborate with Westerners are at risk if the political atmosphere worsens (Whyte 1992b: 322). The cases have been labelled merely the Beijing and Shenyang residential areas and the Shenyang factory. Also included are the Beijing factory studied in 1991, which is referred to as the 'district factory', and a second Beijing factory studied in 1992, referred to as the 'Beijing factory'. While the details of the location of the cases and the names of the factories and residential areas are not disclosed, the fact that all three factories were successful state enterprises is important for an understanding of the interaction between women and birth planning workers and of women's management of policy consequences.

While the Shenyang factory had been designated a model unit in both production and birth planning work, in fact all three factories and the Shenyang residential area claimed to have 100 per cent one-child rates and no unplanned births. Even though a critical stance should be taken towards such official statistics, since it is unlikely that birth planning workers would admit to there having been unplanned births, I do not find the high one-child rates and rates of planned births unlikely as the women interviewed supported the claim. It has often been a problem for foreign scholars studying China that they are allowed access only to model units, i.e. units that have been designated by an authority as worthy of emulation by other units. In the case of this study it has not been a disadvantage as the aim was precisely to study the context in which the implementation of the one-child family policy works, i.e. where the policy goal of only one child per couple is achieved.

Not only are all births first-parity births and unplanned births more or less non-existent in these model units, the work of birth planning workers in implementing the policy is also exemplary. As one Shenyang woman described the situation: 'Because this street committee has been appointed a model unit within birth planning, birth planning workers are very attentive and thoughtful in carrying out home visits.' This apparently well-functioning interaction between women and birth planning workers is an important aspect of the very phenomenon that the project seeks to understand.

The examples of problems between birth planning workers and women were given by women from the two residential area cases who did not work in model units. This leads to the question of whether a more valid representation of consequences of the policy for urban women would be obtained by studying immigrants in Hong Kong because they would be free of the constraints of being obliged to voice opinions following the policy. However, interviewing immigrants would not give an answer to the research question posed for this study as the aim is to understand how women perceive and handle the one-child family policy *in their everyday life context* . As the study is concerned with how women perceive and manage the policy within the framework of the political and cultural context in which they are located, interviewing for instance immigrants to Hong Kong would not meet the purpose of the study. My contention is that the study of the implementation of the policy and of women's management of consequences in model units will reveal a cultural pattern that due to its very distinction from the situation of the majority of the Chinese population, may to some degree explain the urban demographic success of the policy.

计划生育

Demographic Change in the People's Republic of China

> Because the present number and composition of women of reproductive age is a historically created objective fact, the most important task for birth planning work is to work hard to lower the total fertility rate in order to meet the objectives of controlling population increase.
>
> *Peng Peiyun 1991: 10*

The one-child policy is closely linked with the post-Mao development strategy and as such has its roots in the quest for modernization. Since 1949 the size and growth of population have been a political issue in China with leadership opinions differing as to the necessity of restricting population increase.[1] During the first two decades of the People's Republic, opinions within the leadership varied from the extremes of population growth being viewed as a great danger on the one hand and as a positive contribution to the development of the nation on the other hand. Early PRC population policies were advocated in terms of better health for mothers and children. However, predating the one-child family policy was a distinctly quantitative population policy, known as the *wan-xi-shao* policy, introduced in the early

---

1. For a study of population development in China prior to 1949, see Ho 1959.

1970s. The explicit aim of this policy was to limit fertility and curb the population growth rate.

In this chapter a broad picture of demographic change in the People's Republic of China from 1949 to the early 1990s is drawn. The large socio-economic variations among the provinces and the demographic implications of these are not taken into consideration.[2] Rather, the overall demographic change – leading to the situation which implementation of the one-child policy was meant to address – is summarized. Emphasis is put on the cultural and political context in terms of the links between gender ideology, population policy ideology and demographic development. The three central elements of the chapter are thus demographic change, population policy ideology and gender ideology.

Basically, demographic change is influenced by the three components birth, death and migration. Since 1949 migration has had only a minor effect on demographic development in the PRC, whereas changes in mortality rates have had a significant bearing on population growth rates. Politically as well culturally, birth has been the central component of population change in China since 1949. At the level of the family as well as at the level of leadership policy formulation, birth in China cannot be understood without considering the gender ideology of the Confucian family tradition. Furthermore, birth is the main demographic component that can be manipulated by population policy in order to regulate population size.[3]

A population policy is formulated on the basis of a politically based ideological interpretation of the demographic situation in question. The implication is that population policies are politic-

---

2. For a full analysis of demographic developments in the PRC, see Banister 1987. Banister's book is the first major study of the Chinese population prepared in the West since the 1982 PRC census. Demographic statistics used in this chapter are based mainly on Banister's analysis of official data as well as her own calculations which are based on official data, her cut-off point for incorporation of data being January 1985. Demography as an academic discipline was re-established in China in the late 1970s. Since then institutes of demography have been established at major universities. For an overview of the institutional structure and substantive content of demography in China see Greenhalgh 1988. For accounts of provincial variation in demographic change see Banister 1987, Peng Xizhi 1991, Tien 1991 as well as the China Population Series mentioned in Chapter 2 of this volume, footnote 2.

3. In 1990 Maurice King suggested that preventive health care programmes in poor countries be reconsidered as they seemed only to contribute to tightening the 'demographic trap'. Until then it had not been deemed ethically *comme il faut* to view mortality as a factor that could be manoeuvred to reduce population growth rates. See King 1990.

ally defined by the government in office and as such the economic and social desirability of a population policy target is politically motivated. At the root of a population policy is of course the demographic situation itself. However, the interpretation of the causes of whatever aspect of the demographic situation being viewed as a problem, rather than the demographic situation as such, ultimately determines the formulation of the policy (Tien 1973). The overall framework of the interpretation of and solutions to the 'population problem' is referred to as the population policy ideology. Once the problem has been identified, the formulation of a quantitative or demographic population policy, whether pro- or anti-natalist, will include the various targets stipulated by government for the size and composition of the population as well as the means to achieve the targets (Matthiessen 1984: 179). In sum, a population policy is ultimately politically defined, and as such is an expression of both a political ideology and of power relations within the leadership group that formulates the policy (Tien 1973).[4]

A population policy aimed at restricting fertility is also defined or at least influenced by cultural assumptions of gender. One of the central problems encountered by the one-child family policy has been that traditional Confucian son-preference has worked against the policy. Son-preference exists in terms of the need for practical and economic support of parents in old age and as a cultural assumption. Demographic change in this chapter is viewed in the context that a population policy is politically defined as well as deeply rooted in cultural assumptions, including gender assumptions. The first two sections of this chapter present an overview of changes in mortality and fertility levels as well as population policy prior to the one-child family policy. The third section of the chapter delineates the formulation of the one-child family policy. In the fourth section the problem of a gradually increasing sex ratio at birth which has arisen in the 1980s as a consequence of the policy is discussed.[5]

---

4. Commoner 1975 as well as Lappé and Schurman 1990 summarize various interpretations of the cause of the 'population problem' as well as the remedial measures and actions consequently implemented to resolve the problem.

5. Demographic consequences of the policy that are not directly related to cultural gender assumptions, as for instance the skewed age-composition of the population are not addressed here. For studies on the ageing population, see for instance Tu and Ting 1988 and Zhou *et al.* 1990.

Mortality Decline: the First Two Decades 1949–70

Are people primarily *hands*, i.e. producers – in Chinese, *renshou* (people hands) – or are they first of all *mouths*, i.e. consumers – *renkou* (people mouths)? This was the basic issue of the dispute that characterized formulation of a population policy from 1949 to 1970 and severely influenced demographic change as a result. Population policies of the period did not manage to direct demographic development. However, while the dispute raged as to whether a large population was an asset or a great danger to overall development of the nation, quite a considerable population increase took place. During the first three decades from 1949 to the end of the 1970s, an immense demographic change took place as China completed her demographic transition from high to low fertility and mortality rates.

Mortality rates began declining in the 1950s. Owing to the conclusion of many years of war, maintenance of public order, redistribution of agricultural land, distribution of grain to areas of the country that lacked sufficient supplies and the establishment of an extensive preventive health care system, mortality rates declined markedly until the Great Leap Forward in 1957.[6] The Great Leap was followed by several years of natural as well as man-made calamities leading to famine and increased mortality levels. After the famine, health conditions returned to previous levels within a couple of years, and since then mortality levels have remained relatively low. As fertility remained high during the first two decades, China's population increased markedly. By 1970, during the course of only twenty years, it had thus increased by some 300 million to 820 million. The population policies formulated in the 1950s and 1960s were first of all directed by overall political and economic ideologies, rather than by the actual demographic situation. Thus the development of population policies during the first twenty years of the PRC reflected a basic controversy between a Marxist and a Malthusian interpretation of the population issue.

With hindsight one could speculate that, had the leadership not entrenched itself so deeply within Marxist and Malthusian ideologies that it lost sight of the demographic realities of China, it might in fact have been able to prevent the rapid population

---

6. For a detailed account of preventive health care services, which since 1949 made significant inroads on disease and mortality, see Banister 1987, Chapter 3.

increase that took place up until the 1970s. It was this increase in the first twenty years of the PRC that led to a doubling of population in forty years, from 559 million in 1949 to 1.13 billion in 1990. Such hindsight would, however, imply that one could disregard the historical and cultural context of the desire for many children as well as the social and economic conditions of fertility.

In what was probably his first announcement on the population issue, Mao Zedong stated in 1949 that, 'Of all things in the world, people are the most precious' (Mao 1969: 1401). As H. Yuan Tien has noted, this would remain the leading premise of numerous subsequent pronouncements on the control of population numbers (Tien 1973: 179). It remained so during the first thirty years of the PRC, until the death of Mao Zedong in 1976 and the subsequent formulation of the one-child family policy by his successors.

In 1949, at the founding of the People's Republic of China, the total population stood at 559 million. In August 1949 the United States Department of State, in a White Paper on *United States Relations with China*, had advanced the opinion that the Chinese population, due to a doubling of population numbers during the eighteenth and nineteenth centuries, was 'creating an unbearable pressure upon the land' (quoted in Tien 1973: 177). Chairman Mao Zedong's statement on people being the most precious of all things was issued as a response to this claim. While stating that a large population was an asset to the economic development of China, Mao disputed the Malthusian argument that food production could not keep pace with population increase and maintained that, 'It is a very good thing that China has a big population. Even if China's population multiplies many times, she is fully capable of finding a solution; the solution is production' (Mao 1969: 1400). During the first years of the PRC, the issue of population numbers was not regarded by the leadership as a problem. However, in 1953 an emerging acknowledgement within the leadership of the existence of a 'population problem' could be discerned, and a period of dispute and indecision within the central leadership concerning the population issue set in (Aird 1963: 40).

Why was a 'population problem' recognized at this time and how was the problem defined? Varying reasons for the recognition of a problem have been suggested. Food shortages and unemployment highlighted the discrepancy between population numbers and resources (Aird 1963: 46–49, Aird 1990: 20). Recognition may also have been associated with the experience gained from the policy of stabilizing the urban population, keeping the rural population in the rural areas, and encouraging migration to thinly populated regions of the nation (Tien 1973: 189). A speech by Shao Lizi, a non-party member of the State Council before the First National People's Congress, on 18 September 1954, in which he called for birth planning to be implemented, indicated that a change in attitudes to the question of population was taking place within the leadership. According to H. Yuan Tien, 'Shao introduced the subject in language that discredited Malthus and argued for birth control in terms of the welfare of mothers and children during the transition to socialism' (Tien 1973: 176). John S. Aird notes that Shao Lizi had been an advocate of birth control before 1949, and that 'Shao reiterated Mao's argument that a large population was a good thing but, citing recurrent natural calamities and the slow pace of economic development in China, he added that 'in an environment beset with difficulties, it appears that there should be a limit set' (Aird 1973: 445). Shao, and thereby presumably the leadership, were thus dissociating themselves from Malthusianism, while at the same time acknowledging that there was indeed a conflict between population and resources.

On the one hand, the leadership had to recognize that there was actually a problem in the balance between population numbers and the allocation and distribution of resources. On the other hand, due to the Marxist state ideology the problem could not be addressed in a manner at all related to Malthusianism. This was the core of the dilemma confronting the leadership in its formulation of a population policy. The fluctuating and conflicting statements and attitudes from the leadership during the 1950s and 1960s have been interpreted by Western scholars as the result of a Marxist lack of a theory on population. As John S. Aird puts it, the problem was essentially that:

> Convincing the orthodox Marxists was made all the more difficult by the doctrinaire line taken by the Party leaders in the past and by the lack of any good Marxist peg on which to hang the rationale for a family limitation campaign. (Aird 1973: 448)

On the one hand, the ideology of Malthusianism was not compatible with the view of people as primarily producers and therefore as the most precious things in the world. On the other hand, Marxism lacked a theory of population that could be applied as a rationale for limiting population growth. Except for the concept of 'relative overpopulation' in capitalist society, Marxism does not include an actual population theory. Marx repudiated Malthus's theory that the root of poverty was overpopulation and asserted that poverty was a built-in effect of the capitalist system, which maintained a surplus labour force in order to keep production costs down, thus generating a relative overpopulation. Malthus related population and population growth to consumption, whereas Engels and Marx related them to production. The fundamental disagreement between the Malthusian and the Marxist positions concerns the interpretation of the root cause of the 'population problem'. The Malthusian position is that the 'population problem', which is viewed as a lack of balance between resources and people, is caused by too large a number of people and too rapid a population growth. Whereas the Marxist position is that the cause of the imbalance originates in socio-economic conditions and particularly in the way in which the resources of capitalist society are managed with high fertility being a symptom of overall developmental problems rather than a problem in itself.[7]

In spite of the dilemma facing the leadership, a policy on the planning of births was formulated and a provision on birth planning was included in a draft twelve-year plan for agriculture in January 1956 (White 1994: 268). Tyrene White argues that at this point a significant change took place in the meaning and implication of birth planning. Intellectual, urban and politically active women had since the early 1950s pushed for access to and legalization of contraceptives, with a view to individual control of their fertility. Meanwhile, the inclusion of the planning of fertility into the overall economic planning amounted to a shift from the objective of securing qualitatively improved reproductive health to the objective of reducing fertility quantitatively to fit into the overall development strategy (White 1994).

Although a change had taken place, a general agreement on the interpretation of the 'population problem' had not been reached within the leadership, and the population policy controversy with its abrupt changes in official statements on whether or not there was a population problem became quite obvious during the Hundred Flowers Campaign (1956–57). During this campaign the population issue was openly debated. The campaign initiated an

---

7. For an account of the controversy between the Malthusian and the Marxist version of the population issue, see for instance Bondestam 1983.

intellectual debate within the fields of literature, art and natural sciences. The aim was to stimulate new solutions to the economic problems China was facing by encouraging the participation of the intellectual elite in an open debate. During the Hundred Flowers Campaign, warnings against further population increase were put forward by a number of Western-trained social scientists. Prominent among these was economist Ma Yinchu who in his 'New Population Theory' (*Xin renkou lun*) argued that China's huge population and its rapid growth rate were the chief obstacles to economic development (Ma 1957). In September 1957 the intellectuals who had stated themselves in favour of population regulation were subsequently denounced as 'bourgeois rightists', and Ma Yinchu was criticized for applying a Malthusian theory of population based on capitalist society to a socialist society where it could not be valid (Chen Zhongli 1979). The debate between Ma Yinchu and the Marxist theoreticians continued until 1960, when Ma Yinchu was dismissed from his post as President of Peking University, marking the end of the two-sided phase of the debate (Freeberne 1965: 7, Aird 1963: 54).

The criticism of Professor Ma Yinchu, which in all probability was linked to the launching of the Great Leap Forward in 1957, illustrates how the policies on population were primarily directed by the overall political and economic ideologies. The criticism of Ma Yinchu for putting forward the view that mechanization would result in surplus labour was linked to a need for labour during the Great Leap Forward. The year 1957 marked the end of the first five-year plan, during which the Soviet pattern of con-centration on the development of heavy industry had been emulated. In China the result had been a starving out of agricultural resources. In order to end this trend and to initiate an increase of agricultural products, the Great Leap Forward was launched. The main aim was to increase agricultural production. By the end of 1957 and early 1958 large campaigns were initiated to build irrigation systems and water reservoirs. The mobilization of huge numbers of people resulted in a great demand for labour. Thus, the issue of controlling births was dropped, and the population came to be regarded as an asset rather than an obstacle to the development of the economy, and in the official view, the problem of population once again ceased to exist (Aird 1963: 51).

During 1962, following the Great Leap, which resulted in a serious economic crisis as well as famine and increased mortality rates, a population policy was again formulated (Aird 1973: 457).

It is unclear whether the objective of the 1960s policy was to protect the health of women and children or to control population growth as the official opinion that a large population was an asset was put forward simultaneously with women being advised to use contraceptives (Freeberne 1965: 7). Possibly a combination of the two was the aim, as indicated by the following quotation from a 1962 newspaper:

> There is a distinction in substance between *planned childbearing* and birth control or sterilization advocated by the Stoics. *We are not overpopulated; on the contrary, we need people.* Ours is a vast country; more labouring heroes are needed to construct it into a richer and stronger country. *In our country, men are precious. It is just because of this that it becomes more important to improve the physique of the next generation through planned childbearing.* (*Yang-cheng Wen-pao*, Canton 2 March 1962, quoted in Freeberne 1965: 12)

The second population policy phase continued until the inception of the Cultural Revolution. During the Cultural Revolution (1966–69) there was some confusion as to whether birth planning was to be considered a Maoist or a revisionist policy, and the conclusion was finally reached that it was a Maoist policy (Aird 1973: 459–460). Meanwhile, during the first decades of the PRC at the micro level of the family, planning of family size took place within the cultural context of a Confucian family tradition.

If the objective of the two first population policies was aimed at reducing fertility in order to limit population growth, they were not successful. Fertility rates had begun rising in the late 1940s reaching a total fertility rate (TFR) of 6.14 in 1949. During the 1950s, TFRs rose unevenly from 5.81 in 1950 to 6.40 in 1957, with a fertility peak from mid-1954 to mid-1955, and a slight dip in births from mid-1955 to mid-1956, and another peak in births from mid-1957 to mid-1958. During and after the Great Leap, TFRs fluctuated reaching a low 3.29 in 1961 with a negative rate of natural increase. After the crisis of the Great Leap Forward there was an unprecedented surge in fertility from mid-1962 to mid-1964. However, except for the years of disaster and calamities during the Great Leap Forward, population increased significantly during the period from 1949–70, from a total population of 559 million in 1949 to 820 million in 1970 (Banister 1987).

The increase in population numbers was mainly due to two factors. The first was the decline of mortality rates. During the 1950s there was a drop by almost half of the mortality rate of the population as a whole from a crude death rate of 38 in 1949 to 22.06 in 1959. The post-Leap famine led to a sharp rise of mortality rates to 44.60 in 1960, after which the downward trend continued (Banister 1987: 352). The other reason for the huge population increase during this period was that the overall socio-economic situation made the realization of the cultural tradition of many children an advantage to the rural family. The demographic change that took place during the first two decades of the PRC was thus influenced mainly by such tangible factors as the decrease of mortality rates and by economic circumstances, making it possible and advantageous for the rural majority of the population to have many children. However, the more elusive cultural aspects of family tradition and gender relations must be included in any analysis in order to grasp the context in which these factors resulted in high population growth rates.

Confucian Basis of the Population Increase

Prior to 1949 the main difference in family size and structure was between social classes. The well-off families had been large in size and composition, whereas family sizes for the poor majority of the population had been small. After 1949 the pattern changed from a difference between social classes to a rural–urban difference, and by the end of the first two decades urban families were becoming smaller while more children were surviving in rural families (Croll 1985a). There are no accurate data for the child mortality rate before 1949, but it is estimated to have been between 30 and 50 per cent (Croll 1985a: 10). According to a study of landless families in a Yunnan province village in the late 1930s, only one child survived of the six or seven born to every landless family (Fei Hsiao-tung and Chang Chih-i 1945, quoted in Stacey 1983: 88). Lower mortality enabled rural families to accomplish the Confucian ideal of a large family with many sons. The major problem in implementing the one-child family policy can be traced to this enduring traditional Confucian son-preference. Young parents are unlikely to accept only one child if the child is female. The reasons are socio-economic, just as they have historical and cultural roots in the traditional Confucian patriarchal family system.[8]

8. Although there is no static *traditional* Chinese society or family, as both have developed and changed over centuries, the term 'traditional' is applied here as an abbreviation for some general tendencies which none the less do exist.

In order to shed light on population development during the first decades of the PRC and as a background to understanding the reaction of the populace to the one-child family policy, we shall now look at how the Chinese family developed in the relationship between ideal family size and composition and the possibilities for realizing the ideal.

Based on centuries-old Confucian precepts concerning family size and function, the extended family was an ideal shared by all and was as such the ultimate aim of all families, whether or not they were in reality able to realize the ideal. In the extended family, several generations of married couples live with their children under one roof, sharing the joint responsibility of family political, financial and social functions as well as securing continuous ancestor worship (Baker 1979: 1–2). Confucianism is practically synonymous with traditional Chinese society in so far as over the centuries Confucianism has developed an ideology and a social system striving to sustain a society of harmony and hierarchy in which every individual knew his or her place (Stacey 1983: 30). The family was the basic unit of society, and directives for well-ordered relations in both family and society at large were laid down in *the five human relations*. If the rules were adhered to, conflict between members of the family as well as between family and state authorities would be avoided. Each member of the family and of society was strictly bound by the obligations and obedience owed to other members. Confucianism was a protocol regulating all social relations in the family and in society at large, based on a patriarchal, patrilineal and patrilocal family system.

The hierarchical rules governing social relations in the family were based on generation, age and sex, with the elder dominating the younger, and men dominating women (Baker 1979: 20–21). It was the responsibility of the eldest male as patriarch of the family to maintain an unbroken family line and to ensure that the family stayed together on the soil of the ancestors. Hence ancestor worship was an expression of and contribution to stability and family continuity. Since continuity could only be ensured by male offspring, the preference for sons was strong. The family was patrilineal and the fundamental family group was based on men. For men and women this resulted in two totally different perspectives on the family. Women lived their lives in two families, first in the family into which they were born, and then in the family into which they married. For a man the family structure was an unbroken line from his ancestors to himself and on to his descendants, in which power, property and status were passed on from generation to generation. In contrast to the unbroken male family structure, women were never full members of a family and could not inherit property (Stacey 1983: 38–39, Wolf 1972).

The subordination of women in the family and in society in general is symbolically illustrated by the practice of footbinding. In all social classes, the feet of young girls were mutilated and bound in order to realize an ideal of beauty.[9] One explanation of the practice of footbinding is that bound feet were a condition for women to marry into a family of higher social status in a stratified system that was open to class mobility (Stacey 1983: 40–42). Within the Confucian family system, a woman's only prospect to achieve security and respect was to marry. This right to marriage was honoured universally (Stacey 1983: 51–52).[10] Because her main function in life was to produce sons for her husband's family, whatever status and influence a woman could hope to achieve were connected with her role as the mother of sons. As Francis Hsu writes in a description of marriage, based on a study of a semi-rural community in southwest China in the early 1940s:

> The emphasis is not upon partnership between the man and his wife, but upon woman's duty to her husband and especially to her parents-in-law. The woman is obliged to produce sons, which are her indispensable contribution to matrimony. (Hsu 1949: 105)

The extended family was an ideal. In reality, however, it existed only among the rich elite. There was a direct link between wealth, high socio-political status and extended families on the one hand and between poverty, low socio-political status and families with low fertility and less complexity on the other (Croll 1985a: 6, Stacey 1983: 56). This became particularly evident at the beginning of the twentieth century when China was in crisis. The last dynasty had fallen and, while threats from the Western powers and Japan loomed on the horizon, an agricultural crisis that undermined the material and ideological foundation of the family

---

9. The practice of footbinding started during the Song dynasty (960–1279) and was probably linked to a revival of Confucianism and the establishment of greater gender difference.

10. One study found that in the late 1920s 'fewer than one in a thousand women and three in a thousand men never married'; see Barcley, George *et al.* 1976. A Reassessment of the Demography of Traditional Rural China. In *Population Index.* Vol. 42, No. 4, 606–635, quoted in Tien 1991: 30.

system developed. For the peasants of China the agricultural crisis became what Judith Stacey has termed *a realization crisis* in so far as the majority of the rural population was unable to survive materially and was forced to take measures contrary to the principles of Confucian family life.

High death rates influenced both the size and the complexity of the family. The elder generation did not survive long enough to live together with both children and grandchildren, fewer children were born to poor families and fewer survived. Girls were the first victims when food became scarce since boys were needed in their natal family to provide labour and old age security for their parents and to continue the family line. Girls would in any case leave their natal family at marriage, whereupon their obligations were towards the family of their husband. Child mortality was highest among girls, notably because they received less than their share of food, but also because of female infanticide; this was considered a legitimate way of ensuring the survival of other family members. All in all, it was viewed as a simple necessity (Baker 1979: 6). One village study during the crisis at the beginning of the century showed that, in the age group of zero to 5 years there were only 35 girls to 100 boys (Fei Hsiao-tung 1939, quoted in Croll 1985a: 11). The sex ratio of a population is defined as the number of males per 100 females. It varies among population groups due to differential migration by sex or differential mortality by sex. The sex ratio among live births is biologically very stable and under normal circumstances is between 105 and 106 boys per 100 girls (Johansson and Nygren 1991: 35–36); if unbiased health conditions and more or less equal nutrition is provided to males and females, male mortality rates are higher at every age from zero to the highest age attained (Coale 1991: 518).

The family form which took shape under the leadership of the Communist Party emanated from the cooperation between party and peasants. This cooperation was initiated in 1927, when the CCP was driven out of the cities to the rural areas. The peasants' realization crisis and their desire to regain their family form became the backbone of CCP family policy. In the words of Judith Stacey, peasant patriarchs moved 'backward towards revolution' as they were prepared to revolt in order to regain family forms according to Confucian prescriptions (Stacey 1983: 104–105). Because the CCP implicitly accepted the family form of the peasants, the peasants came to shape and realize the CCP family.

With the 1950 Marriage Law and the reforms in agriculture, which were the CCP response to the crisis in agriculture, the family was transformed and reconstructed. Following the resolution of the crisis in agriculture and the distribution of land, many rural families came closer to realizing their family ideal. Improved health and hygienic conditions, increased stability in food distribution for the majority of the people as well as improved medical supplies throughout the country resulted in diminishing malnutrition and illness leading to lower mortality rates (Croll 1985a: 15). The rural family became larger both in size and complexity, while at the same time a series of economic factors made a large family an advantage. With collectivization of rural land, the individual peasant lost ownership of the land. However, the family continued to be the basic unit of production as well as consumption, moreover the family economy became dependent on the number of members available not only for collective production but also for production on the private plot (it was here that vegetables and other food to supplement basic grain rations were produced for the family itself as well as various sideline products for sale).

Marriage and the birth of children were the only ways of optimizing the family economy – simply by having more hands working. Also, young children contributed to the family economy by taking on light tasks and thereby releasing adult labour for heavier or more complicated work processes. Grain distribution also favoured large families (Banister 1987: 129). In addition, the family still had good reason to prefer sons to daughters. Although a daughter could contribute to the family economy and her position in the family was improved both socially, economically and legally, a woman earned less than a man and marriage was still patrilocal, meaning that daughters would leave their parents while sons would stay and secure the parents' old age.

In urban China several socio-economic factors combined to limit fertility. The need for family labour decreased with the establishment of state and collective enterprises, and as the main element of CCP policy for gender equality, women entered the labour market. Parents were induced to have fewer children as child mortality rates decreased while expenses for support of each child increased. Competition for entrance into the few educational institutions as well as for health services and material goods also increased. A fixed salary and pension scheme for employees of state enterprises furthermore meant that parents would not be economically dependent on their children in old age. Compared to rural China, the economic dependency between parents and child was less strong in urban areas and the need for labour in the family was significantly lower in urban than in rural China. The combination of these factors lowered urban fertility rates, while rural families enlarged their families both to fulfil the Confucian ideal and because the new economic situation allowed them to do so.

In sum, China's mortality transition took place most rapidly in the 1950s. In response to socio-economic influences, fertility decline began in China's cities during the mid-1960s. A parallel fertility decline did not take place in rural China until much later when, in the 1970s, the government initiated a population policy with the explicit aim of reducing fertility.

Fertility Decline: the 1970s

In the early 1970s a population policy with the explicit objective of reducing population growth was initiated. The measures implemented to reduce fertility were summed up in the slogan 'later-sparser-fewer' (*wan-xi-shao*) signifying later marriages and child-bearing, longer intervals between children, and fewer children. The policy is thus often referred to as the *wan-xi-shao* policy. During the 1970s, in the course of less than a decade, fertility rates declined at rates unprecedented in a primarily non-industrialized agricultural nation. By the end of the decade, women were having half as many children as earlier. Birth rates declined from 37 per 1,000 in 1971 to 21 per 1,000 in 1978, corresponding to a decline in the total fertility rate from 5.82 in 1970 to 2.85 in 1977, reaching 2.72 and 2.75 in 1978 and 1979 (Banister 1987).

Whereas scholars by and large agree that the demographic results of the *wan-xi-shao* policy are impressive, views differ as to the methods by which these results were achieved. There is also disagreement about how the political ideology underlying the policy should be interpreted. Although clearly the aim of the policy was to reduce the population growth rate, the official ideology of 'people as the most precious of all things' was maintained. The official population policy ideology during the 1970s was that people were the decisive factor in the productive forces, being first of all producers and secondly consumers. Human beings were viewed as the most important resource in developing and expanding production and thereby raising living standards. Based on the experience in China since 1949, the official view was still to reject Malthus's theory that the production of food would not be able to keep up with human reproduction. A basic argument put forward by the leadership was that, although China was a developing nation with a low standard of living, hunger as well as unemployment had basically been eliminated. Since 1949 China had not become poorer despite an increasing population, but on the contrary had become richer and the standard of living had been raised. Thus planned development of the population was China's policy, under the assumption that, if the material production is planned, then human reproduction would and could also be planned (Yu [1973] 1980 and Chi [1973] 1980). Planned population development was to take place in the following way:

> In order to realize planned population growth, what we are doing is, on the basis of energetically developing production and improving the people's living standards, to develop medical and health services throughout the rural and urban areas and strengthen our work in maternity and child-care, so as to reduce the mortality rate on the one hand and regulate the birthrate by birth planning on the other. (Yu [1973] 1980: 95–96)

While the objective of the official population ideology of reducing population increase through a dual planning of production and reproduction was ideologically supported by the writings of Friedrich Engels, China concurrently accused the United States and the Soviet Union of forcing population control on the nations of the South (Banister 1987: 166). In 1974 at the United Nations World Population Conference in Bucharest, a representative of the Chinese delegation said:

> The superpowers raise the false alarm of a 'population explosion' and paint a depressing picture of the future of mankind ... The pessimistic views spread by the superpowers are utterly ground-less and are being propagated with ulterior motives ... Any inter-national technical cooperation and assistance in population matters must follow the principles of complete voluntariness of the parties concerned, strict respect for state sovereignty, absence of any strings attached, and promotion of self-reliance of the recipient countries. We are firmly opposed to the superpowers intervening by any means in the population policy of other countries on the pretext of what they call 'population explosion' or 'over-

population'. We are firmly opposed to the attempt of some international organizations to infringe on the sovereignty of recipient countries by conditioning aid on restricting their population growth rate. (*Peking Review* 1974, quoted in Banister 1987: 166)

Why was China advocating domestic fertility limitation with the explicit aim of curbing population increase, while simultaneously condemning the attempts of the United States of America and the Soviet Union at limiting population growth rates? Judith Banister interprets the views that were being voiced internationally by the Chinese delegation as being simply a political rhetoric employed to disguise what was actually a coercive policy implementation practice in China. According to Banister, 'Some time early in the 1970s a strong element of compulsion was incorporated into the family planning program, thus setting it apart from every other family planning program in the world' (Banister 1987: 165). The view of coercion as a significant factor in reducing fertility rates during the *wan-xi-shao* policy is shared by John S. Aird (Aird 1978). An opposing view is that fertility was mainly reduced by way of socio-economic improvements including the improved role and status of women. Thus the *wan-xi-shao* policy and the ideology of people as the most precious asset have together been emphasized in the international debate on the population problem as being an example of a policy that succeeded in achieving an impressive fertility reduction; primarily by improving living standards and the status of women rather than by imposing isolated quantitative quotas for fertility reduction and applying coercive measures to fulfil these (see for instance Egerö 1980: 204, Lappé and Schurman 1990: 60, Pradervand 1980).

A similar set of opposing interpretations pertains to the question of the transition from the *wan-xi-shao* policy to the one-child family policy. Did an essential change of population policy ideology take place with this transition or not? According to the most common version of the transition, the one-child family policy is basically an intensified continuation of the *wan-xi-shao* policy. The main difference between the two policies is that the fertility limit set by the leadership policy was tightened from two children to one child. State intervention, national fertility plans and the setting of quotas are common to both policies (see for instance Aird 1990, Banister 1987 and Hou 1981: 69). In contrast, another interpretation views the transition from the *wan-xi-shao* policy to the one-child family policy as an expression of a definite shift in population policy ideology, this being reformulated in 1978–79 by the post-Mao leadership. Malthus was resurrected and population growth itself came to be perceived as the main obstacle to improving standards of living (Keyfitz 1984: 23–24). Symbolic of this shift in ideology, Professor Ma Yinchu was rehabilitated. This shift led to a reformulation of the role of the population problem in China's development strategy, and new policy objectives as well as to new measures of policy implementation. All in all, it remains unclear whether the tightening of targets and measures was a matter of a qualitatively distinct policy or if the apparent differences are limited to the level of rhetoric. At present, the political ideologies of the two policies in a comparative perspective and the implementation of the *wan-xi-shao* policy have, to my knowledge, not been thoroughly studied. The issue of the role of coercion in lowering fertility during the 1970s and the issue of whether a shift in population policy ideology did in fact take place in the late 1970s remain unresolved.

Changing roles and the higher status of women have been emphasized as a central force behind the lowering of fertility rates in the 1970s. Notwithstanding the enormous advances that have taken place in regard to education and paid employment of women, there is also evidence that a quantitative measure of two children per couple was advanced as far back as the early 1960s (Freeberne 1965: 12, Kane 1977: 208). This might imply that the promotion of the health of mothers and children was to some degree political rhetoric rather than a primary goal. The *wan-xi-shao* policy also included an attempt to implement a national plan for the annual number of births according to a quota system (Croll 1985a: 21), and at local levels it is likely that there was widespread use of birth quotas based on local population plans (Aird 1978: 239). The promotion of better health for women and children would then have been promoted with the primary goal not of fulfilling the needs and interests of women and children but rather as an instrumental means of achieving overall developmental goals. Empirical studies retrospectively investigating at the micro-level the interaction between birth planning institutions and the populace during the *wan-xi-shao* policy may some day enlighten us to the facts that are well known, first of all to the women who gave birth to their children under that policy. However, there is no doubt that, regardless of whether or not a change of ideology took place, both targets and measures of the population policy were tightened up with the transition to the one-child family policy.

The One-Child Family Policy

As we have seen, in 1978–79 China's population policy was reformulated by her post-Mao leadership. The population problem recognized in the late 1970s was based on the demographic fact that during the period from 1949 to the end of the 1970s China had completed her demographic transition from high to low fertility and mortality rates. Prior to the formulation of the one-child family policy, the population policy of the 1970s had led to a remarkable decline of total fertility rates from 5.81 in 1970 to 2.72 in 1978. However, despite the relatively low total fertility rate, population increase would continue for many years to come due to the demographic momentum. Demographic momentum implies that a population will continue to increase long after replacement level fertility has been achieved, because the young age structure of the total population will produce large cohorts in the childbearing ages for decades to come. Surveys in the late 1970s indicated that 38.6 per cent of the population was 15 and below, while 65 per cent of the population was born after 1949 and was aged 30 and below. Based on this age structure, calculations indicated that, if every woman gave birth to two children, the population would continue to increase over a 72–year period (Tien 1981: 44). The introduction of the one-child policy was explained by the demographic facts of the young age structure and of the number of women entering their childbearing years that would rise from the beginning of the 1980s, as well as by what was seen as new knowledge about the consequences for economic development of population growth and by a clarification of population theories.

The Eleventh Central Committee Third Plenary Meeting in 1978 marked the change to a new development strategy emphasizing the Four Modernizations. The meeting may be regarded as the event marking the transition from the previous population policy of the 1970s to the one-child family policy. In June 1979, CCP Chairman Hua Guofeng officially presented the revised population policy and stated that reduction of the population growth rate was of 'strategic importance' to the development of the Four Modernizations (Hua 1979). In applying the culturally encoded political term 'strategic importance', the leadership was emphasizing the extreme importance of the policy to the safety and continuity of China (Potter and Potter 1990: 226).

An early elaboration of the post-Mao population policy was a 1979 *People's Daily* article by Chen Muhua, then leader of the State Council Birth Planning Group.[11] She stated that it was necessary to acknowledge that, under the present conditions in China, the development of the national economy and improvement of living standards and the employment situation were being impeded by the rapid population growth rate. She repeated Chairman Hua Guofeng's message that the issue at the time was not whether more or fewer children should be born, but rather 'an important strategic question' *(zhanlüexing de da wenti)* related to the productive forces, the development of the Four Modernizations and the construction of socialism. The new population policy was thus based on the interpretation that continuous population growth would hamper the development of the Four Modernizations, since additional population would consume capital that could otherwise be accumulated for investment. According to this interpretation, the aspect of human beings as consumers will be predominant where production is relatively low, as human beings will consume the bulk of their production in order to support themselves and leave little to be accumulated by society (Chen [1979] 1981: 2).

Indeed, population numbers in China have increased rapidly since 1949. At the beginning of the century, China's population stood at about 400 million. Over the next fifty years up to 1949, the population increased by some 100 million to 559 million. Then, from 1949 over a period of only twenty years, China's population increased by some 300 million reaching 800 million by the beginning of the 1970s – 820 million in 1970 and 842 million in 1971. Her population at the 1982 census stood at a total of 1,008 million. By the 1990 census, the number had increased to 1,133 million, reflecting a growth rate of 12.45 equivalent to a mean annual growth rate of 1.48 per cent (*Zhongguo renkou ziliao* 1991: 1). If the present fertility rate continues, according to estimates made by Song Jian and Yu Jianyuan in 1991, China's population will reach 1.3 billion by the

---

11. The State Council Birth Planning Group was established in the 1970s. In 1978 the Group was strengthened with the appointment of Chen Muhua, a Vice-Premier and member of the Central Committee, as its head. In 1981 the Group was reorganized as the State Family Planning Commission (Wong 1984: 221–222).

end of the century, 1.5 billion by 2020, 1.7 billion by 2050 and the growth trend can never be halted (Song and Yu 1991).

The demographic population policy target set in 1979 aimed to limit population numbers to *within* 1.2 billion and to reach zero population growth by the year 2000.[12] When, by 1986, it had become clear that the target was likely to be exceeded, the limit was adjusted to *about* 1.2 billion. 1990 census results, however, led Chinese officials to adjust the goal further to approximately 1.3 billion (White 1992: 6). While the demographic targets and specific birth limits changed during the first ten years of the policy, the substance of the population policy first formulated in 1978–79 was reaffirmed when in 1988 the Standing Committee of the Politburo convened for the sole purpose of re-examining the existing policy on birth limits. It chose to maintain the existing policy, but called for better enforcement of that policy (White 1992: 5). In 1991 the demographic aim stated in the Ten-Year National Economic and Social Development Program and in the 8th Five-Year Plan (1991–95),[13] was 'to strive to control annual population growth rate to within 12.5 per 1,000 in the next ten years'. Again the population policy was reaffirmed with fulfilment of the target being viewed as vitally important to safeguarding the realization of strategic goals of the modernization construction. Implementation of the population policy was assigned an importance equal to the economic construction work (*Zhonggong zhongyang* 1991).

The post-Mao population policy is generally termed the one-child family policy because the main remedial measure for reaching policy goals is to 'encourage every couple to have only one child' (*tichang yidui fufu zhi sheng yige haizi*). This measure for meeting the population policy goals has been maintained as the official policy since 1979, although in reality a two-child policy has become more widespread. The original decision to apply the one-child-per-couple measure was based on projections as to how many births annually China would be able to bear in order to keep within the target limit of 1.2 billion, with calculations indicating that if couples had more than one child, the target would be surpassed (Chen [1979] 1981).

---

12. An optimal population size for China has been calculated to be between 650 and 700 million (Song Jian 1981).
13. The 8th Five-Year Plan started in 1991. This was also the first year of China's Ten-Year Programme for National Economic and Social Development.

not necessary para

According to projections by Susan Greenhalgh and David Bongaarts published in 1985 and 1987, there was in fact an alternative to the one-child-per-couple measure. They suggested that the implementation of a 'stop-at-two and delay and space' measure could be as or even more effective than the one-child measure, not only demographically but also socially and economically. The key element of their proposed alternative, one among several they considered, was delayed childbearing and spacing combined in a different way than during the earlier 1970s policy. The main difference was that a minimum age of marriage should be replaced by a minimum age of first birth. Thus age at marriage would be separated from age at first birth, which would have an effect on fertility as the majority of first births in China occur during the very first years of marriage (Bongaarts and Greenhalgh 1985, Greenhalgh and Bongaarts 1987).

In fact, realization of population policy objectives has been negatively influenced by a decline during the 1980s in the age of women giving birth for the first time, with births being concentrated in the 20–29-year age group. In 1981 this age group accounted for 75.07 per cent of the total number of births nationally. In 1986 its share had risen to 77.07 per cent. The younger age at first birth was related to a tendency to marry earlier, with the average age of marriage having declined following the revision of the Marriage Law in 1980. Although the Marriage Law *increased* the minimum age of marriage by two years to 20 for women and 22 for men, in practice the age limits were lowered. As the relationship between age at marriage and age at first birth is very close, the decline in average age at marriage caused a change in the age pattern of fertility between 1981 and 1986. Fertility in the 15–24-year age group increased, especially in the 15–19-year age group (Zhu 1990).

According to the estimates made by Greenhalgh and Bongaarts, it would have been possible to limit the population to less than 1.2 billion in the year 2000 by enforcing a 'stop-at-two' measure with a minimum age of first birth as low as 25 years. With a minimum age of 27 years there would only be minor differences between the one-child measure and the 'stop-at-two' measure up to the mid-twenty-first century. Provided that the one-child measure on the one hand and the 'stop-at-two' measure on the other hand proved equally efficient in meeting the population target and that the two measures therefore were equally acceptable politically, in the opinion of Greenhalgh and Bongaarts there was little doubt that many Chinese couples would prefer the 'stop-at-two' alternative (Bongaarts and Greenhalgh 1985, Greenhalgh and Bongaarts 1987).

Following a preliminary phase of vigorous one-child family policy implementation from 1979 to the early 1980s, enforcement of the one-child measure has been relaxed in accordance with the reality of (especially rural) local conditions by giving greater latitude in the regulations for special circumstances when a second child may be permitted. Studies of policy implementation have documented that localities are able to exercise substantial autonomy in devising local fertility policies and that higher levels have been obliged to adjust the overall policy accordingly (Greenhalgh 1989: 135, Freedmann and Guo 1988: 135).

While the lowering of fertility during the 1970s has been interpreted as acceptable to the Chinese people with families being prepared to reduce fertility to three or even two children, rural resistance to the one-child norm has been widespread (see for instance Banister 1987, Freedmann and Guo 1988). The requirement that one couple have only one child has in rural China given rise to protests in the form of attempts to avoid policy fertility limits as well as penalties. During the early years of one-child family policy implementation, the desire for more than one child was denounced by the leadership as 'feudal mentality'. However, gradually it has been recognized that rural families have actual problems of labour and old age security and that there are no effective means to achieve the goal of rapid fertility decline to below-replacement levels contrary to the needs of the populace in rural China at present. The result has been an incremental expansion in exceptions that allow for the birth of a second child (Greenhalgh 1989: 51–52). This implies that the one-child family policy is not actually being implemented nationally, but rather in urban enclaves while the majority of the populace is eligible for permission to have a second child. Thus the one-child family policy is promoted as the norm, with the possibility of permission for a second child in a series of special circumstances.

The main change from the original policy formulation is that the birth of a girl as the first child has gradually been accepted among the exceptions that allow for permission for a second birth. Since 1988 this has been confirmed as a national policy for the rural areas in general, except for the municipalities of Beijing and

Shanghai and the provinces of Sichuan and Anhui (Davin 1990: 84). Susan Greenhalgh reports from her study of the province of Shaanxi that the conditions under which couples could have a second child were gradually expanded over time with the most compelling reason for wanting a second child – first child is a girl – from 1986 being placed on the list of exceptions from the one-child rule for rural areas – officially, the reason is that the 'couple has real economic difficulties because its first child is a girl' (Greenhalgh 1989: 26).

One of the main reasons that the one-child limit has been difficult to implement in rural China is that rural reforms have been working directly against the population policy, having profoundly disruptive effects. Following the establishment of households as independent economic units, the economic value of children was strengthened and it became more difficult for the government to control peasants (Davin 1985).

Demographic Consequence of the One-Child Family Policy

In China discussion as to the necessity of the one-child measure has continuously taken place, not openly, but within the leadership, with certain groups advocating a stricter one-child limit while others are proponents of a universal two-child policy as more acceptable to the population (Croll 1983: 100, Dai 1990: 192–193 and White 1992: 6). Owing largely to an effective system of political and administrative control the one-child policy has, none the less, succeeded remarkably in keeping fertility relatively low. However, the demographic success is limited to urban areas, whereas one-child policy implementation in rural China has been far from successful. Furthermore, higher mortality rates for female children as well as higher than normal sex ratios at birth are consequences of the one-child family policy. These problems indicate that female children are being discriminated against, a situation that has given rise to concern both inside and outside China.

High sex ratios at birth have not been a persistent phenomenon in China. Although the 1953 and the 1964 censuses did not publish data on the sex ratio at birth, sex ratios for the age group of zero-year-old children were registered. In 1953 and 1964 these sex ratios were 104.9 and 103.8 respectively. The 1982 census sex ratio for this age group was 107.6 (*Zhongguo funü* 1991: 36). Based on the data from several surveys, the problem of high sex ratios has been recognized and the association with the one-child family policy discussed by both Chinese and foreign scholars (Arnold and Liu 1986, Banister 1987, Gao 1993, Hull 1990, Johansson and Nygren 1991, Johansson 1993, Liu 1986, Tu 1993 and Wang 1985). Although attention had been drawn to the high sex ratio during the 1980s, it was not until the 1990 census results were released that the leadership in China acknowledged the existence of a serious problem (Johansson 1992). The 1990 census data revealed that the sex ratio at birth had been gradually rising during the 1980s. In 1990 the ratio had risen to 111.7 (Tu 1993). The sex ratio among infant deaths in China for the 1982–87 period as reported in the Two-Per-Thousand Fertility Survey carried out by the State Family Planning Commission was 114. According to Sten Johansson and Ola Nygren, however, this is lower than the normal ratio of 130, which they have assumed on the basis of international data, implying that there are excess female infant deaths. Johansson and Nygren estimate that the excess female infant deaths number about 39,000 per year, or about 4 per thousand live-born girls (Johansson and Nygren 1991: 50).

Addressing the issue in a 1993 *Renkou Yanjiu* article, Tu Ping of the Population Institute at the People's University acknowledges that the main characteristic of the sex ratio in China is that it is extremely high. Data from the One Per Cent Sample of the 1990 census shows that the sex ratio at birth rose from 108.5 in 1981 to 114.7 in 1989. This is about nine male children more per 100 live female births than there would be according to the usual sex ratio of 105.5 (Tu 1993).

A second characteristic of the sex ratio in China is that it varies according to birth parity. Under normal circumstances the sex ratio at birth does not vary greatly with regard to parity (Hull 1990: 67). However, in China the 1989 data indicate that on the contrary the sex ratio rises for second and higher-parity births. The sex ratio of first-parity births is quite normal at 105.5. At second and higher-parity birth, the sex ratio is 120.6 and 130.7 respectively. This pattern of a rising sex ratio by birth parity is repeated also when 1989 births are broken down into place of residence, by nationality, by educational level of mother, and by occupation of mother. Geographically the sex-ratio imbalance exists in all parts of China. The highest sex ratios, exceeding 120, were found in the provinces of Henan, Jiangsu, Guangxi and Ningxia as well as on Hainan Island. In twenty areas sex ratios between 107.5 and 118.7 were registered. Only in the five areas of Yunnan, Inner Mongolia, Heilongjiang, Tibet and Qinghai were sex ratios between 102.9 and 106.3. The highest sex ratio registered was for higher than second-parity births in Tianjin with a ratio of 200.0! Generally the sex ratio at first birth is lower than the sex ratio of succeeding births, with sex ratios rising proportionately with the number of births (Tu 1993).

Under-reporting of mainly female births is one of the main explanations of the present sex-ratio imbalance. When the 1981 sex ratio at birth is compared to the sex ratio of 8–9-year-olds in 1989 (i.e. the sex ratio of the same group of children), a decline in the sex ratio can be noted. According to calculations by Tu Ping, there was an under-reporting of 866,000 births for 1989 in the 1990 census. Of these 625,000 were girls and 241,000 were boys. However, even after an estimated under-reporting of births has been calculated into the census data, with the result that the 1989 sex ratio at birth declines from 114.7 to 110.8, this is still a marked sex-ratio imbalance. Another explanation is female infanticide. However, although female infanticide may explain the sex-ratio imbalance in some parts of rural China, the explanation is dismissed by Tu Ping as an explanation of the sex-ratio imbalance in China as a whole, with reference to the fact that the sex-ratio imbalance exists at all levels of society and in all parts of the country, both in rural and urban areas.

The missing link that Tu Ping points out as the main factor that will explain the sex-ratio imbalance is gender-specific abortions. According to Tu Ping, the technology that is the prerequisite for gender-specific abortions, primarily ultrasound equipment, with which it is possible to detect the sex of a foetus, has been widely disseminated in China during the past several years. Tu Ping supports his argument by referring to the fact that in 1979 the first B-scanner went into operation in China and since 1982 a series of B-scanners produced in China as well as imported scanners have been available. In 1987 there were about 13,000 B-scanners in Chinese hospitals, which amounts to an average of six scanners in every county. By 1991 the largest producer of B-scanners in China was able to produce 5,000 B-scanners annually, enough to equip the more than 2,000 counties in China with an average of about two scanners. At present every county has B-scanners, and relatively well-off township hospitals and birth planning service stations are also equipped with B-scanners (Tu 1993). Foreign scholars have, however, dismissed gender-selective abortions as an explanation for the higher-than-normal sex ratios among reported live births in China as other than very marginal. Their argument is based on the fact that the required medical technology 'for early diagnosis of the sex of the fetus' has not been widely enough available in China to have had any impact (Johansson and Nygren 1991: 43). According to Tu Ping, this is not the case; on the contrary, although the government prohibits the practice of identifying the gender of the foetus with the purpose of practising gender-specific abortion, and although the B-scanners at the birth planning service stations are usually only used to check up on IUDs and pregnancies, there is as yet no supervision of the purchase and use of the B-scanners (Tu 1993).[14] The fact that sex ratios at all parity births are higher in urban than in rural China (Liu 1986), and that it is in urban areas that the availability of technology for determination of the sex of the foetus is higher, would seem to confirm the practice of gender-selective abortion.

High sex ratios are doubtlessly linked to persistent son-preference in China, though opinions diverge as to whether it is as a direct result of the one-child family policy that son-preference is practised to the extent that it leads to high sex ratios. The sex-ratio imbalance has been explained not as a specific problem that is the consequence of the one-child family policy, but rather as a general phenomenon prevalent in East and Southeast Asia. However, the relationship between the one-child family policy and the high sex ratios has been documented by a study that compared sex ratios for planned and unplanned births. The study concluded that:

> the sex ratios are generally within or fairly near the expected range of 105 to 106 boys per 100 girls for live births within the plan. They are, in contrast, clearly far above normal for children born outside the plan, even as high as 115 to 118 for 1984–87. That the phenomenon of missing girls in China in the 1980s is related to the government's population policy is thus conclusively shown. (Johansson and Nygren 1991: 40–41)

---

14. The disagreement as to the extent of the use of technology in determining the sex of the foetus may be due to Johansson and Nygren referring to 'technology for early diagnosis', probably meaning amniocentesis, while Tu Ping, who does not specify any time limit, is obviously referring to the use of ultrasound scanners.

Discussion

This chapter has been concerned with links between gender and population policy ideologies and demographic development. Over the years the Malthusian–Marxist population policy controversy over the issue of people as primarily producers or consumers has strongly influenced CCP formulation of population policies. Another basic issue that influenced policy formulation at least in the early years of the PRC was the demand from women within the CCP that they have access to contraceptives. Women wanted control over childbearing decisions, including not only access to contraceptives, but also to abortion and sterilization (White 1994). The rapid drop in birthrates has not only been related to better health and a drop in mortality rates with more children surviving; it has also been facilitated by women's wish to be free of prolonged periods of childbearing and childcare. Hill Gates's study of urban petty-capitalist women shows that women who bore their children before the one-child family policy often voluntarily limited births to three, two or even one child (Gates 1993). Even though the motive underlying the fertility limit set by the population policy of the 1970s was not based on the needs, interests and desires of women, the limit of two children did probably correspond to the limit many urban women and their families were themselves opting for. Women's preference for a smaller number of children was linked to the difficulties they were having in managing their combined working and family life. Families were likely to opt for fewer children due to their overall economic situation and the advantages of concentrating resources on fewer children.

In setting a limit of one child, the present policy no longer corresponds to the fertility preferences of the majority of women and their families whether in urban or rural China. The main reason, especially in rural areas, is that their option for having a son has been severely restricted. The instrumental use of women in reaching overall developmental aims inherent in the 1970s as well as in the succeeding one-child policy is implicit in cultural assumptions of gender. In the 1950s and 1960s there were urban women in China demanding access to fertility regulation because they wanted to manage their own fertility. Since then the availability and distribution of contraceptives have come to be motivated by population control policies that coerce fertility regulation upon women. This shift is far from unique to China; on the contrary it follows an international trend. Had women not been subjugated by unequal power relations within the family and in society in general, population control might never have emerged. The formulation of a population control policy is dependent upon the prior existence of gender relations in which women are subjugated (DuBois 1991: 16–17). In this respect, whether or not the two policies diverge in their interpretation of the 'population problem', the gender ideologies of the *wan-xi-shao* policy and the one-child family policy are essentially identical.

The explicit objective of the 1970s *wan-xi-shao* policy was, as is the case with the one-child family policy, to reduce fertility with a view to limiting population increase. As the majority of the Chinese population is rural, whatever problems exist in implementing the present population policy are heavily concentrated in rural China. The population policy ideology of the leadership no longer adheres to the principle of people being the most precious of all things in the world. However, to the rural majority of the population, children – especially male children – would still seem to be the most precious things in the world. The one-child family policy has, in demographic terms, successfully limited further population growth, although far from the degree to which it was intended. At the same time the Chinese leadership as well as Chinese and foreign scholars are, especially since the release of the 1990 census data, aware of the gradually increased sex-ratio imbalance that is a consequence of the policy. The imbalanced sex ratio as well as female infanticide and son-preference inherent in this phenomenon are regarded as 'a reflection of remnants of a feudal mentality' (Zhu 1991: 306). And it is recognized that rules and regulations for controlling the practice of gender-specific abortions alone will not solve the problem (Tu 1993). The reason is that son-preference and female infanticide are more than a remnant of the feudal mentality of 'exalting males and demeaning females' (*zhong nan qing nü*). These phenomena are visible indicators of a gender discrimination reflecting more profound unequal gender relations in China.

Only once previously has the CCP intervened as directly into the sphere of family life as in the case of the one-child fertility limit set by the present population policy. In the early 1950s following promulgation of the Marriage Law under which it became legally possible for a woman to request divorce, large numbers of rural women divorced their husbands. Following the protests of the rural patriarchs whose support the CCP needed, rules on obtaining divorce were revised and restricted by the central leadership. Because the CCP equal rights policy was threatening established gender relations, the CCP was forced to concede to the demands of a rural patriarchy not prepared or inclined to accept such drastic change (Stacey 1983). Although the one-child policy is still being stressed as the overall national policy, the central leadership has once again been obliged to concede to the demand of the rural patriarchy, with a second child being permitted in most of China when the first child is a girl. In so doing, the leadership – because after all it operates from within the same cultural assumptions on gender as the populace at whole – has affirmed the importance of the family point of view and weakened the official position of the state by acknowledging a gender preference contrary to stated PRC policy on gender equality (Potter and Potter 1990: 229).

CCP policy on gender equality has a history of being subordinated to the overall development strategy. In the case of the population policy, the leadership has been at pains to promote work supporting gender equality because gender discrimination is obstructing implementation of the one-child family policy. The irony and paradox is that the CCP push to eradicate the discrimination of women inherent in traditional gender relations is motivated by the population policy. The primary goal in pushing for gender equality is to limit population growth, rather than to achieve gender equality. As such, gender equality is being promoted as a means to an end rather than as an end in itself. The one-child population policy's instrumental use of a gender equality policy, as well as the targeting of women, is rooted in cultural assumptions of gender relations in which the needs and interests of women themselves are of minor importance.

Fertility Preferences and Policy Acceptance

Q: Why do you have only one child?
A: I have answered the call of the nation.
Beijing woman, May 1992

As mentioned in Chapter 2, nearly all women in the city districts of Beijing and Shenyang who have given birth during the one-child family policy have only one child. At the same time numerous surveys have shown that two children is the preferred number in rural as well as urban China. How many children would one-child mothers in Beijing and Shenyang then prefer? Is there an inconsistency between the preferred number of children of the women studied and the one child they have?

In raising the question of a preferred or ideal number of children, it should be considered that there may be a divergence between the ideal number of children and the number of children the women would have had even without a one-child family policy, since in any case the family is not necessarily able to realize its ideal. Therefore, when about half of the women surveyed state that they would have preferred two children had there not been a one-child family policy, it is not directly possible from this response to deduce that the very low fertility of only one child is solely determined by the limit set by population control. There may well be other determinants, for instance socio-economic, that prevent the family from fulfilling their fertility preferences. However, even though there may be a discrepancy between the number of children viewed as an abstract ideal and the number of children a family is able to realize based upon its actual economic capacities, the distinction will not be maintained in the following. This is because, first of all, the aim here is not to specify the relative weight of fertility determinants. Second, it is practically impossible in the city district context of tight control for women to give birth to more than one child no matter what their fertility preferences might be. This means that the final determinant of low fertility in the urban context is in any case the one-child limit set by the policy.

The aim in this chapter is to explore the relationship between the preferred number of children and the mandatory one child as far as this relationship pertains to policy acceptance. In doing so, I shall first examine whether or not there is a discrepancy between the preferred number of children and the one child. Due to the sensitivity of the issue, as a response indicating a preference of more than one child is obviously contrary to the national policy norm, several questions explicitly or implicitly referring to the preferred number of children were included in the survey as a supplement to the main question on family size preference (see Box 1 below). The aim was thus to view the question from several angles in order to reach a valid representation of the ideal number of children and the possible discrepancy between the ideal number of children and the actual one child. In this first section of the chapter, validity is discussed in relation to, first, question wording and, second, the perspective from which women are responding. It is argued that the varied and conflicting responses to the survey questions and statements on the preferred number of children are influenced by question wording and are the result of respondents applying various perspectives to the questions when responding. The fertility preferences being expressed vary depending on whether women are responding from their own, their family's or their child's perspective or from the perspective of the nation.

In the second part of the chapter, I discuss the consequence of the relationship between the ideal number of children and the actual one child in terms of policy acceptance. In other words, how is policy acceptance influenced by a consistency or inconsistency

Box 1: List of questions and statements included in the survey concerning preferred number of children:

1. 'Without taking into consideration the influence of any factors, how many children would you like to have, in your whole life?'

2. 'Even if there were no one-child family policy, I would have only one child.'

3. 'Even if there were no population policy I would myself limit births.'

4. 'One boy and one girl is perfect.'

5. 'It is beneficial for the development of the child to have a companion.'

6. 'It is best for a woman to have only one child.'

between the preferred number of children and the one child? Three circumstances are taken as the point of departure for this discussion. First, several studies have indicated a discrepancy between the ideal number of children and the one child that urban women actually have in accordance with the one-child family policy (Choe and Tsuya 1991, Feng 1990, Wolf 1985, Xu and Yu 1991). Second, the fertility limit decreed by population policy has been pointed out as the main factor determining this discrepancy between the preferred number of children and the actual one child (Cai *et al.* 1991, Guo and Choe 1990, Feng 1990).

The third circumstance is the existence of diverging conclusions in terms of policy acceptance drawn from the above two circumstances. Xu Gang and Yu Jingwei base their analysis on data from the second phase of the In-Depth Fertility Survey (IDFS). They conclude that most women prefer two children and that certain differences exist between the current policy and the preference of people. They further conclude that 'Urban people have answered the call of the government' (Xu and Yu 1991: 186). Albert I. Hermalin and Xian Liu base their analysis on a comparison of IDFS first phase data from Shanghai and data from the Shanghai Survey of Desired Family Size. They find that women with two or fewer children express a desired family size of around two rather than higher. And they conclude that, 'If this is a valid representation of preferences, it suggests that while *the one-child policy is not widely accepted*, relatively few Shanghai couples in the early stages of family building would exceed two children, even without government restrictions' (Hermalin and Liu 1990: 352, emphasis added). Both analyses conclude that the preferred number of children is not one but two. Xu and Yu then state that *people have responded to the call of the leadership.* While Hermalin and Liu declare that *the policy is not widely accepted.* Hermalin and Liu specifically state that people do not accept (i.e. they do not agree with or consent to) the policy. Contrary to this interpretation, Xu Gang's and Yu Jingwei's conclusion would seem to indicate that, contrary to their expressed fertility preferences, people do support the policy.

The question is what 'answering the call of the nation,' a concept which was also used by women in the qualitative interviews of this study, actually means. In this chapter a preliminary definition of the meanings of acceptance is outlined. I will argue that, although it is difficult if not impossible to reach an unambiguous representation of the preferred number of children when several questions are asked pertaining to this issue, the implication is not that the results are invalid. As responses pertaining to the preferred number of children are varied and conflicting, the consequence is that acceptance cannot easily be gauged from the relationship between the preferred number of children and the actual one child. I will argue that acceptance transcends individual or family fertility preferences when these are in conflict with the policy requirement. Although the policy fertility limit does not correspond to women's preferred number of children, it does not automatically follow that they do not accept the policy.

Preferred Number of Children

The main question on the desired number of children in the questionnaire used for this study was first phrased as a replication of the In-Depth Fertility Survey (IDFS) question on desired family size. In the official translation the IDFS question was: 'If the present government policy had not existed, how many children would you personally like to have, in your whole life?'[1] However, my Chinese associates suggested a more indirect wording, arguing that it would be unwise so directly to refer to the one-child family policy. The question could very well be interpreted as an assumption that there is a discrepancy between the national policy and fertility preferences, and thereby as an indirect criticism of the policy. This could make it difficult to obtain permission to carry out any survey at all. The question was therefore rephrased and became: 'Without taking into consideration

---

1. Questionnaire of the In-Depth Fertility Survey (IDFS), Part 5, Question 514 (*Zhongguo dier* 1989, Vol. 1: 236).

the influence of any factors, how many children would you like to have, in your whole life?' Even though the wording differs, in the opinion of the Chinese scholars there would be no doubt on the part of respondents that the influencing factors being referred to were related to the one-child family policy. Responses to the question were as follows. In Shenyang 49.4 per cent of the women surveyed state that their preferred number of children is two. One child is the preferred number for 38 per cent of Shenyang women. In Beijing a slightly higher 54.7 per cent of women preferred two children, and 21.4 per cent preferred one.[2] However, these differences between Shenyang and Beijing are only one of degree; the pattern of child preference is largely the same (see Figure 7).

Figure 7: Preferred number of children: Shenyang and Beijing (based on answers to the question 'Without taking into consideration the influence of any factors, how many children would you like to have in your whole life?')

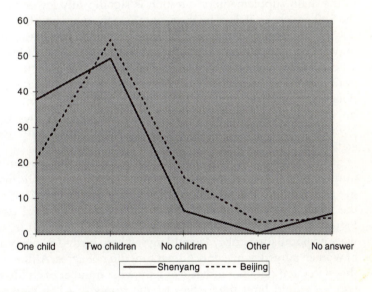

Number of women = 857.

2. In the IDFS, which included both rural and urban women, 66 per cent of women in Beijing and 62 per cent in Liaoning preferred two children, while 20 and 14 per cent respectively preferred one child (*Zhongguo dierqi* 1989, Vol. 1: 139).

The main supplementary question on the preferred number of children was formed as a statement: 'Even if there were no one-child family policy, I would have only one child.' The women were asked to state whether or not they agreed. A total of 62.9 per cent of the women surveyed agreed that even if there were no one-child family policy, they would have only one child, whereas 25.5 per cent did not agree. They would have more than one child if there were no one-child family policy. While the majority of women stated that they would have one child whether or not there were a one-child family policy, about one quarter of the women imply that they are setting aside a personal or family preference by complying with the requirement of the policy that they have only one child. The survey response indicated that for one quarter of the women, there is a discrepancy between their preferred number of children and the one child that they actually have.

However, this discrepancy between the preferred number and the actual one child for one quarter of the women in response to the main supplementary question is significantly lower than the 52.2 per cent reflected by the response to the main question on fertility preference. The diverging responses to the two questions may reflect the different wording of the question. The Chinese scholars did not object to the direct referral to the one-child family policy in the statement 'Even if there were no one-child family policy, I would have only one child,' which probably is due to the implicit and more direct indication in this question that the politically appropriate response would be to agree with the statement.

As the answers to these two questions on the preferred number of children indicate, women do not want many children: the preferred number of children being only one or two. Half of the women surveyed state that two children is their ideal (see Figure 7). In response to an additional statement, 'Even if there were no population policy I would myself limit births,' 84 per cent of women agreed, while only 6.1 per cent did not agree. Although this statement does not indicate exactly what number of children women would limit themselves to, the response when viewed together with responses to the main question and the main supplementary statement does indicate a low fertility preference. Although several of the women interviewed in both Beijing and Shenyang said they would prefer two children, none said they would prefer more than two.

The combination of a boy and a girl is viewed as the ideal by a majority of women, with 72.5 per cent of the women agreeing to the statement that 'One boy and one girl is perfect.' Only 16.8 per cent do not agree. The response to this statement provides yet another indication of the preferred number of children with three-quarters of women indirectly indicating two children as their ideal. Again I would point to the wording of the question as a factor that is most likely to be relevant as an explanation to the divergence of this response from the preceding two responses. In this statement the question of the number of children is detached from any mention of the one-child family policy, as one of seven statements in the questionnaire on the role of children in the family. The point is that, when the question on the preferred number of children is directly linked to the one-child family policy, in an urban context in which it is not possible to have more than one child, the response given will reflect this reality, even to a question where the respondent is specifically asked to disregard the policy in her response. In contrast, it is in fact possible to view the statement 'One boy and one girl is perfect' which does not directly refer to the one-child family policy, as detached from the policy. The effect is a markedly different and (it would seem) more valid reflection of fertility preferences.

Response Perspective

Responses to several statements about women and children support the interpretation of the significance of questionnaire wording for the response. In addition, responses indicate that the perspective from which the question is viewed is decisive for the resulting response. The fertility preferences being expressed vary depending on whether women are responding from their own, their family's or their child's perspective, or from the perspective of the nation. When responding to the questionnaire, the women are being asked to provide their own perspective. Responses from the perspective of the nation, the family or the child are, however, no less valid than responses from the perspective of the women themselves, as all these perspectives exist merged and intertwined in the daily lives of women. Therefore, although the number of children preferred varies from question to question depending on the perspective the women are applying, there is not one measure of the preferred number of children that is more or less valid than the others.

Asked whether they agree or not with the statement that 'It is beneficial for the development of the child to have a companion,' 82.8 per cent of women agreed, while only 9.2 per cent did not agree. As was the case with the earlier statement ('One boy and one girl is perfect'), this statement does not refer directly to the one-child family policy. Another statement, 'It is best for a woman to have only one child', indirectly refers to the one-child family policy. Responses were 49 per cent agree and 37.6 per cent disagree. From the position of the mother, it may very well be perceived by the majority of the women as most beneficial to have only one child. Moreover, the statement directly refers to the policy, which would then tend to result in a higher degree of verbal compliance to policy norms. Nonetheless, quite a number of women did not agree. This would seem to indicate that women's responses were not only directed by what would seem appropriate in terms of the policy, but also by their own opinion. As a minimum, the varied responses indicate that it is not possible to reach an unambiguous measure of the preferred number of children. As soon as the perspectives of, say, mother and child respectively are incorporated into the answer, responses will vary.

The point is that even in the questions in which it is not obvious from which perspective the women are actually answering, they are of course answering from a distinct perspective: their own, the child's, the family's or the nation's. An example from the qualitative interviews will serve to illustrate the point, although the question concerns the preferred sex of the child rather than the preferred number of children. Responding to my question of whether *she* during her pregnancy had any special hope that her child would be a boy or a girl, a Shenyang woman answered: 'My husband has four sisters, he is the only boy in the family, so my mother-in-law hoped to have a grandson.' In her response, although being asked about her personal opinion, the woman applies a family perspective. My argument is that none of the perspectives on the preferred number of children supplies a more valid representation of actual fertility preferences than others. Responses from all perspectives are valid. It is extremely complicated to obtain an unambiguous measure of fertility preferences and therefore also extremely complicated to gauge whether or not or to what degree there is a discrepancy between the preferred number of children and the one-child family policy. It follows, therefore, that policy acceptance is not readily gauged by measuring fertility preferences.

Figure 8: Benefit of one-child family (based on answers to the question 'In your opinion, whom does the one-child family benefit?')

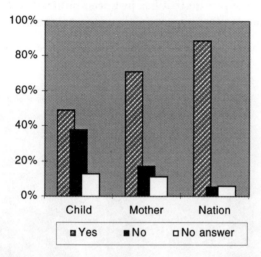

Number of women = 857

In Figure 8 the responses to the question of whom the one-child family benefits illustrates how the response depends on the applied perspective. Half the women believe that the policy benefits the only child. That the one-child family is more beneficial to the mother than to the child is indicated by the 71.3 per cent of women in whose opinion the policy is beneficial to the mother. The policy is seen as even more beneficial to the nation, with 88.6 per cent expressing this opinion.

Norm and Behaviour

Survey responses on the relationship between the preferred number of children and the actual one child would seem to be ambiguous. On the one hand, responses could very well be interpreted as indicative of a disparity between the preferred number of children and the actual one child for between 25.5 and 82.8 per cent of women. Following the interpretation that a gap between the desired number of children and the actual one child indicates non-acceptance, this would suggest that the one-child family policy is not widely accepted. On the other hand, survey data could be interpreted to indicate that for up to 62.9 per cent of women there is no discrepancy between their preferred number of children and the actual one child they have. This would, quite contrary to the picture that has just been outlined, suggest that the one-child family policy is in fact widely accepted.

Figure 9: Summary of questionnaire responses on preferred number of children indicating preference for more than one child

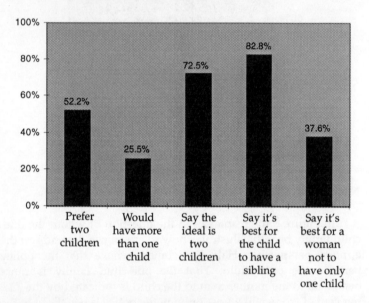

The relatively pronounced divergence between results on the preferred number of children as outlined here would seem to suggest that the representation of fertility preferences resulting from the survey is not valid. As discussed, the expressed number of children preferred varies according to question wording and the perspective applied in responding to survey questions and statements. Furthermore, I would argue that linked to response perspective, the norm-behaviour structure can to some extent explain the quite varied responses on the preferred number of children. The norm-behaviour structure as an issue that is significant in studying Chinese society as distinct from Western society has been referred to by scholars of China as the existence

Figure 10: Summary of questionnaire responses on preferred number of children indicating preference of one child

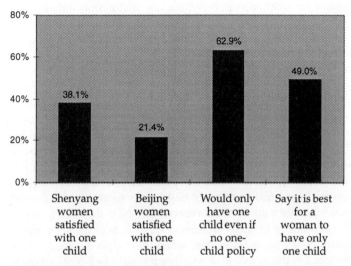

of a pronounced divergence between norm and actual behaviour in Chinese society. This is manifested in terms of a divergence between a clear official ideology on how social structures and social processes ought to function and how they actually function (see for instance Croll 1987, Wolf 1985). Stig Thøgersen argues that the general problem of norm and behaviour is particularly important in China, 'where there seems to exist a set of ready-made, socially acceptable value judgements about almost everything' (Thøgersen 1991: 37). In the realm of population policy implementation there seems to exist not just such a set of ready-made value judgements. On the contrary, ideological education (*xuanchuan jiaoyu*), which involves ensuring that every single member of society is aware of not only policy requirements but also of the significance of the population policy to the overall economic development of China, is a basic element of policy implementation (Chapter 5 will elaborate on ideological education as one aspect of policy implementation). Reflecting on the difficulty of eliciting other than norm responses when conducting interviews in China, Thøgersen calls for precise and concrete questions related to behaviour as a solution to breaking through to a more personal level of reality, thereby revealing actual behaviour as opposed to the norm (Thøgersen 1991: 37).

The connection between norm and behaviour *vis à vis* the population policy would seem to depict a more complex norm-behaviour relationship in which the distinction between norm and behaviour is not simply a question of people rattling off the norms and only revealing actual behaviour if the investigator is able to dig deep enough into concealed layers of reality and meaning. In urban city district China, fertility behaviour corresponds to the policy norm of one child. However, one-child mothers, as illustrated by the survey results of this as well as by many other studies on the preferred number of children, may very well operate with an additional (family) norm that does not correspond to the state norm or to their own behaviour. The case of the 82.8 per cent of women who agree that it would be beneficial for their child to have a sibling will illustrate this point. Their response is an indication that the ideal number of children is more than one child, at least when they apply the perspective of the child to their response. The behaviour of these women corresponds to the state one-child family policy norm. However, when they apply a family norm in response to the question of whether it would be beneficial for their child to have a sibling, it becomes evident that their stated ideal number of children is not in accordance with the policy norm nor with their own behaviour.

Therefore, by 'revealing' behaviour as opposed to norm responses, a more valid representation of reality is not necessarily obtained. In the case of the urban one-child family policy, behaviour corresponds to the official norm. Women may, nonetheless, operate with another set of norms which does not correspond to their behaviour. The norm-behaviour structure thus goes the other way round in so far as the difficult aspect to 'reveal' – or, more precisely, to grasp the meaning of – is not actual behaviour but 'actual' norms, as opposed to policy norms. When fertility preferences do not correspond to fertility, these 'actual norms' become visible.

Policy Acceptance

The two sets of norms, relating to the policy and the family respectively, are of course an aspect that is considered in surveys of fertility preference in China during the one-child policy. These invariably reflect on the issue of verbal compliance to the policy as well as the risk of under-reporting of actual fertility preferences. In this section, the issue is further developed to include a discussion of the definition of policy acceptance. The pivot of the discussion is that appraising acceptance is a more complex matter than a quantitative measure of correspondence between preferred number of children and the actual one child. In other words, acceptance is not necessarily automatically linked to the question of whether or not fertility preferences have been fulfilled. The central issue is not to what degree women are willing to report fertility preferences contrary to the policy limit. More relevant than the issue of under-reporting of fertility preferences is a discussion of how acceptance is defined.

Responses to the questions on the preferred number of children are extremely varied because women are responding according to at least two perspectives that relate to two distinct norm sets. One norm is the state one-child family policy norm. The other is a family norm. While the family norm does correspond to the policy norm in the case of some women, it obviously does not do so for all women. It should also be considered that there may be a discrepancy between the family norm, which is based on family interests as opposed to the interests, desires and needs of the individual woman. However, no distinction between the interests of the woman and the family is maintained here as family interests remain predominant in the Chinese family. The scope of the individual woman for maintaining personal interests, should these diverge from family interests, is limited. The interests of the individual woman as to the number and sex of her children will most often in practice be identical to family interests. The case of a Beijing woman who married in October 1982 at the age of 25 illustrates the case. She and her husband agreed to postpone childbearing for some years. When the newly married woman became pregnant she therefore made an appointment at a hospital to have an abortion. However, as her parents-in-law did not agree to her having an abortion, she gave birth to her child in October 1983, exactly one year after having married.

In their responses to the survey questions and statements, the women alternate between the two perspectives and norm sets pertaining to the state and the family respectively. Before filling out the questionnaire, the women were informed that responses from their personal point of view were being requested. Additionally, some survey questions had been formulated in such a way that the perspective from which the response was expected was explicitly apparent, as for instance 'Do you or don't you agree with the following sayings? State *your personal view*' (emphasis added). However, the perspective applied by the women in responding was not necessarily an individual perspective. Nor was it necessarily a family perspective. It may just as well have been the perspective of the nation. When women respond based on the perspective of the nation, their response may well be contradictory to family perspectives and norms. However, the application of two sets of norms or a double-norm is not necessarily viewed as a contradiction by the women. This is where the norm-behaviour structure becomes more complex, as the women for whom the family norm and the policy norm do not correspond operate with two sets of conflicting norms simultaneously, based respectively on a family and a state perspective. Responses based on one perspective and its corresponding set of norms are not necessarily perceived by women as either more or less valid than responses based on the other perspective and set of norms.

My contention is that urban city district women, when they apply the perspective of the nation, are not merely parroting slogans, but that many actually agree with the CCP population policy. Moreover, this is the case even when the fertility require-ment of the policy is contrary to their own and/or family norms. I would argue that the variation reflected in the questionnaire responses should not only be addressed as an issue of under-reporting fertility preferences or of verbal policy compliance and thereby as an issue of questionable validity. The variation should also be viewed as a reflection of the fact that whether or not there is a disparity between the preferred number of children and the actual one child, the one-child family policy is generally accepted by city district women as a necessary policy due to the economic and demographic situation in China. Thus, disparity between the preferred number of children and the one child is not a precise measure of acceptance.

Responses to the survey question 'With our nation's present population characteristics, which of the following opinions do you agree with?' illustrate the apparent inconsistency that arises from the double-norm attitude (see Figure 11).

Of the women surveyed, 42.4 per cent agree that 'The number of children is the choice of the individual,' whereas 45.9 per cent do not agree. However, at the same time as many as 82.8 per cent of women agree that the leadership has no option but controlling

Figure 11: Placement of fertility decisions at national or individual level (based on answers to the question 'With our nation's present population characteristics, which of the following opinions do you agree with?')

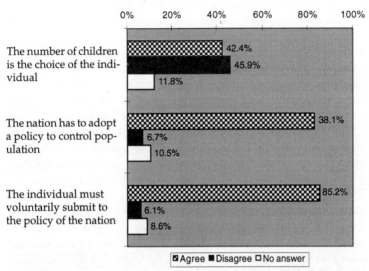

Number of women = 857.

population growth. This could be interpreted as an expression of verbal compliance to the policy norm. However, it might be interpreted as an indication that there is general agreement that solving the national population problem must be given priority over individual wishes. This interpretation might also be applied to the response to the question of whether the individual should voluntarily submit to the policy. Here 85.2 per cent agree.

The wording of the statement 'The number of children is the choice of the individual' conspicuously reflects the problem of formulating a questionnaire from a Western cultural perspective for application in a Chinese context. In the Chinese family the scope of individual self-determination in deciding on the number of children as a personal matter is limited. The number of children is considered a family matter relating first of all to social relations rather than to the feelings of individuals. Thus, when 45.9 per cent of the women indicate that the number of children, in their opinion, is not the choice of the individual, it is not possible to determine whether they are referring to the fact that decisions concerning a woman's fertility have traditionally and are still to a large degree the domain of the husband's family rather than of the woman herself and her husband. Or whether they are, as was the intent of the question, reflecting their attitudes to the fact that fertility decisions under the one-child family policy are the domain of the state. I have, however, chosen to retain the question and include the responses in the analysis in spite of it being posed from a Western individual-centred perspective and in spite of the uncertainty as regards the perspective from which women respond. The reason for retaining the question is that the responses reflect that a significant number of women (42.4 per cent) are in opposition either to the family or to state control of fertility.

Even though social relations are dominant and to a high degree do determine the actions of the individual in fertility matters, this does not necessarily imply that the individual woman does not at all give thought to her individual preferences. The case of the woman, just mentioned, who married in 1982 and wanted to postpone childbearing illustrates how she planned to act according to personal interests, though these were finally overridden by family interests. The 42.4 per cent of women who state that the number of children is the choice of the individual possibly indicates that, in the view of many women, fertility choices ought to belong to the personal domain as opposed to either the family or the state domain or possibly to the family as opposed to the state. The view that the number of children is the choice of the individual or even the family is clearly in contradiction to present reality in which fertility choices are relegated to the domain of the state.

However, this actual dissenting view does not necessarily result in non-acceptance. The majority of women agree that 'The nation has to adopt a policy to control population' and that 'The individual must voluntarily submit to the policy of the nation.' Responses to the first statement together with responses to the two following statements reflect how the response depends on the perspective being applied. Together, the three responses reflect that the individual perspective is less important than the perspective of the nation; the national perspective – and thereby what is perceived to be the interest of the nation – carries great weight. The three responses together also reflect that the two perspectives of family and state can and do occur simultaneously. Although this would seem to be a contradiction, it is not necessarily perceived as such and therefore does not give rise to non-acceptance of the policy. The response of a Beijing woman to the question of her opinion of the national birth planning policy will illustrate this point. She said:

> Population numbers in China are large and there are both advantages and disadvantages in having only one child. The advantage is that when two people care for one child, they will have more time to concentrate on the child's education. They would not be able to cope with two or more children. On the other hand, the only child will be lonely and selfish as there will not be other children in the home. Two children is better. From the perspective of the nation, population numbers are large, and one child is a benefit to future development. To the nation there are definite advantages in having only one child.

The point that the two perspectives and norm sets of the family and the state respectively are able to function side by side with the main attitude of the women being acceptance of the necessity of the policy was supported by the qualitative interviews. In the qualitative interviews women present just as manifold and varying responses to the issue of fertility preferences as is the case in the survey. The women expressed the view that the leadership, owing to the seriousness of the population problem, does not have any alternative to strictly implementing the one-child family policy. This view was expressed both by women who stated that they themselves wanted only one child in any case and by women who would have preferred two children, had there not been a one-child family policy. Some of these women were probably verbally complying with the policy norm but others were expressing genuine agreement with the policy.

Except for a few women who explicitly said they did not want more than one child, practically all the women interviewed explained the reason for having only one child by saying, as the woman cited at the beginning of this chapter, that they had 'responded to the call of the nation'. To the question of how they had planned the number and timing of their children, most answered along the lines of the following examples: One Shenyang woman who gave birth to her child in 1983 when she was 29 said 'At an early stage I was aware of the notion of only one child, since one couple, one child is the national policy. When I made up my mind as to how many children I wanted, this was already the official policy.' A Beijing woman said: 'The national policy allows the birth of only one child. This is the requirement of the nation.' While yet another woman said that 'One child per couple is taken for granted as something we all know.' And a Shenyang woman said that, when she gave birth in 1981, birth planning had been advocated for a long time, 'so from the beginning we planned to have one child'. The following exchange was characteristic of the responses given by women:

Q: How did you plan the number of children you wanted?

A: We only considered having one child.

Q: Why only one child?

A: This is the national policy, so we all respond to the call of the nation and have only one child. Moreover, we have received higher level education. The national policy is relatively foresighted, as population numbers are large whereas territory is limited, a large population is not sustainable, so it is necessary to control population increase. The policy is beneficial to the nation and to the people.

(from interview with a Shenyang woman, April 1992)

Some women quite openly stated that they have one child mainly due to the severe policy implementation. A Beijing woman who married in 1983 said: 'We did not discuss how many children we wanted, because only one child is permitted.' Planning a family of only one child has, as one woman said, become 'quite natural', and as another woman said, 'We did not think about it specifically, but now the policy is one child per couple. Also we did not want more than one child, we just wanted one child.' These responses reflect obvious compliance to the policy requirement, more visible in the following example than in the above. A Beijing woman, who had just said that she believed most women would prefer two children and that two children is a suitable number, was asked how many children she herself would then prefer. At first, she said that she did not want more than the one child she already had, and then she said: 'I [pause] ought to say I do not want more [pause] I do not really want ... ' She then laughed and did not complete the sentence, thus making it quite obvious that she did want more than one child but that she was not going to say so.

There is beyond any doubt a discrepancy between fertility preferences and the one child for many of the women. It is also obvious from the responses of women that they are fully aware that it is not possible for them as city district residents to have more than one child. However, at the same time the women in general actually support the rationale underlying the policy. Through their responses women expressed their knowledge of and support for the interpretation of rapid population increase as the cause of socio-economic problems.

Conclusion

The aim of this chapter has been to appraise the degree of one-child family policy acceptance among city-district women in Beijing and Shenyang. The point of departure was to estimate the extent of acceptance by ascertaining how many children the women surveyed would prefer and thereby whether there was a discrepancy between the policy requirement of one child and the preferred number of children, with discrepancy being viewed as a measure of non-acceptance.

Overall, the responses to the questions and statements on the preferred number of children are varied and manifold, the extremities being the 25.5 and 82.8 per cent who either would have or say it is best to have more than one child. In other words a significant number of women would prefer two children. There is a discrepancy between their fertility preference and the actual one child they have, from which it would follow that the one-child policy is not widely accepted. However, 62.9 per cent of the women agree to the statement: 'Even if there were no one-child family policy, I would have only one child.' Thus it would seem that, on the contrary, the policy is in fact widely accepted.

The wording of the questions undoubtedly has an effect on responses, with questions directly referring to the one-child family policy more easily eliciting responses that are in accordance with the state policy norm. Furthermore, although the women are being asked to provide their personal perspective in the survey, responses from the perspective of the nation or of the child are no less valid than responses from the perspective of the women themselves, as all these perspectives in the daily lives of women exist as merged and intertwined. Therefore, although the preferred number of children varies from question to question depending on the perspective the women are applying, there is not one measure of the preferred number of children that is more valid than the others. As it is impossible to reach an unambiguous representation of the preferred number of children, it is, therefore, also impossible to determine precisely for how many women there is a discrepancy between their preferred number of children and their actual one child. Although the varied and inconsistent responses to the questions on the preferred number of children would seem to indicate that the one-child family policy does not correspond to fertility preferences, the precise scope of the discrepancy cannot be measured. Therefore, the extent of policy acceptance is not readily gauged by measuring fertility preferences.

More importantly, even when there is a discrepancy between the preferred number of children and the limit of one child, this does not necessarily give rise to non-acceptance of the policy. The policy is accepted by women who agree that there is no alternative for the leadership other than to impose population control, while many at the same time disagree with the policy's fertility limit as their preferred number of children is two. The meaning of acceptance goes beyond agreement. Hermalin and Liu conclude that the one-child family policy is not widely accepted by Shanghai couples. The meaning of acceptance in their use is conceived of as equivalent to coherence between fertility preference and actual fertility. Following this line of thought, mandatory one-child mothers do not accept the one-child policy, they *comply* with the policy. My point is that even though there may be a discrepancy between fertility preference and the actual one child, the policy is nonetheless widely accepted by city district women. Even when there is a discrepancy between the preferred number of children and the one child, the one-child family policy can at the same time be accepted. The preferred number of children may be used as a measure of urban population control, in so far as a higher preference than one child indicates that the population policy has been the decisive fertility determinant. However, a preference for more than one child cannot be applied as an accurate measure of non-acceptance of the policy, as acceptance transcends individual and family fertility preferences.

City district women's support of the policy does not necessarily imply an acceptance based on people having absorbed uncritically the CCP norm. Survey responses based on a policy norm and national perspective cannot be understood exclusively as the result or an expression of political pressure, indoctrination or coercion. The policy is based on political pressure and coercion.

City district women have no choice other than to comply. But at the same time women accept the policy in so far as they do not question the ideology of the population policy nor the demographic targets. This study is not able to specify the exact degree to which this form of acceptance is found. Certainly, some women used the term 'responding to the call of the nation' simply as verbal compliance to the policy. Other women used the term to signify genuine agreement that the policy is necessary.

In the following chapters the understanding of acceptance is further developed through the description and analysis of city district women's management of the low fertility imposed upon them by the one-child family policy. The focus is on how urban one-child mothers handle the consequences of the one-child family policy in their everyday lives. In the analysis no distinction is established between women according to their fertility preferences. This is because it is not possible to reach an unambiguous representation of fertility preferences, and because acceptance is not directly linked to a correspondence between the policy fertility limit and family size preferences.

Interaction between Women and Birth Planning Workers

> Birth planning is voluntary, we do not apply force, but of course we have to use ideological education to over-come thousands of years of persistent feudal mentality.
>
> *Beijing city district birth planning cadre, June 1991*

> We have people managing birth planning at all levels. There are no leaks. There are no places without some-one managing birth planning. Why is birth planning in China managed so well? This is the most important aspect – that there is someone managing at all levels.
>
> *Liaoning factory birth planning cadre, April 1992*

Drawing mainly on interviews with birth planning personnel and women in Beijing and Shenyang, this chapter seeks to understand the cultural meanings inherent in the concept of acceptance at the micro level of society by examining the inter-action of urban birth planning workers and women. The first section describes the leadership concept of acceptance and the remedial measures of the one-child policy. The work of the birth planning institution and workers is also outlined. The second section presents women's perception of acceptance based on their experience of the interaction between themselves and birth planning workers. In the third section the cultural meaning of acceptance is discussed. However much it may disturb the Western feminist and/or human rights advocate, the majority of the urban one-child women studied do not define the one-child policy as other than voluntary. Even in cases where the policy is termed coercive by these urban women, they nonetheless accept the control exercised by birth planning workers to ensure that they follow the policy.

Policy Implementation

In cases of conflicting interests between the state and the individual, the latter is expected to acknowledge conscientiously that the interests of the state take precedence over the interests of the individual (Chen [1979] 1981: 11). Commenting on the interaction between the state and the people in achieving 'encouraging results' in population policy, sociologist Dai Kejing writes:

> It was achieved under *the principle of combining State direction with more-or-less voluntary action by the masses*. On the one hand, the State formulates and implements unified regulations to bring down the population growth. It also energetically supports and guarantees the realization of family planning by providing funds, scientific techniques, medical personnel and materials. On the other hand, the general public is called on to discuss the population plans in order to link their own family interests with those of the State's and to pave the way for the realization of the State's plans. Without *people's mainly voluntary and semi-voluntary cooperation*, even the present results would not have been achieved. (Dai 1990: 196–197)[1]

Since the inception of the post-Mao population policy, three measures for policy implementation have been emphasized with the aim of promoting the one-child family norm and reaching the policy target of stabilizing population numbers. These measures are ideological education (*xuanchuan jiaoyu*),[2] supplemented by administrative and economic measures (Wang 1981: 54–55). The essence of ideological education is that leading cadres and birth planning workers will explain the policy to the people in the

---

1. The Chinese word for 'voluntary' here is '*ziyuan*' (personal communication Dai Kejing).
2. Literally *xuanchuan jiaoyu* means to propagate education or propaganda education.

context of the national economic situation and the requirements of the modernization programme. In its 1991 Whitebook on human rights, the State Council thus stresses that: 'China adheres to the principle of combining government guidance with the wishes of the masses when carrying out its family planning policy', and that 'Government officials are required to take the lead in carrying out the policy and set a good example' (*Human Rights* 1991: 67–68). Presuming that leaders and officials do their job well, the people will 'definitely and immediately accept the program for control of population growth' (Chen [1979] 1981).

Former PRC programs leading to considerable social reform[3] have been initiated by nationwide propaganda that explained the need for the program, the problems it addressed, and the value to the nation as a whole.[4] In putting into effect these programs of social change, the state has made use of coercive measures, but education and persuasion have been seen as the more important factors in bringing about compliance. The practice has been to separate the uninformed, uneducated and unwilling population, who are assumed to be susceptible to propaganda, from a small group of those in actual opposition. In the case of one-child family policy implementation, in view of the magnitude of rural opposition, it has proved exceedingly difficult to establish a small group of transgressors (Kallgren 1985: 134–135). In the ideal situation, the majority of the populace will be persuaded by ideological education alone to adhere to the policy of one couple one child. When ideological education is not sufficient, economic measures are resorted to.[5] A 1982 *Directive of the Central Committee of the Communist Party of*

---

3. These included the 1950 Marriage Law, the law regulating labour insurance, the effort to outlaw the use of opium and suppress prostitution, programs of social assistance, as well as efforts to improve health and offer universal education (Kallgren 1985).

4. For a discussion of the campaign to implement the one-child family policy as a continuation of the pre-1978 political practice of mobilization of the party and mass organizations to take a lead in implementation, as well as the skilful and massive use of the propaganda apparatus, see White 1990.

5. In order to obtain a picture of how many couples would in fact be willing to have only one child, the State Council Birth Planning Group in 1978 carried out a series of investigations. Among other results the investigations indicated that in Shanghai municipality 60 per cent of the urban population, about 19 per cent of the suburban population and 1.9 per cent of the population in the outer suburban districts were willing to have only one child. Not surprisingly, the number of couples in rural areas willing to have only one child was quite low. The use of a system of incentives and penalties for policy implementation was then suggested at a national conference of birth planning workers in January 1979 (Li 1980: 5).

China and the State Council of the PRC on Doing a Better Job with Birth Planning Work stressed that birth planning work should rest primarily on ideological education and encouragement and that economic penalties were only to be applied to a minority of the populace, who after patient persuasion were still not willing to adhere to policy requirements. Those who, after repeated education, still do not act according to the birth planning policy should be subjected to the necessary economic sanctions (*Zhonggong zhongyang* 1986: 46).

The aim is, as expressed by the official terminology, to educate people to follow the policy and to ensure that the policy that is based on the interests of the state and the people is not violated. The rationale for applying economic penalties was that couples who have more children place additional financial burdens on the state and the collective. It is a reasonable measure, the argument goes, that they should carry part of that burden themselves (Chen [1979] 1981, Wang 1981: 54).[6] The 1982 directive also states that:

> For state cadres and workers and urban dwellers that have a second child in violation of the plan, the medical attention and general state-sponsored welfare benefits that they would normally enjoy under compliance with the plan should be eliminated. Furthermore, their wages may be reduced or held up proportionately in accordance with the circumstances, or they may be suspended from enjoying subsidies given for special difficulties and for childcare. (*Zhonggong zhongyang* 1986: 47)

Penalties for transgressing the policy are aimed not only at the couple that has defied the policy, but also aimed at the birth planning workers responsible for policy implementation and at the group (the rural village or urban work-unit) to which the couple are administratively attached. The following is an example of group penalties. In a Sichuan township in 1989, if a family had more than one child the fine was 1,000 yuan or more. In addition, birth planning workers at various administrative levels were fined between 50 and 100 yuan. All members of a production team paid 1 yuan annually to a common fund. If one family had more than one child, all families would lose their payments. The system,

---

6. Professor Ma Yinchu applied similar arguments when in his 'New Population Theory' he proposed that, in addition to propaganda and education, 'sterner and more effective methods' should be employed to curb the population growth rate (Ma 1957). When his work was published in 1957 he was thus accused of regarding the people as criminals (Chen Zhongli 1979).

according to local government leaders, implied strong group pressure from the other villagers towards any couple who might contemplate having a second child (Delman 1989).

The collective system of penalties is, in principle, also applied in urban China, although in practice the mere threat of penalties is usually sufficient to ensure compliance with the policy. One study mentions that urban factories may halt payment of one-child benefits to all employees until a woman agrees to abortion (Wolf 1985: 245). At the district factory, each workshop signs an annual agreement to fulfil a series of birth planning targets. The overall objective of the agreement is, according to factory birth planning workers, to strengthen the planned management of births and to keep the total annual number of births in the city district within about 6,000 births. If the targets are reached, a reward is granted; and if not, workshop employees are penalized. The targets include allowing no second births, and achieving planned birthrates, late childbearing rates and late marriage rates at 100 per cent. Targets also include being a 'three no work unit' (*san wu danwei*), which means having no births prior to marriage, no unplanned births and no late abortions. Finally the target includes reaching a long-term contraception rate of 70 per cent. This means that a minimum of 70 per cent of women of repro-ductive age must be either using an IUD or sterilized.

Economic measures also include incentives. These primarily take the form of a one-child certificate (*dusheng zinüzheng*), also called a one-child honorary certificate (*dusheng zinü guangrongzheng*). Once the child is born, parents register for a one-child certificate by pledging not to have more than one child. Thereby it is under-stood that should the woman become pregnant again, she will have an abortion. The one-child certificate entitles parents to a monthly healthcare cash payment until their child reaches the age of 14, as well as to material benefits and privileges that vary from locality to locality.[7] The cash payment is borne on a fifty-fifty basis by the parents' work units. At the two factories studied in Beijing, the monthly subsidy was 10 yuan per child.[8] In addition, there

---

7. For examples of one-child benefits, see for instance Davin 1987: 113–115, Greenhalgh 1993: 238–239, Kallgren 1985: 148 and Saith 1981: 495.

8. According to the birth planning worker at one Beijing factory, in 1991 the Beijing Birth Planning Regulations (*Beijingshi jihua shengyu tiaoli*) stipulated that the monthly one-child cash payment could be increased from 5 to 10 yuan, depending on the economic ability of the work units. The regulations do not, however, mention the amount to be paid.

was a milk subsidy for the child up to 2 years of age (4 yuan a month at the Beijing factory – 2 yuan from each of the parent's work units) and a childcare subsidy as well as priority in free medical care and schooling. According to a birth planning cadre, the aim of applying incentives was to encourage parents to bring up a healthy child and to follow the one-child policy. At the district factory a bonus of 30 yuan was released upon registration for a one-child certificate according to factory rules. At the Beijing factory the bonus for registering for the certificate was 50 yuan. If a couple, after having received the benefits of a one-child certificate, then contrary to the contract do have a second child, the usual practice is that all incentives must be returned.

In contrast to rural China, active opposition to the policy in the city districts has been relatively small. According to one district level birth planning cadre in Beijing, there have been only rare cases of opposition because, as she says:

> The state call for one couple one child is advocated by way of voluntary [*ziyuan*] acceptance. The policy is based on everyone understanding the benefit of the policy for the nation and understanding the burden being placed on society. Also the policy is based on everyone deciding on their own fertility according to their own interests.

In other words, according to this birth planning cadre, in the city districts ideological education as the main remedial measure has been more or less sufficient towards all but a relatively small group in opposition. At the district factory the birth planning cadre, who has been responsible for birth planning work since 1969, found that the early years of one-child policy implementation had been difficult.[9] One-child implementation started at the factory in 1980 when the CCP Central Committee issued its *Open Letter*. The birth planning cadre explains:

> The difficulties were due to the feudal habit of the more children the better. Also people felt one child would be too lonely. Gradually, following ideological education and ideological work, birth planning has become easier as people have become accustomed to the policy. We continuously propagate population theory. We explain that although the territory of China is large, arable land is limited and cannot be enlarged. The more people,

---

9. Birth planning cadres interviewed by Elisabeth Croll in Beijing in the early 1980s had a similar experience of the early years of the policy being the most difficult (Croll 1985b).

the less arable land per person. At our factory people will now answer that they do not want a second child if you ask them ... Before 1980 the policy was 'one is not too few – two is best' [*yige bu shao – liangge zhen hao*]. So after 1980 there were people who still wanted two children. Of course there were problems in the beginning as it takes time to change the attitude [*sixiang*] of people. However, following our work and the efforts made by our work unit, the employees gradually have accepted [*jieshou*] the policy. Certainly not all at once but gradually. It was not very easy to change the notion of two children.

Before turning to a closer study of urban one-child policy implementation, the structure of the urban birth planning institution is delineated using the example of the Beijing Municipality birth planning institution. The birth planning institution is divided into two parallel vertical systems based on area of residence and work unit (see Figure 12). At the highest level the Beijing Family Planning Commission is situated directly under the Beijing Municipal Government.[10] Related to area of residence, each of the subsequent administrative birth planning levels are placed under the authority of government administration at the levels of city district government,[11] street government and residents' committee.[12] Related to workplace, there are birth planning units at the levels of municipal commercial and industrial bureau and departments, municipal enterprises and business units as well as at local level work unit branches and workshops. The levels of the birth planning institution in the city district at the residential area levels

10. For an account of the structure and work of the Beijing Family Planning Commission in implementing the one-child family policy in the early 1980s, see Croll 1985b. I would prefer to translate the Beijing Family Planning Commission (*Beijingshi jihua shengyu weiyuanhui*) to Beijing Birth Planning Commission, not only because birth planning is closer to the literal translation of *jihua shengyu* (planned fertility/birth), but also and mainly because the term family planning as a human right is not compatible with the Chinese concept of birth planning. I have, nonetheless, followed the practice of applying the official Chinese translation in order not to create confusion. For lower levels of the birth planning institution I have, however, used 'birth planning' for *jihua shengyu*.

11. Only the administrative levels of urban and suburban Beijing are included here. The system for the rural counties is identical at the levels of county (*xian*), township (*xiang*) and village (*cun*).

12. *Jiedao weiyuanhui* is translated as street committee and *jumin weiyuanhui* as residents' committee. In 1988 there were 35 street committees and 1,308 residents' committees in the city districts of Beijing. Dongcheng district had 10 and 346 respectively; Xicheng district 10 and 418; Chongwen district 7 and 235; and Xuanwu district 8 and 309 (*Beijingshi shehui* 1990: 7).

are city district birth planning committees, street committee birth planning offices, full-time (*zhuanzhi*) and part-time (*jianzhi*) birth planning cadres, and at the lowest level propagandists (*xuanchuanyuan*).[13] At the workplace, the levels of the birth planning institution are birth planning offices at municipal bureau and department level; birth planning offices at the level of work-units; full-time birth and part-time birth planning cadres; and propagandists.

Figure 12: Structure of birth planning institution, Beijing

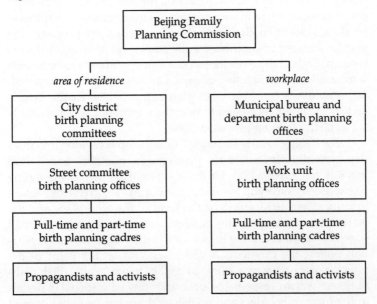

Source: Adapted from Li Muzhen 1987: 412.

The district factory employs 469 workers and administrative personnel, of whom 307 are women. Of the 307 women, 216 are women of reproductive age, in Chinese terms meaning married women who have not yet reached the age of 50. The factory has one part-time birth planning cadre and eight propagandists – one in each of the six production workshops as well as two propagandists

13. Here the term 'cadre' means party and state functionary. In the following the terms 'birth planning cadre' and 'birth planning propagandist' are used to designate two separate levels in the birth planning hierarchy, while 'birth planning workers' is used as a general term to designate both cadres and propagandists when both are involved or no distinction is necessary.

who are responsible for the administrative personnel. The propagandists serve as assistants to the part-time birth planning cadre who assigns them specific tasks. The birth planning cadre at the Shenyang factory had worked full-time at birth planning work since 1982. She is responsible for birth planning work at the factory, which employs 1,300 workers and administrative personnel and supervises the birth planning propagandists in the four workshops and four departments of the factory. When she has attended a meeting at a higher birth planning institutional level concerning policy implementation, she passes on the information to the eight propagandists. They in turn convey the information to employees in their respective departments. One workshop propagandist was for instance responsible for 130 employees of whom 100 were women. Each of the workshops is further organized systematically into smaller birth planning groups. One spinning workshop with 400 employees has four birth planning activists. At the Beijing factory the union representatives in the workshops simultaneously act as birth planning propagandists.

The Beijing Family Planning Commission is divided into three departments responsible for propaganda, planning and liaison work (Croll 1985b: 198). Of these three areas of birth planning work, propaganda and ideological education are given the highest priority (Shen 1990: 60).[14] At the level of the workplace and the residential area birth planning ideological education is first of all based on communicating information on the need for the population policy, the problems it addresses, and on the value of the policy to the nation as a whole as well as to the family. Birth planning workers are responsible for distributing educational materials in the form of booklets and leaflets that are handed out either at meetings held especially at the residential area or at the workplace to study the national birth planning policy, or at home visits, or on the street in connection with large-scale propaganda activities. In Beijing these large-scale activities organized at the level of the District Birth Planning Committee take place two or three times a year. Typically the times are the Spring Festival (Chinese New Year); in April–May when there is usually a surge of weddings and in October up to and following the National Day on 1 October, when many weddings also take place. Large propaganda bill-

---

14. For an overview of propaganda and education work within the framework of the population policy, see Shen 1990: 57–69.

boards are set up in the streets, and birth planning workers hand out pamphlets to passers-by, who can also put questions to propagandists.

In 1989 the Beijing Family Planning Commission arranged three large-scale birth planning ideological education activities covering the whole municipality. Additional ideological education activities were for instance a radio program in cooperation with the Beijing People's Broadcasting Station. Also, more than 300 articles and radio/television features distributed by the Beijing Family Planning Commission were carried by newspapers, magazines, radio and television and, in cooperation with the Beijing Population Society, ten well-known population experts were invited to give talks at every city district, suburb and county on the population situation and on population theory (*Beijingshi shehui* 1990: 160–161). The scope of the birth planning institution in carrying out large-scale activities such as Birth Planning Month (held annually in January) is indicated by the more than 15 million cadres and propagandists, as well as about 700,000 medical personnel that took part in the 1983 activities nationwide (Shen 1990: 61).

To a large degree, birth planning cadres at the factories and residents' committees base their ideological education work on the newspaper *China Population* (*Zhongguo renkoubao*), published bi-weekly by the State Family Planning Commission, as well as on other newspapers such as *China Women's News* (*Zhongguo funübao*). At the Shenyang factory, the full-time birth planning cadre subscribes to *China Population*, and in addition she buys materials such as posters and leaflets from the Shenyang Educational Centre. At the district factory, a weekly newspaper carrying excerpts from *China Population* and *China Women's News* is published. The factories also use their internal radio systems to transmit propaganda. Furthermore, information is carried on blackboards and printed materials are distributed to all employees.

At the Beijing factory in 1990 the factory branch of the CCP and the factory birth planning office checked up on the knowledge of factory Party and Youth League members on the population policy using a written one-page test. At the Shenyang factory, the birth planning cadre felt that birth planning work had been carried out quite well during the past ten years. The factory had been made an 'advanced birth planning unit' at both city district and municipal levels; there had not been many difficulties, because the attitude of the employees was relatively good. As in Beijing, propaganda emphasis was placed on the principle of focusing on ideological work supplemented by the practice of a regular effort, meaning that it was important to carry out birth planning work every single day, not only on special occasions such as the New Year. Until a couple of years ago the Shenyang factory arranged an annual propaganda event in the streets aimed at all young people over 15 years of age. The event was arranged in cooperation between the factory and the residential area in which the factory is situated.

Such cooperation is part of a wider pattern of integration. The work unit and the residential area birth planning institutions work together in a system of 'combined line and area' (*tiaokuai jiehe*),[15] in which the work unit provides vertical control from above to below while the residential area provides overall daily surveillance with its residents. Although the residential area does not have as much control over the lives of its residents as the vertical work unit system, it works in close cooperation with work units and is able to report to the work units if there are aspects of her life a resident is attempting to conceal. Residential area and work unit work is thus coordinated in monitoring the contraceptive practice of women. If there are any difficulties, the work unit will make contact with the residential area to coordinate their work.

Control is not only administered downwards from birth planning cadres and propagandists towards the women within their jurisdiction; birth planning workers themselves are also controlled. Just as the propagandists are under the supervision of the birth planning cadre, birth planning cadres are subject to the supervision of higher levels of the birth planning institution. The Beijing factory birth planning cadre felt that higher levels handle birth planning implementation 'relatively severely' and she felt stressed by all the meetings she had to attend. She takes part in two regular monthly meetings, one at the company to which the factory is affiliated and one at the district level. The objective of both meetings is mutual exchange of information. The birth planning cadre reports on the situation at her factory and receives assistance if she is having any problems, and she receives information to pass on to the women at her factory. She remarks that, during the

---

15. See Lee 1991: 359–360.

monthly meetings, higher-level birth planning cadres emphasize that the birth planning cadres at the work unit level must under no circumstances allow unplanned births. The Beijing factory birth planning cadre hands in a monthly report to the district birth planning administration concerning the contraceptive practice of all married female employees who have already given birth. The report functions not only to control the contraceptive practice of the women, but also to control the work of the birth planning cadre. The monthly report includes information on the number of women of reproductive age employed, their contraceptive practices, the number of only children and their sex. The Beijing factory birth planning cadre says her work is quite bothersome. There are too many forms to fill in. She registers employees for marriage; employees must have a permit to be allowed to give birth; and when their child has been born, the parents must be registered for one-child certificates. The birth planning cadre is responsible for birth planning work on a part-time basis but feels the job ought to be full-time, as she is also the factory doctor and has to take care of the general health problems of employees.

According to one birth planning cadre, the rare problems encountered in the city district are usually related to either the older generation insisting on having a grandson to carry on the family line or to second marriages. When grandparents pressure the younger generation to have a grandson, birth planning workers will visit the home of the grandparents to convince them and to explain to them that 'men and women are equal' and that a daughter as well as a son can support parents in old age and carry on the family line.[16] The problem in relation to second marriage occurs when someone who has been married earlier and has a child from the previous marriage, remarries and the newly wed couple wish to have a child. According to a district level birth planning cadre, birth planning workers try to convince the person who does not have a child to accept the spouse's child as if it were their own. The district birth planning cadre says birth planning workers use Liu Huifang from the TV series *Expectations* (*Kewang*) as an example worth following: 'We encourage them to learn from the spirit of Liu Huifang.' In the popular TV series, transmitted in

---

16. When the Marriage Law was revised in 1980, birth planning became the fifth fundamental principle of the law. Several articles stress that a daughter has the same rights and obligations towards her parents as a son.

Beijing several times in the early 1990s, a young woman by the name of Liu Huifang takes in a child who has no parents. Liu Huifang comes to love the child very much and takes care of her as if she were her own child. The example of Liu Huifang is promoted in the context of the birth planning ideological education so that others can study her example. This is not with a view to having people take in homeless children, the birth planning cadre emphasizes, but is specifically related to the problem of people with one or two children from an earlier marriage re-marrying. The idea is to teach the spouse who does not have a child to accept the child of the partner as their own.

The person or group that does not feel immediately obliged to follow a given policy following ideological education is subjected to persuasion (*dongyuan*). 'To do work' (*zuo gongzuo*) which is short for 'to do thought-work' (*zuo sixiang gongzuo*) is also used to influence and change people's thoughts or attitude. Persuasion as well as thought-work is applied *to cause or induce someone to have a certain belief or to cause or induce someone into a certain action*. In order to draw a very broad distinction between ideological education as opposed to persuasion, one might say that, while ideological education is conveyed to educate the populace in general, persuasion takes place as a direct personal meeting between the birth planning worker/workers and the person/persons unwilling to comply with a given policy. The susceptibility of the unwilling to persuasion depends on the nature and context of the issue in question.

In addition to ideological education and the system of economic incentives and penalties, the third policy measure is the administrative use of a national quota for annual births. In urban China the annual quota of births is distributed from the highest levels of birth planning administration downwards in a system where birth planning personnel at workplaces and residential areas work in close cooperation.[17] Birth planning cadres at the level of the work unit and the residential area manage the distribution of the annual quota of births to women in their jurisdiction. Before she becomes pregnant, a woman must apply for a share of the quota. First, the woman must apply to her work unit for a certificate confirming that she has reached the age of late

---

17. The planning department of the Beijing Family Planning Commission is responsible for setting the goals for each administrative level during the coming year (Croll 1985b: 198).

birth. The residential area Birth Planning Office then issues an official document granting her permission to become pregnant (for application procedures according to the Beijing Municipality Birth Planning Regulations, see Box 2). When she does become pregnant, the woman will need the document to gain access to pre-natal services. As the birth planning cadre at the Beijing factory notes, a woman will not obtain permission to become pregnant without agreement from both the residential area and the work unit, because childbearing must be planned. Until recently (as far as the Beijing factory birth planning cadre remembers this was until 1990), the residential area would more or less automatically issue a birth permit to any woman whose work unit had confirmed that she fulfilled the late childbearing requirement. Since then, however, the work unit has had to coordinate more closely with the residential area, as the residential area will only issue a birth permit if the quota has not been used.

Box 2: Birth quota application procedures

Question: Who can apply for the birth planning quota?

Answer: Couples in which both the husband and the wife are married for the first time, who comply with the requirement of late age at birth of child may apply for the one-child birth plan quota.

Couples of reproductive age who comply with the conditions for giving birth to a second child may apply for the two-child birth plan quota.

Question: How should one apply for the one-child birth quota?

Answer: All first-time married women of reproductive age registered in this district who have reached the age of late childbearing, who are not yet pregnar t and whose work unit has issued a birth plan certificate, should during the specified time limit procure a quota at the residents' committee. Following the inspection, approval of and endorsement by the residents' committee, the woman is permitted to become pregnant upon return of the endorsed certificate to the work unit. Otherwise the the pregnancy is considered as outside the plan.

Source: *Dongchengqu jihua shengyu bangongshi, jihua shengyu xiehui*

The following example illustrates a case of relatively un-complicated persuasion related to the distribution of birth permissions. When in 1988 the Beijing city district had a surge of women born in the 1960s applying for birth permits, they were asked to queue according to their age. The birth planning cadre explains:

We let the eldest, the 28-, 27-, and 26-year-olds give birth first, and persuaded the 24- and 25-year-olds to wait for two years. After we persuaded them, they agreed to wait and we did not give them a permit. If, for example, we have three women applying for a birth permit but we only have a quota of two, we will persuade the youngest woman to wait until next year. We discuss the situation with her taking her personal situation into consideration, saying for example: 'You are still studying or you have just started working, so you need to make a special effort at school or at work. Don't you agree?' And she will agree to wait another year. This is the way we persuade. Birth planning work is precisely to persuade people. We make everyone understand, make them support and agree with the policy. We do not apply force.

According to the birth planning cadre, if a woman who does not have a child becomes pregnant without a permit and she is 24 years old or older, which is regarded as late childbearing, a birth permit will usually be issued to her. If she has not reached the age of late childbearing, she will be persuaded to have an abortion.

If someone is not immediately susceptible to being persuaded, cadres will continuously visit the reluctant person or persons and will explain the reasons that it is necessary to comply with the policy until the person is ready to accept the policy. This form of persuasion is not an innovation of the new order, but is a traditional process that was also applied before 1949 (Potter and Potter 1990: 65).[18] Cases of women who give birth to more than one child with or without permission are, as noted in Chapter 2, rare in the city districts of both Shenyang and Beijing and only occur under special circumstances. The following cases of Beijing city district births without permission, i.e. *unplanned births*, serve to illustrate the extreme situations that do give rise to births outside the official quota. In one case the woman was a private entrepreneur. The penalty of firing her from her job could therefore not be applied. Furthermore, her family of private entrepreneurs was able to pay the fine for having a second child. While the older generation and second marriages are the main problem areas within the work unit, private entrepreneurs and immigrants, the so-called 'floating population', are the more serious urban problem groups. The emergence of a 'floating population' of rural migrants to urban areas, where they cannot obtain permanent residence,

---

18. For a description of how the practice of persuasion was applied in a village during the collectivization process, see Potter and Potter 1990: 65.

has been one of the consequences of the economic reforms. The 'floating population' is difficult to control as they are not registered at the main urban birth planning control posts – the work unit and the residential area.

The effect of economic penalties towards private entrepreneurs has been eroded as they are often willing to pay the sizeable fines incurred. In 1992 the fine for having a second child in Beijing was between 5,000 and 50,000 yuan and between 20,000 and 100,000 yuan for a third child (Beijing birth planning worker, June 1992 and personal communication from Chinese scholar). These are quite substantial sums compared to a normal monthly salary of approximately 200–300 yuan. According to the Beijing factory birth planning cadre, penalties as stipulated by the 1991 Beijing Birth Planning Regulations are far more severe than the penalties that were in effect up to 1991 as stipulated by the previous 138 documents, according to which birth planning work was implemented prior to the promulgation of the Beijing Municipality Birth Planning Regulations. Now management of birth planning implementation is more meticulous. Economic penalties have increased to fines of up to 100,000 yuan for the birth of a third child compared to a few per cent of monthly wages earlier. The reason for the change is, according to the birth planning cadre, that some people did not care about small fines. She views the increase of the fines as an indication of the policy being implemented more severely, as ordinary people absolutely do not have that much money. The precise amount of the fines varies from work unit to work unit. At one work unit the fine for a second child in 1992 was 10,000 yuan. The Beijing Regulations do not, however, specify the size of fines.

Another case of a child born without permission concerned a woman who married a divorcee who had a child already. According to the 1991 Beijing Birth Planning Regulations, a re-married couple could be permitted to have a second child if either the husband or the wife has a child, but not if they both do (*Beijingshi jihua* 1991: Section 3, Article 4). However, at this particular work unit regulations were more strict, and as the husband already had a child from a previous marriage, his second wife could not obtain permission to become pregnant. In this case the couple decided to have a child without having received a birth permit. The consequence was that the woman was fined 8,000 yuan and fired from her job. However, although she was officially fired, she kept her job on a temporary contract that did not entitle her to the subsidies she had otherwise been entitled to (personal communication from Chinese scholar)

In another case, a 40-year-old woman, who had married a divorcee with two children, became pregnant. The two birth planning workers at her work unit disagreed as to whether she should have an abortion or not. One was willing to let her have the child, while the other said she could not. However, as she did not have a birth permit, the birth planning cadres eventually compromised. The woman said they 'made her have an abortion' otherwise her bonus would be deducted. Then, following the abortion, they helped her to obtain a birth permit so that she could become pregnant again.

At the level of the work unit and the residential area, the duty of birth planning cadres and propagandists is mainly to carry out ideological education work and to do practical work directed at married women of reproductive age in order to implement the policy. Birth planning workers are responsible for the initial procedures involved in registering women for obtaining permission to marry, and give birth, and for applying for one-child certificates. They also perform a double role of caring for and controlling women as they supply them with contraceptives and monitor their contraceptive practice. Caring includes not only the free distribution of contraceptives, making arrangements for abortions and administering incentives, but also assisting families who, for example, have difficulties in making arrangements for childcare.[19] Once a woman has given birth, her contraceptive practice is monitored at her workplace and at the residential area in which she lives. The extent to which contraceptive practice is controlled and monitored varies, as it is up to the individual work unit and residential area administration to decide on the degree of monitoring necessary to avoid second births.

---

19. Much of the birth planning work is carried out in cooperation with the China Family Planning Association (*Zhongguo jihua shengyu xiehui*) established in 1980. For an introduction to the work of the association, see Zhou 1990. The work of the Family Planning Association has not been included in this study. In urban China the Association is especially engaged in work relating to private entrepreneurs and the floating population, as neither group is covered by the control of the work unit.

Interaction between Urban Birth Planning Workers and Women

At the Beijing factory, women aged 23 and men aged 25 fulfil the requirement of late marriage. These ages are three years higher than those stipulated by the 1980 Marriage Law. At the Shenyang factory a woman must be 21 years old to marry. However, as the age limit for late childbearing is 23, women who marry earlier must pledge to postpone childbearing until they reach the age of 23. A similar system is applied at the Beijing factory. If an employee who has not reached the age limit wishes to marry, the birth planning worker will persuade her to postpone the marriage. The incentive for a postponement is a late marriage reward of ten days' paid postnuptial vacation. There are, however, exceptional cases that the birth planning cadre is willing to make allowances for. For instance if the husband-to-be of a 22-year-old woman is 30 years old, they will be permitted to marry, but on the condition that the woman postpones childbearing. According to the Beijing Birth Planning Regulations, a woman who has reached 24 years of age is considered a late childbearer. At the Beijing factory this is interpreted to mean that a woman must be 24 years old before being permitted to give birth, which implies that if an employee gives birth prior to reaching this age, she will be penalized.

The birth planning worker will not issue a marriage request form, without which residential area officials will not register a marriage, to the 22-year-old woman unless she signs a late birth contract.[20] The contract is made out in three copies of which one remains at the work unit, one is taken to the residential area office and one is for the woman to keep. The woman will not be permitted to give birth without the approval of both the residential area and the work unit. In the words of the factory birth planning cadre: 'The three parties: the woman, the street committee and the work unit must agree before the woman will be allowed to give birth.' This system of approval by the residential area as well as by the work unit before a woman may obtain a birth permit is identical to the previously described quota system that applies to all women.

---

20. According to the birth planning cadre at the Beijing factory, these rules were effective in the four city districts of Beijing. Due to the precarious conditions of data collection it was not possible to confirm this at higher levels of the birth planning institution.

The most important duty of birth planning workers prior to the birth of the first and only child is to ensure late marriage and late childbearing. Once a woman has married, birth planning workers will inform her of the procedures necessary to obtain a birth permit. Generally they do not offer information about contraceptives to women until after they have given birth to their child. As the majority of women plan to conceive immediately after marriage, they do not seriously use contraceptives until after they have given birth to their child. Some feel it would be fine not to conceive during the first year or two, which would give them an opportunity to amuse themselves, but they seldom actually use contraceptives to avoid pregnancy.

Generally women consider marrying in their mid or late twenties to be 'late', 'relatively late' and 'very late', so they plan to conceive as soon as possible. Only in exceptional cases, as for instance if one or both spouses are students or the couple is waiting for better housing conditions, will they be using contraceptives specifically in order to postpone conception. A survey conducted in 1981 in Beijing showed that unmarried women preferred to marry at an average age of 25, and that about half (54 per cent) of the women interviewed thought it would be best to have their child in the second year of marriage (quoted in Tuan 1989: 57). Of the women in this study, 82.2 per cent gave birth to their child within two years of their marriage. Based on data from the 1987 IDFS, a study concludes that, while the proportion of women having their first birth within 18 months after marriage has increased steadily in all provinces, both in rural and urban areas, urban Beijing is the exception. Here there may be an emerging group of women who are postponing the birth of their child deliberately (Choe *et al.* 1991). Whether or not women are interested in using contraceptives and postponing conception once they have married, it is obvious that generally birth planning workers do not take an interest in the contraceptive practice of women until after they have given birth. The objective of their work is decidedly not to support women in planning their family but to ensure that the policy measure of one child is adhered to.

One Beijing woman who did not plan to conceive immediately after marrying was given no information on how to avoid pregnancy. In her opinion, if you had asked the birth planning cadres, they would probably have thought that she and her husband ought to have a child and that they did not need contraceptives. One Shenyang woman thought the reason that birth planning workers had not contacted her when she got married was that it was not necessary for them to start convincing her until after she had given birth to one child. Women had no expectation that birth planning workers would assist and support them with information about and choice of contraceptive method when they married. An employee at the Beijing factory, who married in 1985 at the age of 26 and planned to postpone childbearing for four years as both she and her husband were taking university classes in the evenings after work, said they read books on how to avoid pregnancy. Also they bought condoms at a pharmacy, because both she and her husband found that it was embarrassing to ask for free contraceptives at their work unit. On the other hand, the birth planning cadre at the Beijing factory expects women to contact her if they need her help. She herself does not take the initiative until after the birth of the first child. As one Beijing woman said:

> Now that I have one child I must use contraceptives, whereas when I was newly married and as yet had no child, it didn't matter that I was suddenly pregnant. Now I have to use contraceptives because only one child is allowed and anything else would be a violation of the policy.

In a leaflet in the form of a letter to young people who have not yet married, one Beijing city district birth planning office and Birth Planning Association do however encourage not only late marriage but also postponement of birth for two to three years (Dongchengqu 1990).

The most important part of birth planning work starts after the birth of the first child and is designed to make sure that women do not have a second child. This is done by ensuring that women use contraceptives and apply for a one-child certificate and by constantly controlling and monitoring their contraceptive practice.[21] The Shenyang factory birth planning cadre says:

> Contraceptives are the most important. In order to adhere to the call of the nation that each couple has only one child, it is of utmost importance that all women who have given birth use a contra-

---

21. None of the birth planning workers mentioned that their work was in any way aimed at male employees or residents, just as the women generally themselves took it for granted that they alone were responsible for not becoming pregnant. Information on male use of contraceptives does exist (see Li and Liu 1990).

ceptive method which suits them, first of all IUDs. Prior to the birth of the child the birth planning cadres do not intervene, except of course in regard to women who marry before they reach the age of 23. If women are physiologically suited to using an IUD, they are given an IUD. If they are not physiologically suited to the use of an IUD, we do not force them to use one, but let them use some other form of contraceptive method. We prefer IUDs because they are relatively reliable and do not easily fail.

Once a woman has given birth and is using a contraceptive, she is continuously and closely monitored by both her street committee and work unit. This is where the propagandists in every workshop play a role. If a women gets pregnant without a permit, they will notice and inform the birth planning cadre, who will then contact the woman and make sure she has an abortion as soon as possible.

The most frequently used form of contraceptive is the IUD.[22] At the district factory, 170–180 of 216 married women of reproductive age were using an IUD or had been sterilized, while about ten women were using contraceptive pills. Having an IUD inserted following the birth of their child has more or less become a matter of course to urban women. A worker at the Shenyang factory who gave birth to her daughter in 1986 said:

> I use – the habit in China is to use an IUD. After giving birth to a child you go to have an IUD inserted. The IUD is a good contraceptive method that safeguards the health of women. The work unit makes arrangements for an annual X-ray check-up at the hospital, which is quite convenient. All the women using IUDs go along. Everyone uses an IUD. After the birth of one child nearly everyone uses an IUD and there are no side effects.

The birth planning propagandist at the Shenyang factory confirms that the most-used contraceptive after first birth at the factory is in fact the IUD. As she says:

---

22. In 1981, 69.46 per cent of women of reproductive age in China were using contraception. Of these 50.20 per cent were using the IUD, while 25.40 per cent had been sterilized (tubal ligation). In 1987, 71.21 per cent of women of reproductive age were using contraceptives with 41.48 per cent of these using an IUD and 38.24 per cent having been sterilized. The proportion of men who were sterilized (vasectomy) was 10 per cent in 1982 and 10.99 per cent in 1987 (Zhu 1990: 276). The Chinese IUD has no tail, which means that it cannot be safely removed by the user or by any unskilled person. 'IUDs are not supposed to be forced on women, but removals which have not been officially sanctioned are referred to as "illegal removals", even if they have been sought by the woman herself' (Davin 1990: 85).

The objective is to ensure that every couple has only one child. Not to let anyone have a second child. Usually no one wants a second child. There is no problem. Sometimes, however, the contraceptives fail. But all women conscientiously have an abortion. I do not have to convince them.

Apart from sterilization, birth planning workers prefer IUDs, which are also defined as long-term methods because they only need to be checked once or twice a year. Both at the Shenyang factory and the district factory the check-up takes place by use of X-ray. According to a Beijing birth planning worker, an IUD is usually effective for ten years, but if the woman has any problems, she can switch to another form of contraceptive method. Because the IUD in its most common form has no tail, the IUD user must seek permission for removal of the IUD; it cannot be removed by the woman herself or by an unskilled person. Unauthorized removals are forbidden, but they do take place with a risk to the health of women (Davin 1987: 120).

Women are expected to have an IUD inserted about three to six months following the birth of their child. One woman did mention that she was offered an IUD immediately following the birth of her child by Caesarian. She had not been asked beforehand but, as the doctor said it would save time, she had one inserted then and there. Birth planning workers at both the residential area and the work unit make sure that women do have IUDs inserted. At the Beijing factory it is, according to the birth planning cadre, no longer necessary to persuade women to use IUDs; usually they themselves approach the birth planning cadre. At the Shenyang residential area, birth planning workers visit women about six months after they have given birth to check up on their contraceptive practice. At the Shenyang factory birth planning workers make sure the woman starts using contraceptives when she gets back to work following her 150 days maternity leave. Sometimes, according to a Shenyang birth planning worker, it is necessary to do ideological work, although mostly the attitude of women is very high. Most women make arrangements for IUDs and one-child certificates themselves, so the birth planning workers do not have to persuade them. The hospital that inserts the IUD issues an IUD certificate which the woman must submit to birth planning workers at both the residential area and the work unit as both keep an account of the contraceptive practice of the women of reproductive age in their jurisdiction.

One of the reasons for registration of contraceptive practice at the Beijing factory is that if a woman who is using an IUD does become pregnant there are no repercussions, as an IUD is considered a long-term contraceptive. If the woman has not been using an IUD and becomes pregnant, her bonus will be deducted during the sick leave following the abortion and medical expenses are not reimbursed. If, on the other hand, she has been using an IUD and becomes pregnant, it is not regarded as her own fault so her bonus is not deducted. At another Beijing work unit there are no penalties for the first abortion for a woman who is using an IUD. Even though she is using an IUD, a second abortion or an abortion due to lack of IUD use does result in bonus deductions. Women sometimes have abortions without the knowledge of the work unit in order to avoid repercussions. Since 1992 the Beijing factory has issued a cash payment of 30 yuan to women who have an IUD inserted. The birth planning cadre notes that this makes women more willing to have an IUD. For a sterilization, the incentive is 100 yuan as well as three weeks' paid vacation including bonus payments. However, as sterilizations are not explicitly advocated, none of the younger women at the factory has been sterilized. The birth planning cadre does not encourage sterilization partly due to concern that some accident might befall the one child.

Although penalties for not using an IUD are not applied at the Beijing factory until the woman without an IUD becomes pregnant and has to have an abortion, the birth planning cadre does advocate the use of IUDs as it is her primary responsibility to ensure that women do not have more than one child. Previously, she says, she had to persuade women to have an IUD inserted, but now there are no problems. Employees at the Beijing factory as well as other women confirm that birth planning workers handle birth planning 'relatively severely': 'They request that you use a contraceptive method so that you will not give birth to a second child.' Women of reproductive age who have given birth 'must be sterilized or use an IUD, usually they don't let you use contraceptive pills, usually women use an IUD'. However, they also confirm that 'use of an IUD is voluntary'. In sum, women who have given birth to their first child must use some form of contraceptive method and the IUD is advocated. Most women agree to use an IUD because, as one Beijing woman said,

'The woman herself will suffer if she does conceive.' Another woman expressed her opinion in the following way:

> If a woman already has a child, she will not be allowed to give birth again. She will have to have an abortion, because the national policy does not allow the birth of a second child. But as abortions are extremely uncomfortable, women are urged to use an IUD. Most women agree to have an IUD inserted because abortions are so painful.

Contraceptive use after the birth of the first child is compulsory, but there is a limited extent of freedom of choice as to which contraceptive method to use. By way of incentives and the threat of penalties should they become pregnant without an IUD, women are encouraged to choose an IUD. There are, however, also work units where women definitely do not have a choice of contraceptive method. One Beijing woman describes how she and her husband initially used condoms as she was afraid to use an IUD. When she finally did have an IUD inserted, it was because work unit birth planning workers continuously insisted that she should use an IUD. They were afraid she would become pregnant and not be willing to have an abortion. As they do not allow a second birth, she explained, you have to have an IUD inserted and if, you do not, your bonus will be deducted. Pressured by the work unit birth planning workers, finally she did have an IUD inserted.

Some women cannot use an IUD due to heavy bleeding or other side effects. In this case birth planning cadres say they help them to choose a more suitable contraceptive method. Not very many women at the Beijing factory use hormonal contraceptives because, as the birth planning cadre says, although she cannot openly discourage the use of hormonal contraceptives, in her opinion there are too many side effects and the use of hormonal contraceptives is not recommended for long-term usage. So she recommends the IUD and condoms, and tries to find a method that is suitable for the individual woman. The birth planning cadre at the Shenyang factory confirms the opinion of Beijing birth planning workers that contraceptive pills or other forms of contraceptives are acceptable if a woman is unable to use an IUD. However, in her opinion, contraceptives other than IUDs have a tendency to give rise to unplanned pregnancy. The concern of this cadre is not the hormonal side effects but rather the 'side effect' of the woman becoming pregnant if she forgets to take the pills. For this reason, she says, pills are not good for the health of the woman because she will have to have an abortion.

The argument of birth planning workers is thus that women must use an IUD to protect their own health, as an abortion is a disturbing and painful affair. Their reasoning takes as its point of departure the assumption that the population policy limit of only one child must be followed. Within the framework of this assumption, their reasoning is that the health of the woman is in fact best protected if she does use an IUD subsequent to the birth of her child, except in the case that physiological reasons do not allow her to do so. In this way the role of birth planning workers is not only to ensure that the policy measure of one child per couple is not violated, but also, within the limits set by the policy, to care for the women under their control. Not only do birth planning workers perceive of their duty as caring for women; women themselves also share the perception. This is for instance illustrated by the words of a Beijing woman:

> When you become pregnant, you cannot have the child and must have an abortion. Many abortions are not good for women's health. The birth planning workers are caring (*zhaogu*) for women by applying a method of supervision and urging. They supervise and urge you to use a certain contraceptive method to avoid injuring your health. They are showing concern (*guanxin*)[23] for women by continuous urging. When you have one child and have a one-child certificate, they help you to find a safe contraceptive method to save you from enduring hardship.[24]

The merging of control and care, through which coercion and control become care, operates in relation to several spheres of the duties of the birth planning workers and is an integral part of the tight control system as well as of residential area and work unit

---

23. *Zhaogu* and *guanxin* both mean care. In the *Chinese-English Dictionary guanxin* is translated as 'be concerned with, show solicitude for; be interested in; care for' (*Hanying cidian* 1981: 248). *Zhaogu* is translated as to 1) give consideration to; show consideration for; make allowance(s) for or 2) look after; care for; attend to' (*Hanying cidian* 1981: 881). The distinction between the two forms of care and concern is that *zhaogu* involves a more practical form of care in contrast to *guanxin* which is primarily verbally expressed care. To distinguish between the two forms of care, *zhaogu* is translated as care, *guanxin* is translated as concern.

24. In connection with the concern that women should not be subjected to abortion, it is worth noting that abortion is often performed without the use of anaesthetics. The birth planning cadre at the Beijing factory does not know why anaesthetics are not used. She assumes, however, that the reason is that the pain is not unbearable.

cooperation. It is also part of the basis from which control is established by the birth planning institution. Interlinking ideological education with providing service to people is, according to a 1990 article by Shen Guoxiang, Director of the State Family Planning Commission Ideological Education Department, a new development within recent years in the sphere of birth planning ideological education work. Birth planning service should not only ensure that women give birth according to the policy requirements but also include, for instance, concern for the physical and mental health of women and children and concern for the welfare of the elderly. The objective is to make people realize that birth planning as required by the policy is in accordance with their personal interests (Shen 1990: 69). The 'Five Visitings and Five Enquiries' are one of the forms of combining ideological education with providing care.

The 'Five Visitings and Five Enquiries' include visiting couples who, after the birth of one child, do not request to be permitted second children; visiting family planning role models and active elements; visiting comrades who have undergone birth control surgical operations; visiting comrades who, for all sorts of reasons, have been subjected to punishment; visiting newlyweds; enquiring about people's conditions in the winter, when it is cold, or when it is warm; enquiring after the health of the mother and her daughter or son; enquiring about the financial difficulties in the family; enquiring about people's opinions on the work that is being done (Document no. 7 in White 1992: 38).

Care and control are combined when, as the birth planning worker from the district factory says, she visits a woman who has been on sick leave for some time in her home to bring her medicine and 'to keep an eye on things'. Once they have given birth to their child, women are visited in their home both by work unit and by residential area birth planning workers at varying intervals. At the Shenyang factory a birth planning propagandist says that, when a woman in her workshop has given birth, she will call on her in her home to convey greetings to her, because 'to give birth is a big event in a woman's life, so we must call on her as representatives of the factory to express our concern.' Women are of course well aware that the visits in their homes by birth planning workers are part of the work to ensure policy compliance. This is particularly apparent as one objective of many visits is to fill in forms on the contraceptive practice of the woman.

One Beijing woman remarks of the residential area birth planning workers:

> To me it seems that they are more concerned than my work unit. There is often someone from the residential area who comes to visit. In any case more than the work unit. They first of all ask about contraceptive use. They make out statistics and seem to be more concerned about their statistics than about what contraceptive method I am actually using.

However, women also perceive of the visits as an expression of care and concern. As women see it, the birth planning worker not only visits once or twice a year to check on whether or not the woman is using the contraceptive method she is registered as using. She also visits to check up on her health in general, just as the birth planning worker is concerned with the health of the child. Some women have problems of excessive bleeding due to IUD use, but often they do not feel comfortable mentioning this or going to the hospital. But then the birth planning workers, who are all women, arrive to offer their care. As one Shenyang woman says: 'They urge you to go see a doctor if you are ill and help you to choose another form of contraceptive if you are not able to use an IUD.' The annual gynaecological check-ups for married women of reproductive age who have given birth – these are annual or biannual, depending on the economic capacity of the work unit – are also perceived of as an expression of the care extended by the nation, the work unit and the birth planning workers towards women. They are perceived as care although it is obvious that the primary motive underlying the check-ups is to prevent the birth of second children by making sure that IUDs are in place and women are not pregnant.

The Cultural Meaning of Acceptance

The tight net of control exercised at work units as well as in the residential areas and strengthened by their cooperation underlines the importance of control for the demographic success of the urban one-child policy. During the first years of the one-child family policy there were difficulties in persuading urban women to have only one child, to sign a one-child certificate and to use an IUD. Since then, according to both birth planning workers and women themselves, having only one child, having an IUD inserted following the birth of the first child, and applying for and signing a one-child certificate have all become a matter of course for urban women. The cultural meaning of the manner in which adherence to the policy requirement of having only one child has become a matter of course is constructed within a pattern of control as care.

Urban state enterprise employees are, as Andrew Walder has described, subject to a relatively high degree of dependence upon their workplace because employment plays a welfare role. The state workplace is politically and economically organized to satisfy a broad range of the needs of employees. The needs that are satisfied (or potentially satisfied) at the workplace include not only the monetary wage, but also other economic and social needs such as health insurance, medical care, pensions, housing and childcare. Dependence is further strengthened by the scarcity of alternatives for satisfaction of these needs (Walder 1986). Walder argues that there is a common structure of worker dependency across cultures. However, the meanings workers in varying cultural settings ascribe to the structure, and the cultural maps from which they manoeuvre within these structures, are not necessarily shared. Notwithstanding a recognition of the significance of economic as well as political control exercised by the workplace and the subsequent dependence of employees, an insight into the structure of control mechanisms does not sufficiently explain why women are accepting control to such a degree that they do not perceive of control as coercion but rather as care.

The control implemented to avert the birth of second children is perceived by women not only as control, but also as care and concern, although they are well aware that the main objective of the measures implemented by birth planning workers is to secure policy compliance. However, the role of birth planning workers is more than just to ensure that women within their jurisdiction comply with the policy requirements; it is also to implement the policy based on the interests of women within these limits. It is, for instance, not in the interest of women to have one or several abortions, therefore the main contraceptive method is the IUD, advocated at some work units and compulsory at others. Control is care. Control is an aspect of care and concern. Or one might turn it the other way round and say that care and concern are aspects of control – the two merge and are part of or perhaps the very essence of a reciprocal relationship. Providing care is an integral aspect of the work to ensure policy compliance, in the sense that the motive for providing care is to ensure policy compliance. The work unit supplies care. Employees are dependent upon and subordinate to the work unit. In exchange for care, compliance is expected and control is accepted.

The following four properties constitute the pattern of control as care. First, control and monitoring is taken for granted as a basic element of everyday life. Second, the women being controlled are aware that birth planning workers are just doing their job and themselves are subject to control. Third, control as care is based on cultural assumptions of reciprocity. As long as the work unit satisfies the needs of employees, they will in return comply with the requirements of the work unit. Fourth, women and their families are willing to act contrary to fertility preferences by following the one-child requirement on the condition that the policy requirement is applicable to all city district residents. Together these four interlinked properties shape a pattern of the perception of control as care. The first and second properties are related mainly to taking control for granted, while the third and fourth are related mainly to a reciprocal relationship between work unit and employee. The perception of control as care was expressed by a Beijing woman who said:

> There are unplanned births in Beijing, although very few. There was a woman at my work unit who left to become a private entrepreneur. Her first child was a girl, and I have heard that she has already given birth to three girls. They have money enough. If there are economic penalties, they just pay however much they have to. They are private entrepreneurs, and they want a son who can inherit their property, so she has given birth to several children without permission.

> I don't know whether the nation has any measures towards this kind of people. If there are not any special measures, then, as far as I can see, people who have the economic means can have as many children as they like as the economic penalties do not bother them. From my point of view the nation should apply measures to prevent this. They have money and they don't care about penalties. The nation ought to ensure that even though they have money, they should not have as many children as they please. They should understand that this is not their personal concern, this is the concern of a whole people, of a whole nation. There are many private entrepreneurs, and if they all act like this, it will amount to only us ordinary people complying with the call of the nation as we don't have the money to do otherwise. Implementation of the

policy is voluntary, but if we compare with them – they also live on the land of this nation, they ought also to observe the policy of the party. They should not have as many children as they please just because they have the economic means to do so. From the point of view of the nation, coercive measures ought to be applied towards them. Even though they have money they should follow the call of the nation.

The problem is not only the private entrepreneurs in the cities but also the rural population. If I, as an employee in a state enterprise, give birth to a second child, I will be fined maybe 5,000 yuan. I couldn't pay that much money in a whole year. At present, the coercive measures work only with employees in state and collective enterprises. At the shop where I work I would be fired immediately if I gave birth to a second child. This is what the penalty would be. I have only my basic salary, so even though in our hearts we might want another child, we do not dare to. I have to protect my job, if I am fired I wouldn't have the money to support the child, so I would not dare to have another child. This is a form of coercion that does not exist towards private entre-preneurs. It is possible to control staff and workers in state and collective enterprises relatively severely. You can have a child if you want, but if you do, you will be fired.

This woman conveys the core of the meaning of acceptance of the policy. She says the policy is voluntary (*ziyuan*). At the same time she defines the measures applied to enforce the policy as coercion (*qiangzhi*). Furthermore, she acknowledges that the reason private entrepreneurs are able to avoid policy implementation is that they are not subject to these coercive measures. It would seem that her statements are self-contradictory as she says both that the policy is voluntary and that it is coercive. Her referral to the policy as voluntary might then be interpreted as an expression of verbal compliance. The alternative would be to assume that she actually perceives of the policy as both voluntary *and* coercive. Instead of dismissing her statements as verbal compliance, the task is then to understand the meanings she ascribes to voluntary and coercive. One aspect of her perception of voluntary and coercive is that she takes for granted the fact that her scope of choice is limited. She moreover considers it to be her choice either to keep her job and comply with the policy or to quit her job and have a second child, even though the option of leaving her job is not economically realistic. She chooses to keep her job in view of the consequences of living without the welfare pro-

vided by the work unit. Thereby she chooses to follow the requirement of only one child regardless of her fertility preference. This
is a parallel to the way in which women choose an IUD because
there is no alternative within the framework of the policy. They
are complying with the policy. And they perceive of their action
as an expression of acceptance of the policy.

The Shenyang factory, which has improved factory working
conditions as well as wages and subsidies during the past ten
years and has established a system of a monthly 5-yuan pension
supplement for one-child parents, has achieved 100 per cent one
child implementation since 1983. It is part of a cultural assumption
of reciprocity that the work unit has the right to control the people
within its care. Women perceive of the policy as voluntary in the
sense that they take control for granted. This follows the logic
that, as long as they remain within the structure of the work unit
and work unit welfare system, they must also accept control; they
are indebted to the work unit. Indebtedness, as described by
Lung-kee Sun, is central to the pattern of control as care. Following Sun's analysis, in the Chinese culture a person is motivated to
serve and make sacrifices by means of a sense of indebtedness:

> If, as a Western philosopher points out, reciprocity is a matter of
> returning good 'in proportion to the good we receive', and of
> making 'reparation for the harm we have done', then what
> amounts to 'sacrifice' is a form of compensation for a beneficence
> one has already received. In other words, *so-called sacrifice is a
> matter of mutual benefit in a relationship based on reciprocity.* (Sun 1991:
> 35–36, emphasis added)

Sun further emphasizes that not only is reciprocity in Chinese
culture institutionalized as a formal obligation, in contrast for
instance to American society where reciprocity is also a social
reality, but also that inherent in reciprocity is the implication of
expectation and control (Sun 1991).

Women do not find having to apply for permission to give
birth at all peculiar or offensive. When a criticism of the quota
system is voiced, it is not of the system as such, but rather of what
is perceived as an unfair implementation of the system. The
system was for instance perceived of as unfair in the case of a
woman who married a divorcee who already had a child from a
previous marriage and thus could not obtain a first-child birth
permit. In another case a Beijing woman was obviously angry on
behalf of her friend at what she perceived as the unfairness of

policy implementation. Her friend was a 40-year-old unmarried woman who wanted to adopt her brother's child so that he and his wife could have her share of the birth plan quota and give birth to a second child. As an unmarried woman she herself was, however, not eligible for a share of the quota. Here women do not question the structure of policy implementation itself, but they do question local-level implementation practice.

The only possible way of avoiding control is to leave the work unit. Control and monitoring are an integral part of everyday life, which women do not question, and with which they are familiar as the tight system of control from above to below and upwards again in the form of reporting on colleagues and neighbours is a reproduction of the overall political organization at the workplace.[25] Women felt that birth planning work was being handled 'relatively severely' and 'very severely' both at residential areas and work units. However, they were also aware that birth planning workers were merely doing their job according to orders they had received from higher levels. Just as women felt that birth planning workers handle policy implementation severely, the Beijing factory birth planning cadre felt that higher levels of the birth planning institution were handling work severely in the sense that she was being controlled by them. Responding to the question of what she thought about the visits in her home to monitor contraceptive practice, one Beijing woman said: 'I do not have any opinion, usually I am quite cooperative, as this is just routine business.'

The system of penalties is not questioned either. Penalties are accepted as a logical consequence of the overall policy requirement of only one child. As the overall policy framework is accepted without question, so is the system of penalties. Just as women choose to stay within the work unit and therefore to accept the control that is part of work unit care, women choose to use an IUD based on a weighing of the consequences of not following the directions of birth planning workers. Women do not question the system of penalties; they adapt their actions to fit the system in the sense that if a woman wants to avoid penalties, she must use an IUD.

---

25. For an account of the political control system at the workplace, see Walder 1986: 19. For how the work unit political control system has changed from the Mao to the reform era, see Walder 1991. Although political control mechanisms have changed, the basic structures of control are still being used within birth planning work.

Control as care is a reciprocal relationship. The women are subject to the political authority of the state and work unit, and they are economically dependent on the work unit. Structurally, they are forced to comply with the policy. Furthermore, they feel culturally obliged to be compliant. The care provided by the work unit towards its employees includes work unit responsibility for the actions of its members. If an employee does give birth to a second child without permission and is fined an amount exceeding the capacity of an ordinary worker, the work unit will be responsible for payment of the sum. If the birth quota is exceeded by a worker at a factory, the factory director and the work unit risk being penalized and the factory will not be given the status of a model unit regardless of how well it does in reaching production quotas. The functioning of the reciprocal relationship is dependent not only on the work unit supplying care, but also on a perception of equity implying that, as long as control is universal, the reciprocal system is accepted.

The significance of the equity issue has been mentioned in quite a different context by Andrew Walder. One of the factors that gave rise to worker support of the 1989 student movement was that workers were dissatisfied as they felt that other groups – private entrepreneurs, suburban peasants, and cadres and their families – had better work, better wages and benefits than the average worker (Walder 1991). Sulamith Potter and Jack Potter write of population policy implementation in the village of Zengbu that:

> no one should receive an unfair advantage. This is a crucial element of the villagers' definition of justice. They will accept an unpopular policy if the hardship appears to be equally shared. However, if they think that some people are receiving privileges denied to others, they will resent it so much as to threaten the possibility of enforcing the policy. (Potter and Potter 1990: 238)

In this context it is significant that birth planning workers are themselves the mothers of only one child, as women would be unlikely to accept being controlled by someone who had not herself had to comply with the policy. On the other hand, there is little sympathy for those women who attempt to have a second child. One woman related the story of a woman who, confronted with the threat of losing her job, consented to having an abortion in the eighth month of her pregnancy. Whereas I found the story gruesome, the woman who told the story shrugged and said that the pregnant woman could just have had her abortion earlier. Another woman mentioned a case at her workplace where a woman had successfully managed to hide her pregnancy and had given birth to a second child. However, because she had been lacing herself in to conceal the pregnancy, the child was damaged and died shortly after.[26]

When private entrepreneurs are able to have more than one child, not only because they have the economic means to pay the penalties but also because they are not subject to a reciprocal relationship with a work unit, the result is dissatisfaction among those who are subject to these limits. While the woman cited earlier did not question the fact that she herself was subjected to control, what she did question was the fact that private entrepreneurs were able to evade control. The ultimate consequence of policy evasion by a minority is that the majority will feel released of their cultural obligation of reciprocity. Control is practised to ensure that the individual woman does not give birth to more than one child. Control is also practised to avoid the situation that those who have only one child become dissatisfied with having to follow the policy while others are exempt from the policy requirement of only one child. In this way the control being exercised is also an expression of state and work unit care towards employees, because tight control ensures that everyone is subject to the policy fertility limit. Furthermore, tight control and the insurance that everyone is subject to the policy limit is a prerequisite for the functioning of the cultural assumption of reciprocity.

For the majority of the women studied, control is experienced as care. Strict control of only one child per couple has in the course of the 1980s come to be taken for granted in the context of a reciprocal relationship between employee and work unit and in terms of control being universal. The women whose children are about 10 years old or older would not be likely to have a second child, even if a change of policy did take place, whereas many of the younger women whose children are small would have a second child if it were possible. One woman estimates that 85 per cent of women at her workplace would prefer two children, and the Beijing factory birth planning cadre says that sometimes women

---

26. Both these stories were told by Chinese friends whom I have no cause to disbelieve. However, whether they are true or not is irrelevant to the fact that the women relating the stories quite clearly did not in any way sympathize with the women who were attempting to evade the policy requirement.

jokingly whisper to her that if the policy is relaxed to allow for the birth of a second child, she must let them know first. The importance the nation attaches to the population policy is recognized and the necessity of the policy accepted by women. Nonetheless, as one woman remarks, 'If birth planning workers don't keep a strict eye on the signing of one-child certificates and contraceptive practice and you yourself are not quite attentive, it is easy to become pregnant.' In other words, national interests and the population policy are accepted only in so far as the state, represented by the work unit and residential area control network, is strong enough to ensure policy compliance.

Since the early 1990s restrictions have been tightened. One of the reasons is, according to the Beijing factory cadre, that some people would pretend to be ignorant of the rules in order to evade them. For instance, a woman who was marrying for the first time would not inform birth planning workers that her husband was marrying for the second time and already had a child from the previous marriage. Now, with the new rules on tighter control, not only the woman but also the man she plans to marry must obtain a certificate from their respective work units specifically indicating whether or not the marriage is a first marriage. As the Shenyang factory birth planning cadre noted, the control system is effective because there are no leaks. However, as soon as there is a weakness in the system, a leak or a crack, it will be used. And if there is a hole through which someone manages to pass, others will follow because the basis for the culturally assumed reciprocity will then have been undermined.

Cultivation of the Perfect Only Child

> A girl is her mother's cotton padded winter overcoat.
>
> A boy is his mother's down jacket.

As we have seen, urban women accept as a matter of course the one-child family policy as necessary, given the present demographic and economic situation in China. Not only do women accept the demographic and economic rationale underlying the one-child policy; most also accept the control with which the policy measure of only one child per couple is implemented. And on condition that the policy applies unequivocally to all city district citizens, they are willing to comply with the policy, at least in so far as policy evasion is made impossible by strict control measures. However, regardless of women's compliance with and acceptance of the call of the leadership to have only one child, the one-child family policy is a radical break with tradition. One consequence of this break is that parents' prospect of establishing an intergenerational contract as the basis for their own support in later life is weakened. This contract is established as a reciprocal relationship between parents and child and is an important aspect of the objective of child-bearing (Ikels 1993). This chapter is about the consequences of this break with tradition and about the management strategy applied by urban women in order to adjust to these consequences.

One of the reasons urban women are willing to accept the one-child limit is that in any case they have neither the funds nor the energy to support more than one child. The economic situation of the urban population has improved during the 1980s, and the supply of and the demand for consumer goods have increased significantly. However, the budget of urban one-child families is stretched by considerable expenditure to cover the material needs of the only child plus a range of spare-time educational activities. Rather than being a solely economic phenomenon, the expenditure related to the only child should also be understood in the context of the one-child family policy and of what I have termed *cultivation of the perfect only child*. Much attention has been focused at the demanding and selfish only children who become 'little emperors' (see for instance Bian 1987 and Poston and Falbo 1990). Børge Bakken argues that there is no basis in the vast research literature on the only child to justify conclusions such as the only child being selfish, wilful, maladjusted, etc. (Bakken 1993). Here the issue is not the psychology of the children, but their mothers' management of the policy.

Parents devote a great deal of money, and especially mothers focus a great deal of time and energy, on developing the perfect only child. For one-child mothers, cultivation of the perfect only child is a way in which they cope with one consequence of the policy – that their prospect of fulfilling the objectives of child-bearing and -rearing has been weakened by the one-child family policy. In cultivating the perfect only child, women adjust their actions to accommodate the new situation.

The cultural and structural context from which cultivation of the perfect only child is adopted by urban women as a management strategy is discussed in this and the next chapter. The first section of this chapter focuses on the financial and energy constraints to which women ascribe their acceptance of the policy. Urban one-child mothers seek to cultivate their child to perfection by concentrating money and energy on her/him. They make arrangements for the child to take music lessons and to attend painting, drawing, dancing or drama classes, and they provide their child with toys and books to an extent previously unknown for Chinese children. The family focus on the development of the child is supported by the work of the birth planning institution. The second section of this chapter is about the active role of the birth planning institution in promoting cultivation of the perfect only child. The third section is concerned with the cultural context of securing care and with how cultivation of the perfect only child is an element of the building of a reciprocal relationship between parents and child. The fourth section discusses the importance of continuing the family line for women's choice of management strategy.

Limits of Funds and Limits of Energy

A recurring theme in the interviews was that women would say that they had neither the economic means nor the energy to support more than one child. Of the women surveyed, almost three-quarters stated that their family could only support one child, only few being able to support two children, and almost none able to support more than two children (see Figure 13).

Figure 13: Number of children the family is able to support (per cent) (based on answers to the question, 'According to your present economic situation, how many children would your family be able to support?')

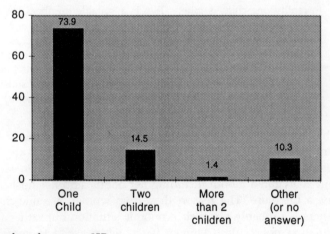

Number of women = 857.

During the 1980s the economic situation of urban residents improves with wages trebling between 1978 and 1989 and living standards increasing. The variety and availability of consumer goods increased and household appliances such as colour televisions, refrigerators, and electric fans became commonplace household items (Davis and Harrell 1993: 3). Although inflation meant that real wages only increased by 50 per cent over ten years, nonetheless, the nationwide picture does reflect an increase in wages and living standards. There are, however, wide local level variations in wages and living standards. For instance, a study of urban workers in Tianjin in 1986 indicated that for this group, although nominal wage increases were large, they barely outpaced the rate of inflation for the decade from 1976 (Walder 1991: 471–472).

The present study has not measured to what degree the family economy of the women studied improved during the reform period, because the aim has been solely to convey women's experience of their family economy in relation to the one-child family policy. Perception rather than fact is important here, as is the circumstance that – whether or not women perceived an improvement in their family economy – they were using a substantial amount of family income for expenses related to the only child. The case of a Beijing worker will illustrate this point. She said:

> In reality one child is lonely. Two is a suitable number. But the government policy does not allow more than one child, nor will our economic situation. We do not have more than we need as it is, and our income is too low ... Commodity prices have increased in Beijing, especially cereals are expensive. My husband and I both receive a 5-yuan cereal subsidy each month, but no cereal subsidy is issued for our child, even though we use most of our money on her.

Both this woman and her neighbour, who accompanied her to the interview, agree that the situation is that while prices are increasing, salaries are not. Her friend, who is also a worker, earns about 200 yuan a month including her bonus, and her husband earns a bit more. The reason these two women are one-child mothers is probably not their economic situation but rather the population policy. Both women laugh when asked to confirm that their economic situation would not then allow them to have more than one child. They agree, but add that with the help of their families they would be able to manage, just as their families helped out when they got married. The larger family probably also contributed when one of these two women bought a 2,000-yuan keyboard for her daughter.

The weight of the policy limit rather than family economy is also reflected in the case of a Shenyang woman. Her family was quite well-off and she only needed to work four hours a day as a saleswoman. Responding to the question of how many children the family would then be able to support she said:

> My family would be able to support [she then hesitated] now it is only one child [and she giggled]. I have not thought about having more children, because one child is very good. It is good for the nation and it is also good for oneself.

She was probably on the verge of saying that her family could very well support more than one child but then apparently thought better of it.

In general, one-child mothers feel there is a notable difference between the material and educational requirements for a child today compared to the situation during their own childhood. Based on her 1980–81 study, Margery Wolf noted that urban children had little space and few toys and books (Wolf 1985: 118). However, during the 1980s the situation changed as a surge of consumer goods and activities for pre-school and primary school children emerged. Since the late 1980s large urban department stores generally have special counters selling children's toys, and in Beijing several stores marketing toys exclusively have been established. In ten years the Beijing Children's Department Store on the main shopping street Wangfujing has changed its selection of goods, from primarily underwear and padded cotton jackets to a large variety of toys and colourful clothing. Urban children no longer have just a few toys stored in a shoebox, and there is a tendency for parents to spend a comparatively large amount of their monthly income on their child.

Survey data indicate that the vast majority of parents spend more money on their child than on themselves. Only for some is the situation reversed (see Figure 14). Prices are high, with the support of one child often equaling the income of one parent. According to a Beijing woman, clothes are expensive, with one set of children's clothing costing about 60 yuan. And while parents used to pass on clothes from one child to another, now both parents and children compare clothes to see who has the best, and no one wants hand-me-downs. An employee at the Beijing factory spends the equivalent of one salary per month on her 4-year-old daughter. She and her husband earn about 200 yuan each. Of this,

Figure 14: Consumption related to only child (based on answers to the question, 'Do you spend more or less on your child than on the grown-ups of the family?')

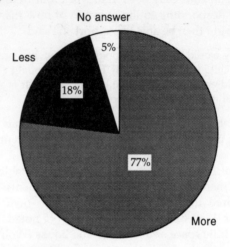

Number of women = 857.

kindergarten fees amount to 120 yuan. A substantial but unspecified amount is spent on clothes for the child, as the mother finds it important that the child is well dressed.

There are several types of expenditure related to the child. Parents buy toys and books for their child because they are economically able to do so and because they have only one child, just as they are willing to spend extra money to send their child to a better than average kindergarten. Most of the women interviewed send their children to pre-school classes and later, when they have started school, to extra-curricular music, painting or drama classes. A typical example is the 8-year-old son of a Shenyang woman. The mother says she pays much attention to her child's schooling and spare time education. The boy takes part in extra-curricular English lessons at school three times a week, and also three times a week he takes painting classes. Many children take music lessons, primarily learning to play the piano and the violin and parents make sure that they practise every day. An example of the expenses related to the child is given by a Beijing mother: school fees are 10 yuan and school books 30–35 yuan per semester, extra-curricular classes are 5 yuan a month, and periodicals 3 yuan a month. Perhaps more illuminating than the actual expenses is her experience that she is 'always paying for something'.

Not only is the family economy stretched by the material requirements for the single child, but parents, especially mothers, put a lot of energy into caring for and educating their child and they feel pressured by the requirements related to being responsible for the education of the child. While some parents shared the duty of accompanying the child to and from school and extra curricular activities, many of the women interviewed had sole responsibility for these duties. The mother of a 6-year-old first-grader, who achieved a result of 100 points at his latest exam, says that she helps her son do homework every evening. The following expressions used by women indicate that they feel pressured by the responsibilities attached to caring for and edu-

'Go play the piano!' Cartoon by Jiang Fan, reproduced from Beijing Family Planning Propaganda and Education Centre and Beijing Family Planning Association (eds). *Population and Birth Planning Cartoon Series.*

cating their child. One mother said she definitely did not want more than one child 'because this child takes up too much of my time, too much of my energy'. Another woman said:

> I do not have the energy for more than one child. I am very busy at work and I am already very busy with one child. At the moment, great importance is attached to educating children, both by society and by the family. Everyone hopes their child will do well in her studies, and specialize in some field. So both parents are busy and are not able to manage more than one child.

The various types of concentration of energy on the child include accompanying children to and from kindergarten, school and extra-curricular activities, minding the child and the home and helping the child do homework. Though both parents are often engaged in these activities, the main responsibility falls on the mother.

The Birth Planning Institution: Improved Childbearing and -rearing

The birth planning institution plays an active role in promoting the development of the only child. With the transition from the *wan-xi-shao* policy of the 1970s, eugenics became an integrated element of the present population policy. The new policy slogan became late marriage, late childbearing, few births and quality births (*wanhun-wanyu-shaosheng-yousheng*) (Yang 1982: 143).

At the Liaoning factory the birth planning cadre explains that birth planning work starts when women have married with information being given on eugenics and improved childbearing. She offers information on the optimal time of conception, followed by information to pregnant women on how they should take care of themselves during pregnancy, on nutrition, as well as information on prenatal education (*taijiao*). As the Beijing District factory birth planning cadre explained, although the difficulties in policy implementation are not the same now as in the early years of the policy, there are still difficulties. The requirements have become more detailed and intense in the form of promoting eugenics, improved childbearing and improved childrearing in order to develop the child to become talented for the sake of the nation. Now birth planning work is no longer, as it was in the early years of the policy, concentrated on convincing people to have only one child, but instead includes supporting the improvement of births and child education. Now her efforts are concentrated on more intense ideological work related to improved childbearing and -rearing.

The ideological education work of one-child family policy implementation has from its inception been accompanied by a series of information material on both eugenics and the correct care and education of the single child.[1] The contents of this material range from practical physical aspects of infant care such as bathing, feeding and so on to more complex educational matters. One of the main factors mentioned in the early years of one-child policy implementation as important for the policy's acceptance by parents was that the child be healthy and certain to survive. This was especially relevant in rural China, where the health system is less developed than in urban China, but was also relevant in Beijing. Here, for instance, some army hospitals established special clinics specifically for only children, increased the number of hospital beds reserved for only children and established a special system of health check-ups for only children (Song Zicheng 1981: 5–7). Since then, according to the Beijing District factory birth planning cadre, concern in urban China has shifted gradually from centring on the physical health of the only child to centring on their mental health and intelligence.

The propagation and marketing of toys and extra-curricular classes are aspects of the focus being placed on the mental development of the child and are clearly linked to implementation of the one-child family policy. Books on child development are typically published by birth planning institutions and distributed by birth planning workers. Often one book will contain information on the population policy and/or contraceptives, sexual life, pregnancy and birth and then continue with information concerning the development of the child.[2] Thus a relatively important part of the information work that the birth planning institution carries out in relation to parents, and aimed at especially women as mothers, supports the tendency to cultivate the perfect child. This work is also carried out by the Women's Federation. In 1981, a few years after the initiation of the one-child family policy, the Liaoning Women's Federation established a Children's Department. The department is engaged in educational

---

1. For an example of this form of educational materials see Zhang 1989. A 1965 booklet on child care was reprinted in the early 1980s – see Lin 1981.
2. See, for instance, Cao 1990.

activities relating to the physiology, psychology and health of children and aimed at parents of children aged up to 14 years. The department also organizes extra curricular classes for children in painting, calligraphy, music, dancing and sports.

The strategy on the part of the leadership in implementing the one-child family policy is to apply ideological education to persuade every family to focus their resources on the development of one perfect child. The state birth planning institution, which holds the main responsibility for policy implementation, plays a leading role in the creation of a one-child ideal as an alternative to the ideal of several children. The focus of the new ideal family is the physically and mentally perfect only child. Birth planning workers give parents advice on nutrition for the child, on how to prevent illness, and they provide information on 'scientific methods' of child education to parents, grandparents and others who mind children. The birth planning institution furthermore offers courses to work place employees in the form of, for instance, films on improved childbearing and -rearing. These are shown at the workplace during working hours to teach parents to educate their children based on scientific methods. According to the Beijing district level birth planning cadre, during recent years ideological education work in the district has been centred mainly on presenting to the populace calculations illustrating the necessity of the one-child policy and increasing the standard of medical security so that women will understand the benefits of giving birth to fewer children. The birth planning cadre gives an example of the calculations that are passed on to the population:

> If each of the grown-up children from a family of three children themselves have three children, the result will be an exponential growth of nine children. If each has only one child, there will be only three children to support. The expenses for the support of nine children is much larger than that for three children. Using the method of calculations, we raise the knowledge and understanding of the people, that is why the main focus of our propaganda work is this form of calculations. We make clear to people that the funds needed to support one child for one year are 10,000 yuan, five children would then need 50,000 yuan. If all 50,000 yuan are concentrated on the one child, this makes a sizeable sum. Part of the money can then instead be used to develop the nation. From this kind of calculations the people really comprehend the reasons for controlling rapid population increase.

At the Shenyang factory, calculations that compare the living standard of a family with one child with the living standard of a family with more than one child are, as in Beijing, applied to illustrate the benefits of having only one child. A Shenyang birth planning worker says:

> By using calculations and comparison we illustrate that one child is best and that there is no use in wanting more children. So in the minds of people the concept of one child being good is established.

In the summer of 1992 the Ministry of Public Health, the State Education Commission and the Beijing Municipal Government arranged *the First National Exhibition on Eugenics, Improved Child-bearing and -rearing* in Beijing. At the exhibition the link between the one-child policy and the development of the perfect only child was emphasized. At one exhibition booth, doctors from the National Defence Scientific Working Committee No. 514 Hospital Clinic offered visitors the opportunity to test a computer program that, given an input of information on the intellectual, physical and emotional cycles of future parents, could calculate the optimal time of conception with the objective of giving birth to an intelligent and healthy child (Guofang 1992: 2). Thus parents can initiate the development of the perfect only child before the child has been born. The walls of the booth were decorated with pictures of chubby, smiling only children – the evidence that the resulting computer children were a success.

At another booth, medical doctor Liu Zelun from the Beijing Medical College exhibited his music tapes for development of the perfect child. The music in the set of three tapes is western classical music. The first tape is to be used by the parents before conception, because the state of mind of the parents even before conception will influence the mentality of the child. The next tape is intended for use by the pregnant woman who listens to the music together with the foetus. The foetus listens to the music through a special set of 'earphones' placed on the belly of the mother. The music influences the mother to the advantageous development of the child. On this tape the music is interrupted by the woman telling her husband that his smoking will influence the physical health of their child negatively. The third tape is intended for the child, who continues to listen to the music during his or her first years. In developing the tapes, Liu Zelun has undertaken studies of the children whose parents, as well as the children themselves, have listened to the tape. Results based on studies that have followed the children over a period of several years indicate that the development of these children takes place more rapidly than does the development of non-music children. The music children are more intelligent and they learn to stand, walk and perform other motor functions earlier than other children (personal communication, see also Liu Zelun 1991).

The objective of the birth planning institution in cultivating the perfect only child is to develop a qualitatively more perfect generation of children and to avoid the birth of more than one child per couple. The objective of the parents and especially the mother in cultivating the perfect only child is to build a reciprocal relationship of an 'intergenerational contract'.

The Cultural Context of Securing Care: Cultivating Reciprocity

The immediate objective of mothers in concentrating economic and energy resources in the form of music during pregnancy, toys and extra curricular activities on the child is to produce a child who is bright, clever and intelligent. The keywords used by mothers in relation to the economy and energy focused on their child were intelligent (*congming*) and talented (*rencai*). Parents and especially mothers concentrated their funds and energy resources on their child in order to enhance the intelligence of their child. Mothers preferred for instance to pay to let their child attend kindergarten rather than let grandmothers or uneducated personnel mind the child, because they were anxious that they would negatively influence the education of the child. Several women had paid attention to their nutrition during pregnancy with the explicit aim of producing an intelligent child, and in order to 'develop the child's character'. The women had read books on pregnancy and childbirth to obtain information on how to make sure they would have not only a healthy but also an intelligent child.

Although only a minority of women were actually presented with music tapes at the clinics where they attended pregnancy check-ups, knowledge of the tapes had spread and they were generally well known. One woman had been informed of the tapes by birth planning workers at her work unit and had then bought the tapes. Many of the younger women interviewed had listened to music during pregnancy, some without precisely being aware of the objective. Others had listened to music with the specific aim of influencing the child's intelligence, and several commented that their child had in fact turned out to be very intelligent. One woman who was pregnant in 1981 had listened to music during her pregnancy because 'people said the child would become intelligent if I listened to music.' Regardless of whether or not she did in fact listen to music when she was pregnant in1981, her attitude to the tapes and her conclusion that her child was born very healthy and intelligent reflects the significance being attributed to developing the perfect only child.

Several of the mothers interviewed emphasized the importance they attached to their child receiving an advanced level education and some had high ambitions regarding the future education of their child. One of the incentives attached to one-child certificates in the early years of the one-child policy was that the only child was given priority to entrance to the best schools. However, as practically all city district children are now only children, the incentive has lost its value. There are, however, still work units that give special care to those of their employees whose child is female, for instance in entering kindergarten and school. Even though it is important for parents to ensure that their child does well at school, this is not the only motive underlying cultivation of the perfect only child. The objective is above all linked to the objective of childbearing and -rearing itself. It is to ensure support and care for parents provided by the child. Cultivation of the perfect only child is a strategy for securing care. Whether or not the long-term objective of cultivating the perfect only child has been reached will be evidenced when the child has grown up and the parents themselves have grown old.

In Chinese society the objective of childbearing and -rearing has traditionally first of all been to secure continuity of the family line which, according to tradition, only sons can do. Moreover, the objective has been that children would support their parents economically in old age, which according to tradition is also the duty of sons. For the rural majority of the Chinese population, the economic obligations of especially sons towards their parents remain important. Despite a system of social security for the aged that is independent of any support from their offspring, the rural aged are dependent on their children both economically and practically. For the city district population, who are often covered by pension schemes, the economic aspect is weaker, though the urban aged are dependent on the practical help provided by their children. Although the generations of many urban families live in separate households, they are attached to each other functionally, with childcare, cooking, care of the elderly or disabled, and monetary transfers frequently taking place among geographically divided branches of families (Ikels 1993 and Zhou *et al.* 1990).

Childbearing and -rearing is thus related to the objective of securing the practical and economic assistance of children towards their parents. According to Sulamith Heins Potter and Jack M. Potter, these two functions cannot be understood without taking into consideration the two aspects of the economic realities and of the cultural realities. The cultural realities are based on the assumption that the aged will receive appropriate care from their offspring. The Potters base their argument on the fact that both children and the aged have a need of care. But where the need of children is emphasized in American society, which they use as a point of comparison, in Chinese society it is the need of the aged that is the more legitimate. Should the aged in China not receive care, the consequence will be a great sorrow. This sorrow is not only related to the miserable, practical, economic situation in which the aged who do not receive care may find themselves. Sorrow is also related to not having fulfilled the moral obligation of having secured care. Parents who have not secured practical, economic care have themselves failed morally and culturally. In the context of the cultural reality of securing care, 'Childcare is a means to an end, a form of long-range self-interest' (Potter and Potter 1990: 228–229).

In a context where the economic aspect – as well as continuation of the family line (an issue covered next in this chapter) – has come to be less practically important to the urban population, the importance of the cultural aspect persists. Although urban parents are less likely to depend economically on their child in old age, they are still dependent on their child to supply security and care.[3]

---

3. Pensions in urban China normally range from 60 to 80 per cent of pre-retirement pay. A state-sector retired couple will often earn more than a married child and his/her spouse. However, though there are high rates of pension receipt by urban inhabitants, retirees from collective enterprises (these are mostly women) are not entitled to pensions. A 1984 survey in Tianjin found that 55 per cent of the elderly without incomes depended on a spouse's income, while 44 per cent depended on support from children or grandchildren (see Unger 1993). A Shanghai study of the monthly incomes of urban elderly indicates that the higher the education of the elderly, the less dependent will they be on the help of their children and that the majority of the elderly are highly dependent on their offspring (Liu 1993).

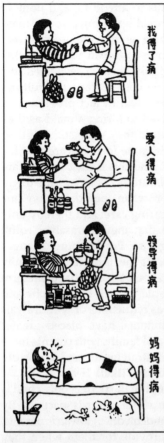

我得了病

I am ill.

爱人得病

My wife is ill.

领导得病

My superior is ill.

妈妈得病

My mother is ill.

Mother who does not receive care from her son. Cartoon by Li Shimin, reproduced from Beijing Family Planning Propaganda and Education Centre and Beijing Family Planning Association (eds). *Population and Birth Planning Cartoon Series.*

And they are morally and culturally obliged to ensure that their child provides them with care. The present generation of one-child mothers provide care to their parents' generation. In the case that the elder generation is in need of special care, it is of course an advantage if several siblings can provide care. A Shenyang women illustrated the case with the example of her parents-in-law. As both her parents-in-law are crippled, her husband and his six brothers and sisters had taken turns caring for the old couple until the task became too time-consuming. All seven sons and daughters and their spouses had jobs to attend to, and none of them lived with the parents. They ended up hiring a young maid to live with the old couple, but as long as they themselves were providing the daily care, it had of course been an advantage that they were seven siblings who could take turns. The element the Potters add to this form of visible practical care is the cultural reality of ensuring that one's children will in fact provide care. Although these seven siblings resorted to hiring a maid as they could not cope with the practical work, they were still fulfilling their obligation to provide care. This is the form of care that the parents of only children also expect. And this is the care they are grooming their child to provide. Naturally, parents find themselves in a more vulnerable position when they only have one child to invest in with a view to securing care, and thereby only one child through which to secure that they themselves fulfill their cultural obligation of securing care. Furthermore, changes during the reform period are reinforcing the importance of family support. Ikels' study of urban Guangzhou indicates that the reform period opportunities for young people to seek distant jobs and move into separate housing, as well as reductions or withdrawals of state subsidies from urban inhabitants, have placed greater financial responsibility on the individual family, with parents more than ever finding it necessary to think strategically and to nurture a sense of filial obligation in their children (Ikels 1993).

An important objective of developing the perfect only child is to cultivate the gratefulness of the child towards parents. By establishing the child in a position of indebtedness towards parents, parents ensure that the child will provide for them when they become old. When there is only one child to provide care in the old age of the parents, they will invest money, time and energy to ensure that the only child does in fact provide the necessary care. Parents are building up the reciprocal relationship of an 'intergenerational contract', thereby laying the foundation for their own support in later life (Ikels 1993).

Xiao Hong (pseudonym) is a middle-school teacher in Beijing. In the mid-1980s she was saving money to buy a piano for her 5-year-old daughter. According to Xiao Hong, the long-term purpose was not primarily that she wanted her daughter to learn to play the piano. The actual purpose of investing in the piano was to convey to the child the experience that her parents were saving their money in order specifically to please her. As Xiao Hong explained the situation, the purpose was that the daughter would become as grateful to her parents as Xiao Hong herself had been to her own parents when, during her own childhood, they used their savings to buy a musical instrument for her; a child who is grateful to her parents should provide care. Xiao Hong, who was in her mid-thirties when she told me about the piano, has no brothers. Together with her two sisters she will care for their parents. This is probably the reason that she was able so precisely to express the meanings inherent in cultivating the child to ensure the providence of care. The fact that the essence of care is not only practical but also related to the cultural meaning of having ensured care is also illustrated by the example of Xiao Hong, which shows that up until then her parents were providing more practical assistance to her than she was providing to them. In the mid-1980s she and her daughter were living with her parents all week except Sundays, because her own apartment was too far away from the school where she taught for it to be practical to commute. With the parents lived also the youngest unmarried daughter. Xiao Hong's mother was still working, but as her father had retired, he provided everyday practical assistance to his two daughters, especially helping Xiao Hong by accompanying her daughter to and from kindergarten every day. And he was the one who did the family shopping. In the long run, however, because she is indebted to her parents, Xiao Hong will care for them.[4]

The repeated use of the term 'a girl is close' (*nühai tiexin*) and the accompanying explanatory commentary provide additional evidence of the importance of securing care. Several women said they would prefer a daughter to a son because as they were only going to have one child, they felt a girl would be closer to them than a boy. This was reflected by the 70.2 per cent of the women surveyed, who agreed to the statement that a girl is close. Some 16.8 per cent did not agree. As 429 women (corresponding to 50.1 per cent of the women surveyed) have a son, it is worth noting that not only the women who have a daughter but also many of the women who have a son agree that a girl is close. The Shenyang woman who had used music tapes during her pregnancy but

---

4. Xiao Hong told me her story in the mid-1980s several years prior to the initiation of this study. However, it was not until I was analysing the interview data of the present study that I actually realized the full implications of the reciprocity which Xiao Hong had in fact quite clearly been illuminating for me.

could not exactly explain why, was probably nearer to an awareness of the underlying motive of cultivation of the perfect only
child than other mothers. She did not, as the other music-tape
mothers mention, use the tapes to achieve an intelligent child.
Instead she said that perhaps the objective had been to ensure that
the child would love her mother. Encouraging love for the mother
is also a way of developing reciprocity and thereby securing care.
Another Shenyang woman mentioned that she thought it was even
better to have a girl than a boy, because boys misbehave while
girls are close and easier to educate. What she may indirectly have
been saying was that girls are easier to cultivate to providing care.

When women said their husband and his parents wanted a
son to carry on the family line they may very well have meant to
ensure care in old age, because ensuring care has traditionally
been the responsibility of sons. While parents-in-law view the
ensuring of future providence of support and care as directly
related to their sons and grandsons, the mandatory one-child
mothers see a possibility of ensuring care not only from a son but
also, and perhaps even more so, from a daughter.

Management Context: to Continue the Family Line

> To give birth to a boy or a girl is equal, but to give birth
> to a boy is best.

Although it contains a contradiction in terms, this short statement
given by a Beijing woman contains an extremely precise articulation
as well as quite an adequate description of the movement that
has taken place in urban China away from the traditional son-
preference. The statement reflects that urban son-preference has
diminished but still exists, just as it reflects the friction between
the People's Republic norm of gender equality and the
traditional patriarchal male primacy. The survey response of 83.1
per cent of women who agree that 'giving birth to a boy or a girl
is equal', with only 5.9 per cent disagreeing, is definitely in
agreement with the gender equality norm. However, according
to the Confucian patriarchal tradition, a family must have sons to
carry on the family line. This traditional concept is weaker in
urban than in rural China, where tradition is emphasized by at
least two socio-economic aspects. One is that rural families need
the labour of sons in order to sustain daily life, the other that
parents depend on their sons for economic support in old age.

Because of son-preference, an immediate consequence of the one-child family policy has been the physical maltreatment of women who give birth to a girl plus a gradually rising sex-ratio resulting from female infanticide, gender-specific abortions and under-reporting of female births. Son-preference in urban China is, however, not as directly related to the labour or the support in old age by the male child as it is in rural China.

Diminishing son-preference in urban China is illustrated by the preferences women have for the sex of their child.[5] In response to the survey question of whether the woman, when she was pregnant, hoped to give birth to a boy or a girl, more women said that they hoped for a boy than for a girl, but about half were unconcerned as to the sex of their child (see Figure 15).

Figure 15: Preferred sex of child (based on answers to the question, 'Did you hope to have a boy or a girl when you were pregnant?')

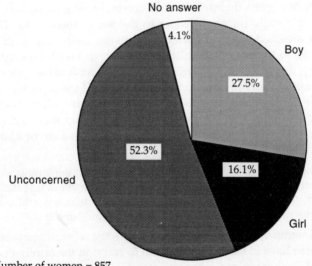

Number of women = 857.

The lack of strong son-preference is also reflected by the sex-preferences expressed by the 250 women (29.1 per cent) who, in response to the main question on the preferred number of children

5. Data from the 1982 One-Per-Thousand National Fertility Sample Survey indicates that Beijing and Shanghai are the only areas of China in which couples do not appear to have a preference for sons (Arnold and Liu 1986).

discussed in Chapter 4, stated that they wanted only one child. Of these, 127 women preferred a boy, while 123 women preferred a girl. The sex-preferences of the women who wanted two children also reflect a diminishing son-preference, as all preferred a boy and a girl – not, as could be expected were there still a strong son-preference, two sons. A Beijing birth planning cadre maintained that in the early 1980s the policy of only one child was difficult to implement. One of the reasons she mentions was that 'when people had given birth to a boy, they wanted a girl, and when they had given birth to a girl, they wanted a boy.' In other words, people wanted two children – one boy and one girl.[6]

At first glance the survey responses on the preferred sex of the child do not fully correspond to the information obtained through the interviews, as there was a clear tendency that inter-viewees wished for a boy. The preference for a boy was, it turned out, clearly linked to a family or parent-in-law interest, while the majority of women themselves were, corresponding to the survey results, generally unconcerned as to the sex of their child. The women attached more importance to giving birth to a healthy child than to the sex of the child. When they did wish especially for a boy, this preference was not the personal wish of the woman herself but was mainly due to her desire to fulfil the expectations of either her husband and/or of her parents-in-law. When asked about their own view, the majority of women said that to them personally it did not matter whether their child was a girl or a boy. As one woman said:

> I hoped for a girl. My husband hoped for a boy. I think most men want a son. I suppose the reason is the tradition of exalting males and demeaning females (*zhong nan qing nü*) which is still very prevalent in society. Boys can continue the family line.

It is still significant for the elder generation – the woman's parents-in-law – to have at least one grandson to carry on the family line. A young Beijing woman whose husband is an only child said:

> I have a good relationship with my husband, so I feel I ought to give birth to a son for him. My mother-in-law wants a grandson. To me it does not matter whether I give birth to a boy or a girl. My own mother did not want more children after she gave birth to my older sister, but both my father and his mother wanted a boy. They

---

6. The ideal of one boy and one girl has also been found in other studies, for instance Davin 1990: 85 and Xu and Yu 1991: 184.

told her the next child would probably be a son and then she gave birth to me. As soon as my grandmother heard I was a girl she didn't even want to see my mother or the newborn child – me. This was exalting males and demeaning females, though my father was quite nice to me. So I have decided that whether I have a boy or a girl, I will take good care of my child.'

Based on her personal experience of not being the boy that her father and grandmother had planned and expected her to be, this woman emphasizes that for her personally the most important aspect is not whether her child is a boy or a girl. However, because she loves her husband and is fully aware of the importance he attaches to carrying on the family line, she nonetheless hopes for a son.

The woman mentioned in Chapter 4 who had originally planned to delay childbearing was sure the pressure from her parents-in-law that she give birth was influenced by her husband being the eldest son. If parents-in-law already have a grandson by their eldest son, or sometimes even by a younger son, they are more likely to be content with a female grandchild. A Shenyang woman who gave birth to a girl said she did not have any problems with her parents-in-law, even though her husband is the eldest son, as he had a younger brother whose wife shortly after gave birth to a son. She said: 'So as it happens we have one girl and one boy making our family complete.' Even though it is still important to carry on the family line, a change is taking place. Another Shenyang woman mentions that, although her husband is the eldest of three sons and was the first to have a child, she did not in any way feel pressured by her parents-in-law to give birth to a son, her explanation being that the parents-in-law are young.

A final quote will serve to illustrate the roots of the still existent son-preference to tradition and the change that is taking place towards an acceptance of female children. A Shenyang woman explained why she wanted a son when she was pregnant: 'My husband has four sisters, he is the only son in the family. My mother-in-law wanted a grandson, but when I gave birth to a girl she did not mind, as a boy and a girl are equal.' Why then, if boys and girls are equal, was it important to give birth to a boy? She explains: 'Chinese people have this custom. The old generation has a feudal mentality, but when I gave birth to a girl they did not express any extreme dissatisfaction.' Unlike the grandmother mentioned above who would not even look at her daughter-in-law when she had given birth to a girl, these parents-in-law expressed their goodwill by helping the young parents to prepare a bed for their daughter.

Even though most parents-in-law would still prefer a grandson, the majority of the women surveyed indicated that they had not felt pressured by their husband's family to bear a son. In response to the survey question: 'Were you pressured by your family to give birth to a boy?', the vast majority responded that they felt 'no pressure'. To varying degrees, the rest of the women had felt pressured to give birth to a son (see Figure 16). Although pressure

Figure 16: Extent of family pressure felt by women to bear a son (based on answers to the question, 'Did you feel pressured by your family to bear a son?')

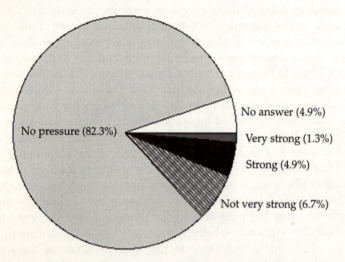

No pressure (82.3%)

No answer (4.9%)

Very strong (1.3%)

Strong (4.9%)

Not very strong (6.7%)

Number of women = 857.

is not extensive, an awareness of the possibility of being pressured was fully present. This was indirectly expressed by several women who during the interviews did mention pressure to give birth to a grandson. When asked about her preference regarding the sex of her child, one woman answered that she was not concerned with the sex of her child, and then she continued to say that she had not felt pressured. Actually she just said 'there was no pressure', without specifically mentioning that the pressure she was referring to was of course pressure to give birth to a boy.

Diminishing son-preference is also reflected in the way women generally did not feel that the sex of their child influenced their own status in the family once they had given birth to their child. Only 17 per cent of the women surveyed said that the status of women who are mothers of a son is higher in the family in urban China than the status of mothers of girls. According to the majority of 76.8 per cent, this was not the case. Likewise only 14.9 per cent agree that 'Giving birth to a boy is honourable,' with a majority (70.4 per cent) not agreeing. One mother of a girl remarked that, although her parents-in-law would have preferred a boy, 'the situation in our family is okay.' Just as in the example above, in which a woman mentioned that following the birth of a grand-daughter, parents-in-law 'did not express any extreme dissatis-faction', this example indicates that although discrimination is not pronounced, and even though the direct and openly expressed wish for a grandson is limited, everyone is well aware of the presence of son-preference, and women themselves feel an obligation to give birth to a boy, regardless of their personal wish for a girl or indifference towards the sex of the child. A Beijing woman men-tioned that the wife of her husband's younger brother was extremely unhappy when she gave birth to a girl. However, in this case it was her mother-in-law who scolded her for being old-fashioned. Even though both of their sons have daughters, the parents-in-law have not expressed any dissatisfaction. Nonetheless, this woman thinks that in their hearts, and regardless of their modern attitude, the parents-in-law would probably have preferred a grandson.

In appraising the degree of pressure to give birth to a son and the possible discrimination towards mothers of female children experienced by women, it should be considered that the issues are extremely sensitive. It is not unlikely that women have neglected to mention instances of discrimination, even though the survey depiction of diminishing son-preference is supported by the inter-views. There were only a few accounts of parents-in-law who did not acknowledge a granddaughter or their daughter-in-law if she gave birth to a girl. That the problem does exist to some degree is illustrated by responses to the survey question: 'Has giving birth to a girl given you any problems?' Of the 393 mothers of daughters responding to the question, only 61 women (corresponding to 15.5 per cent) indicated that they had in fact had problems because their child is female. The majority of women (78.9 per cent) said they had not had any problems (see Figure 17).

Figure 17: Extent of discrimination of mothers of female children (based on answers to the question, 'Has giving birth to a girl given you any problems?')

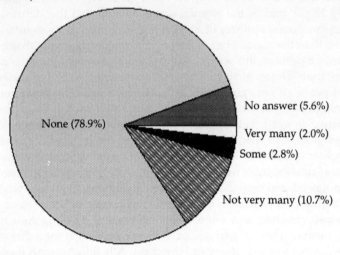

None (78.9%)

No answer (5.6%)

Very many (2.0%)

Some (2.8%)

Not very many (10.7%)

Number of women = 857.

Though the problem does not seem to be extensive, it is also likely that the women have not been willing to expose discrimination either to survey interviewers or to a foreigner. One female survey interviewer in her thirties, who took part in the Shenyang residential area survey, described how the mother-in-law of a woman being interviewed was present during the interview. When they reached the survey question on whether giving birth to a girl had given her any difficulties, the interviewer, aware that the issue could be sensitive, only pointed out the question on the questionnaire without saying anything out loud and the woman answered only by nodding that she had in fact had difficulties. In the few examples of discrimination that were mentioned in the interviews, women would refer not to themselves but to someone they had heard of or were familiar with who had encountered problems. This might be interpreted to indicate that discrimination does take place. One woman mentioned that when she gave birth to her daughter, another woman at the hospital gave birth to a girl on the same day. The other woman's husband and mother-in-law were at the hospital, but left as soon as they saw that the child that had been born was a girl. No one visited the mother of the girl while she was at hospital. Usually, according to this Beijing woman, friends and relatives will bring presents and food to the mother of a newborn child. However, she viewed the incident as an exception from usual practice.

Son-preference, then, has diminished but still exists. A change has taken and is taking place with girls generally being accepted even though the woman's parents-in-law, especially, would in most cases prefer a grandson to carry on their family line. City district women are generally not directly and physically discriminated against for giving birth to a girl, although there is second-hand evidence of parents-in-law who refuse to accept a granddaughter. Responding to the survey statement of whether a good relationship to parents-in-law requires that a woman give birth to a boy, the majority (72.7 per cent) of women responded that they did not agree. Just as the majority of the women interviewed said that they themselves were not directly discriminated against because they had given birth to a girl, but there were examples of grandsons being excessively pampered. Differential treatment would usually not be aimed directly at the mother but rather, in the cases where it did take place, at the grandchildren, with boys being pampered by grandparents. Although the requirement that a woman give birth to a son has certainly not disappeared completely, there has been a movement away from a son-preference that was in essence a distinct son-requirement to a more general wish or actual preference that seldom results in any direct pressure being put on the city district woman.

However, although urban women are not being pressured directly to produce sons for their husband's family, they are experiencing quite another form of pressure. Whether their child is a son or a daughter, women bear the primary responsibility for building up the reciprocal relationship that will ensure that the child will care for the aged parents. It has become less important for women that their child is a son, because they feel that the prospect of ensuring care is not lower, and possibly even higher when the child is a daughter, as expressed by the term 'A girl is close'. In the cultivation of a reciprocal relationship that will ensure that parents receive support and care, girls are being given opportunities equal to those of boys, which may in the long run have extensive consequences in terms of a change of gender relations. But the change will be tough. As the District factory birth planning cadre noted:

In the old days people would say boys carry on the family line, while girls leave their home to get married. Now this idea no longer persists. Now people say a girl is close to her mother's heart. An idiomatic phrase runs: 'A girl is her mother's cotton padded winter overcoat', meaning that the girl is very close to her mother.

However, this new and unusual advantage of girls was immediately neutralized by the counter phrase 'A boy is his mother's down jacket' – much warmer, weightless and more modern than the heavy padded cotton coat.

The Uterine Family

In the traditional Chinese family, women would establish a uterine family in order to cope with their situation as an outsider in their husband's family. By focusing their attention and resources on their own children, first of all on their sons, to build a uterine family based on emotional and loyalty ties, women could achieve a certain amount of influence in their husband's family. The uterine family is the informal linkage of relationships built by women within the traditional patrilineal and patrilocal Chinese family. Margery Wolf used the concept of the uterine family based on studies in rural Taiwan in the 1950s and 1960s. She wrote:

> The uterine family has no ideology, no formal structure, and no public existence. It is built out of sentiments and loyalties that die with its members, but it is no less real for all that ... With a male focus we see the Chinese family as a line of descent, bulging to encompass all the members of a man's household and spreading through his descendants. With a female focus, however, we see the Chinese family not as a continuous line stretching between the vague horizons of past and future, but as *a contemporary group that comes into existence out of a woman's need and is held together insofar as she has the strength to do so, or, for that matter, the need to do so.* (Wolf 1972: 37, emphasis added)

Based on her studies of women in the People's Republic of China in the early 1980s, Wolf concluded that uterine families no longer exist for urban women, because there no longer is a need (Wolf 1985: 206). My contention is that the uterine family still exists. Women adjust to the situation that they have only one child by applying a known sphere of action – the uterine family. The reason women use the uterine family has changed and the way in which it is used has changed to a focus not only on sons but also on the only daughter. Whereas the objective of the uterine family Wolf described was to build reciprocal relationships in order to gain influence in the husband's family, the objective of the present-day urban uterine family is to build a reciprocal relationship in order to secure care. The number of members of the uterine family has been reduced as urban women have only one child and the effort of the mother is focused not mainly on sons but on the only child, regardless of whether the child is a son or a daughter.

The majority of the women surveyed, both mothers of sons and of daughters, agree to the expression that 'a girl is close'. Since several women specifically express the view that it is better to be able to focus efforts on a daughter, urban parents, quite contrary to tradition, may feel more confident that they will receive care from their only child when that child is a daughter rather than a son. The focus on the daughter is a new expression of a tradition of securing care as well as a new way of using the uterine family. Concentrating efforts on the daughter is both a consequence of a weakened son-preference and a consequence of the fact that about half of urban parents do not have a son, and possibly also a consequence of the changes of values that are taking place with modernization in which sons do not necessarily fulfil their cultural obligation to provide care for parents. The stronger socialization of girls to self-sacrifice and self-control may condition women as perpetuators of tradition in the rapid change of the reform period. On the other hand, with girls being assigned the role of the son in the family, the boundaries of culturally accepted gender relations will be questioned and they may change to the advantage of girls and women.

Women say that they have neither the money nor the energy to care for more than one child, and women concentrate money and energy on cultivating the perfect only child to such a degree that they feel pressured by the requirements of being the mother of an only child. Generally, interviewees did not seem to perceive of having only one child as being very easy. On the contrary, women felt that, although they have only one child, they spend more money, time and energy on the child than their own mother spent on several children. Consequently, most women conclude that, although in their opinion two children might possibly be the ideal, they themselves did not feel that they would be able to manage more than one child. A curious form of circular reasoning was applied by several women in explaining why they, owing to limited funds and/or energy, would not be able to manage more than one child. One woman said that it would be intolerable to have to practise the violin with two children every evening, not to speak of the unbearable noise. Another woman said two children was out of the question as they would only fight over the piano. A young Beijing woman said that, as powdered milk and disposable diapers were very expensive, it was economically impossible to support more than one child. Characteristic of all three examples is that the items and practices involved – milk powder, diapers, violin and piano playing – have only become commonplace during the economic reform period and appeared with implementation of the one-child family policy.

The tendency to concentrate both money and energy on cultivating the perfect only child is both an element of the birth planning institution work to implement the policy and it is a management strategy on the part of one-child mothers. From the point of view of the birth planning institution, developing the perfect only child is part of the overall objective of improving the quality of the population, and encouraging parents to focus their resources on the only child is an aspect of the creation of an ideal one-child family as an alternative to the Confucian tradition. For one-child mothers, cultivation of the perfect only child is a way in which they cope with one consequence of the policy, that their prospect to fulfill the objectives of childbearing and rearing has been weakened by the one-child family policy. In cultivating the perfect only child, women adjust their actions to accommodate the new situation, thereby coping with the consequence of the break with tradition.

Cultivation of the perfect only child should be viewed in the broader context of the reform period's modernization, higher material living standards and consumerism, and as a parallel to the behaviour of parents in all parts of the world. However, in urban China these tendencies are being further emphasized by the one-child policy, and cultivation of the perfect only child is furthermore being employed as a management strategy. Urban women are adjusting to the consequence of the one-child family policy that the potential for ensuring care has been weakened, and they are fulfilling the role as good mother in which they are expected to make sacrifices for their child and are evaluated according to their achievements in educating the child. Women's focus of funds and energy on the one child is based on the role of good mother within a known sphere of action – the uterine family. Women are, therefore, not doing anything innovative. Their efforts are, however, intensified and concentrated on the one child. Because they are not doing anything essentially innovative, one-child mothers themselves do not see that they are at all doing anything related to their own role. Even though they are of course aware of the increased range of material goods and spare time activities for children and of the phenomenon of cultivating the perfect only child, they do not view these as linked to their own role and status. Women do not actively question the intervention of the leadership into their fertility decisions, and thereby do not question the policy consequence they react to by applying cultivation of the perfect only child as a management strategy. By managing the situation without questioning the causes, women are accepting the policy.

While family funds for cultivating the perfect only child are allocated by both parents, the energy expended on this is, as far as women experience the situation, primarily invested by the mother. The reason is that, should the child fail or not fulfil the obligation of providing care for parents, it is primarily the mother who will bear the responsibility and burden for not having brought up and educated the child properly. The mother will then have failed culturally and morally and not have fulfilled her role as 'the good mother'. The structure of the social roles as well as the cultural meanings of these, from which women apply cultivation of the perfect only child as a management strategy, will be further elaborated in the following chapter.

CHAPTER 7

婚姻与家庭

The Cultural Assumption of Virtuous Wife and Good Mother

> If you cannot be a virtuous wife, at least be a good mother.
>
> *Shenyang woman, April 1992*

According to a Beijing district level birth planning cadre, one of the main reasons that the group in opposition to the population policy is so relatively small in Beijing is that women's concept of fertility (*shengyu guannian*) has changed as women 'have entered society' (*zoushang shehui*). This expression denotes the structural change that has taken place with women entering the paid labour force following the Communist Party's promotion of the employment of women as the main means to achieving a change in the role and status of women. The birth planning cadre explains:

> Women are no longer subordinate to family patriarchs. Before liberation women did not have self-determination [*zizhuquan*], they were subjected to their husband and the elder generation. Because urban women now are employed and therefore manage all aspects of their own lives, their concept of fertility has

changed. Women's economic position has been raised owing to increased opportunities to engage in paid work. Women do not have to ask their husband for money now that they work and support themselves. Therefore women's concept of fertility has also changed. Now there are only very few women in the whole city district who would have another child. Most find fewer births a benefit to themselves, the family economy, as well as to the child's education. Women's concept of fertility is thus in accordance with the national policy.

This birth planning cadre no doubt hits the mark in saying that most city district women find fewer births a benefit not only to themselves and their family economy but also to the education of their child. The birth planning cadre's conclusion that women's concept of fertility is in accordance with the national policy is nonetheless inaccurate. This study, as well as several other studies, have documented that a majority of urban women would prefer two children. A change of concept of fertility has indeed taken place with women preferring fewer births, but not to the extent that the preferred number of children for the majority of women is in agreement with the one-child requirement of the present population policy. As the birth planning cadre further remarks: 'Now that women are employed, they have to manage both their housework and their job. This has influenced their concept of fertility.' Dual working roles in full-time paid work and domestic work have no doubt had an influence on the number of children that urban women would prefer. However, as described in the preceding chapter, women feel pressured also, and probably even more so, when they have only one child.

This chapter is concerned with the context of the structure of the social roles, as well as the cultural meanings of these, from which women apply cultivation of the perfect only child as a management strategy. The first section is concerned with the structural change that since 1949 has led to the present dual working role of urban women. Though considerable structural change has taken place, women's roles have been expanded rather than basically changed, and a concurrent fundamental change of the underlying cultural assumptions of gender relations has not taken place. The roles assumed by men and women and people's expectations of their behaviour have not basically changed. Moreover, during the reform period traditional female virtues such as women being respectful, submissive and self-sacrificing have been revived (Tan 1991a: 29).[1]

In the second section, which deals with the debatable advantage of being a one-child mother, I will argue that the cultural assumptions of gender relations within which women are evaluated by others and from which women perceive of themselves are integrally linked to the concept of virtuous wife and good mother (*xianqi liangmu*). Consequently, the management strategy of cultivation of the perfect only child is shaped not only within the framework of women's dual working roles, but also from cultural assumptions of the virtuous wife and good mother. This does not imply that culture is viewed as a static framework which shapes the action of women. On the contrary, while most women act within cultural assumptions of the virtuous wife and good mother, there are various interpretations of the concept and others act to change these assumptions. In the third section, the extent of the self-determination women have obtained is discussed. I will argue that the limited scope of expectations women have towards being able to influence their lives based on their own needs and interests shape their employment of cultivation of the perfect only child as a management strategy.

Structural Change: Extended Roles

Elisabeth Croll has summarized what the aim and measures of the Chinese leadership have been in regard to changing the role and status of women:

> After 1949 the new government of China adopted a number of policies and programmes to redefine the roles of women and place them in a position of equal status with men in both the public and domestic spheres. Taken together, the legal, economic and political programmes amounted to a comprehensive four-pronged strategy to: legislate for equality, introduce women into social production, introduce a new ideology of equality and organize women to both redefine and forward their economic, social and political interests. (Croll 1983: 1)

---

1. For a discussion of the rapidly changing role of urban women during the reform period based on the Chinese periodical press, books for women and interviews conducted from 1979 to 1986, see Honig and Hershatter 1988.

There is absolutely no doubt that the roles and status of women in China, especially urban women, have changed dramatically during the first thirty years following the establishment of the People's Republic. The CCP policy on promoting gender equality has viewed the entry of women into the paid labour force as the material basis for realizing equality between men and women in society. In addition, education for women has been and is viewed as an important measure of women's status in society as well as a condition for development of women's participation in society. Based on results from a 1990 survey,[2] the All-China Women's Federation (ACWF) concluded that the policy of engaging women in production as well as increasing the level of education for women had been successful (*Zhongguo funü* 1992).[3]

Nonetheless, in spite of these structural changes in the lives of women, primarily in the fields of employment and education, an accompanying fundamental change of gender relations has not followed. A study of the effects of changes in employment and education for urban women has documented that women's disadvantage is most evident in their severe under-representation in the more powerful, political positions, not just because women receive less education than men, but mainly because a fundamental change in gender relations has not accompanied the structural change (Bauer *et al.* 1992). Scholars who have written on women in the PRC agree that the aim of the leadership, in promoting the entry of women into the paid labour force, was to address what it considered to be the underlying cause of women's subordination – women's lack of access to the economic sphere. They also agree that, contrary to what the leadership had anticipated following Marxist theory, attitudes did not more or less automatically change as women 'entered society'. On the contrary, structural change took place within the old context, and was built on traditional notions of gender relations. Judith Stacey argues that most of the traditional family values and practices which survived the socialist revolution, rather than being anachronisms, were actively defended by the CCP policy through a process that gave them new and sounder structural support (Stacey 1983).

---

2. The study was carried out by the All-China Women's Federation (ACWF) and the State Statistical Bureau among 41,890 men and women aged 18 to 64 years, of which half were classified as urban population.
3. For a detailed study of change in employment and education for urban women based on data from the 1987 One Per cent Population Survey, see Bauer *et al.* 1992.

When women 'entered society', fundamental change within the family did not take place simultaneously. This does not mean that attitudinal change has not taken place at all. As Honig and Hershatter write:

> In the 1980's, young women were no longer told, as were women in prerevolutionary China, that they were worthless and a burden to their families. Yet the message that they were inferior was still communicated to them, and given a scientific gloss that made it difficult to dispute. (Honig and Hershatter 1988: 335)

Culturally, women were still primarily perceived of as minders of the home. Women had been expected to enter the waged labour force on the same basis as men and at the same time continue to service and maintain the household. The family was still the basic unit of consumption and the primary caring unit for the weak, ill or elderly, and its proper functioning was still seen as women's responsibility (Croll 1983: 7, Wolf 1985). Women were still carrying the bulk of domestic chores, though studies have shown that urban men are in fact taking part in domestic chores (Tan 1993: 5). It is, however, not only the practical working load, but the more intangible cultural assumptions pertaining to the proper behaviour and responsibilities of women that constitute the core of the lack of a genuine transformation of gender relations.

Structural change on the one hand and the lack of fundamental change of gender relations on the other hand are reflected in what can be viewed as two parallel, and in fact incompatible, sets of attitudes to equality applied by women to the public and the domestic spheres respectively. On the one hand, women expect a high degree of equality in the public sphere. On the other hand, although many women expect their husband to take part in domestic chores and childcare, the majority of the women interviewed in this study perceive the responsibility for not only practical domestic work but also for maintaining harmony in the family as their responsibility. The structural changes whereby women entered the public sphere were accompanied by a promotion of equality related to the value of the work men and women contribute in the labour force. The CCP has championed equal pay for equal work, and there is no doubt that the attitude of urban women is that there ought to be equal pay for equal work. In practice, however, the fact that aims have not been realized is reflected both in the lack of equal pay for equal work as well as in the lack of equal work, as men tend to be engaged in the better-paid jobs.

The close affinity between women and the domestic sphere is also reflected in the types of employment women are engaged in, as women tend to be employed in 'wife-type' and 'mother-type' jobs (Sun Shaoxian 1993). The traditional division of labour has remained largely untouched despite policies based on the principles of: 'Anything a man can do, a woman can also do;' 'Women hold up half the sky' and 'Equal pay for equal work.' Women workers consequently receive less than equal pay even where they perform the same labour as their male colleagues (Croll 1983: 6). In addition, a majority of men are employed in the state sector that provides the highest wages as well as subsidies, while women are predominantly employed in the collective sector, which pays less and provides fewer welfare benefits (Jacka 1990: 6). The wage difference is reflected in the 1990 ACWF survey, in which the men surveyed earned more than women. Urban men received an average monthly pay of 191 yuan, whereas women received 156 yuan, with women on average earning 81.68 per cent of what men were earning (*Zhongguo funü* 1992: 22).

The equality attitude regarding the public sphere that has accompanied structural change, as well as the practice, which does not fully correspond to the equality attitude and ideal, are also reflected in the survey results of this study. A majority of 91.9 per cent of the Beijing and Shenyang women supported the ideal of equal pay for equal work. This was not always the reality at their workplaces, however. At the workplaces of 81.9 per cent of the women, there was in fact equal pay for equal work, but only at the workplaces of 71.9 per cent of the women were there equal bonus payments (elsewhere the men were likely to receive preferential treatment in regard to bonus payments).

Preferential treatment of men in the public sphere has escalated during the reform period. The tendency since the onset of reform, for urban women especially after the reforms entered the cities in 1984, has been that women in several areas are being pushed out of work sectors in which they thought they had become firmly established in the course of the preceding thirty years. With the reforms, the earlier top-down use of employment to foster gender equality and material security has gone. Emphasis has instead been placed on economy, with enterprises rationalizing and cutting down on employees. Women especially have been affected by these procedures that have brought up and seriously aggravated an old contradiction between the work women do in production and reproduction. During the recent period of reform, enterprises are finding that costs related to female labour are unnecessary, and the inclination towards and practice of laying off and rejecting women employees is increasing (Zhu 1990: 279). Although actual dismissals were rare in the 1980s, enterprises were reducing staff numbers either by giving some workers a form of leave on a proportion of their pay, or by setting up subsidiary collective enterprises and employing them there. Rather than being pushed completely out of the workforce, women were being shifted from the state sector into the collective and private sectors where wages and subsidies are lower (Jacka 1990).

Since the establishment of the People's Republic, the costs related to pregnancy, birth and maternity leave for employees have been carried mainly by individual enterprises as state administrative regulations ensured protection of women. Up till September 1988, married women workers in state and large collective enterprises were entitled to 56 days, paid maternity leave, and to time off during the day for breast feeding. Work units were also required to assign appropriate work to pregnant, menstruating and nursing women. And work units were required to establish breast-feeding rooms, childcare centres and kinder-gartens. In smaller collectives and in private enterprises, welfare benefits and special provisions for women depend on the economic capacity of the individual enterprise. In 1988, regulations on the protection of female workers were revised to ensure better protection (Jacka 1990). However, the revision of the regulations was double-edged, as better protection of women makes women appear even less 'cost-effective' in employers' eyes than previously, with the consequence that they are likely to worsen rather than improve employment possibilities for women (Jacka 1990). Evalu-ating the effects of the reform period on the female population, Professor Zhu Chuzhu writes:

> Economy is ruthless and merciless, and does not talk of morality and justice or show sympathy, but weighs advantages and disadvantages, evaluates benefits according to economic require-ments and therefore chooses men who will be able to give direct profit. The work that women do in relation to human reproduction,

however, is not acknowledged. Human reproduction is a necessity for society, but the unit that carries out this reproduction is the family and it is considered as private. This causes women to meet an increasingly acute conflict between taking part in social production and shouldering the task of human reproduction. In present Chinese society this is the main contradiction seriously influencing improvements in the situation of the female population. (Zhu 1990: 278)

As Chinese women began to have difficulties in maintaining their position in the public sphere, it became obvious to them that a conflict existed between the compensation being given for all social labour and the lack of compensation for the work women do in relation to childbearing and rearing and housework. And it became obvious that, regardless of the structural changes that had taken place, although the reform period competition seemed to be completely equal in so far as whoever has 'strength has possibilities', the underlying conditions for taking part in the competition were nevertheless unequal. This was not only because the educational level of women was still lower than that of the male population, but also because the scope of social activities for women was narrower than for men, giving women an inferior position in competition (Zhu 1990). Employers' rationale for cutting down on the number of female employees is based on a reinforcement of traditional notions that women's primary responsibility is to rear children and to do domestic work.

The reforms aggravated an already existing contradiction between structural change and the lack of change in gender relations and gave rise to a series of visible contradictions and conflicts specifically related to the female population. In urban industry, women were for instance pressured to take extended maternity leave, female employees were required to pass entrance examinations with significantly higher marks than male employees, and enterprises became unwilling to assign work to female university graduates (Honig and Hershatter 1988, Jacka 1990, Tan 1991a).

Because women had come to expect equality in the public sphere, the reforms' negative impact on women's position in employment and education, as well as in other fields, resulted in protests from the ACWF as well as in the establishment of women's studies as an academic discipline (Li Xiaojiang 1991 and

Tan 1991a).[4] During the preceding thirty years of CCP rule, differences between men and women in the public sphere had been, if not eliminated, at least considerably minimized. The aim had been to eliminate differences in order to obtain equality. While differences were ostensibly eliminated, equality did not automatically follow. On the contrary, by obscuring the most obvious differences between men and women in the public sphere, it became possible to overlook the fundamental inequality in gender relations. Women dressed as men in blue and green cotton trousers and jackets, and the models set for women to emulate were Iron Girl Brigades, which managed all kinds of physically strenuous work that had been assumed to be the domain of men. As Li Xiaojiang writes, that women could in fact do whatever men could do became a kind of dream. In a society where the idea of women being inferior to men is deeply rooted, giving women a position equal to men was regarded by women as an immense favour. Women themselves would therefore have been the last to admit that inequality persisted (Li Xiaojiang 1991: 9–10).

The ACWF as well as groups of women intellectuals have since the mid-1980s been engaged in attempts to solve the practical reform problems related to women. Examples of this work are the fertility compensation funds being advocated by the ACWF (Zhu 1992: 28, see also Jacka 1990: 20–21) and the passing of the Law on the Protection of the Rights and Interests of Women in 1992. The reform problems in relation to women have, however, first of all elucidated the consequences of the lack of a fundamental change of cultural assumptions of gender relations parallel to structural change.

Together with their jobs outside the home, which have become an unquestioned part of their lives, urban women acquired a

4. In 1985 the first local organization of women's studies in the form of a women's committee was set up at the Henan Institute of Futurology. In May 1987 the Women's Studies Centre was formally established at Zhengzhou University, Henan (Li 1993:8). The Zhengzhou Women's Studies Centre publishes a series of books on women's studies in China – *Funü yanjiu congshu* (Women's Studies Series). Two books edited by Li Xiaojiang, Director of the Zhengzhou Women's Studies Centre and Tan Shen, a sociologist at the Institute of Sociology at the Chinese Academy of Social Sciences in Beijing present some of the early work done within Chinese women's studies (see Li and Tan 1991a, Li and Tan 1991b). Wang Qi 1991 presents a brief outline of the institutional framework as well as the issues being addressed by the nascent women's studies in China.

conflict that is known by women in many parts of the world – the conflict between their job role and their domestic role as wife and mother. Traditionally in China, a woman's first obligation as a wife was to bear children – especially sons – for her husband's family. This was primarily to continue the family line, but also to supply the family with labour and old age security. Although urban women now work outside the home, their role as defined by society is still principally the role of wife and mother. Writing on the situation in the early 1980s, Margery Wolf describes how women are judged by others mainly according to how they manage their role as wife and mother: 'A fine worker who neglects her husband and beats her children is a bad woman. A fine worker who neglects his wife and beats his children is a fine worker' (Wolf 1985: 182). It is also within this context of the domestic sphere as the responsibility of women that birth planning work is aimed at women. Main birth planning ideological education activities are for instance held on International Women's Day. At one Beijing factory, birth planning workers in 1992 celebrated the day by arranging an exhibition of photographs of the children of all female employees. All were only children except one pair of twins. On the first of July International Children's Day, work units hand out to their mothers gifts and toys for only children.

Not only are women judged by others on the basis of their relationship to the domestic sphere, but also they define themselves in relation to their role as wife and mother. In the context of the study of women's management of the one-child family policy, the focus in the following will be on, first, consequences of the conflict between the job role and the role of wife and mother and, second, consequences of the sustainment of the cultural assumptions of gender relations, related to how women perceive the one-child family policy. The questions that are examined are: To what degree do women identify with either their employment or domestic role? How does their identification with either role influence their perception of the consequences of the one-child policy on their lives? Is there a correlation between a woman identifying primarily with her job role and a positive attitude towards having one child? Or the reverse, with a woman identifying primarily with her domestic role and having a negative attitude to the one-child family policy?

There are no doubt cases of women who view the one-child policy as supportive of their preference of fewer children and who otherwise, had it been possible, would have been pressured by the family to have more children.[5] One initial proposition of this study was that having only one child might support a change of traditional women's roles, with women possibly concentrating more on their job role if they found either that their role as mother was weakened by having only one child or that their household duties were less of a burden. However, findings suggest that this is generally not the case but rather to the contrary – for the majority of the women studied, their domestic sphere role is more likely to be strengthened by the one-child family policy. There is, however, also a minority of women for whom the traditional role has been weakened but this does not appear to be directly related to the one-child policy. Overall it seems that the role as mother is strengthened for the majority of women by the one-child family policy.

The Dubious Advantage of Being a One-Child Mother

In the survey women were asked to state their personal experience in relation to a series of statements on their lives as one-child mothers. The statements, more or less directly taken from birth planning materials and from 1991 interviews with birth planning workers, were: 'The woman uses relatively less time for housework', 'The woman uses relatively less time for childcare', 'It is very good for the health of the woman', 'The woman has better job opportunities', 'The woman has better educational opportunities', 'The woman has more time for rest and leisure' (see Figure 18). All statements denote the situation of the one-child mother relative to the situation of a mother who has more than one child. They do so because this is the form used in birth planning work.[6]

Responses to the statements indicate that, in the opinion of the majority of one-child mothers, there are obvious advantages for them in being the mother of only one child. In sum, 55 per cent of the one-child mothers said that as they have only one child they

---

5. See Hill Gates's study of birth limitation among urban capital owning women (Gates 1993).

6. During the qualitative interviews several women said they could not compare their situation as one-child mothers with the situation of mothers of more children, as their personal experience only covered being the mother of one child, whereas other women compared their situation to the situation of their own mother. However, during pilot-testing of the survey, respondents did not have any difficulties with the statements.

Figure 18: Responses to statements on the advantages of being a one-child mother

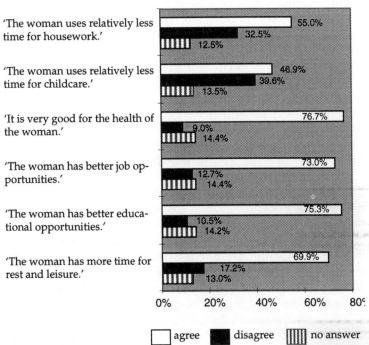

Number of women = 857

use relatively less time for housework and 46.9 per cent said that they use less time for childcare. This was supported by the 69.9 per cent in whose opinion women therefore also have more time for rest and leisure. Furthermore, in relation to job and educational opportunities – the two CCP priority areas relating to achieving equality between men and women in all spheres of life – a majority of the women surveyed find there are better opportunities for them as the mothers of only one child. Moreover, 73 per cent agree that there are better job opportunities and 75.3 per cent that there are better educational opportunities. While relatively few women (12.7 per cent and 10.5 per cent respectively) do not agree that there are better job and educational opportunities for them as the mothers of only one child, the percentage of women who do not find that their condition as one child mothers is relatively improved in the domestic sphere is somewhat higher:

32.5 per cent of the women do not find that they use relatively less time for housework, though they have only one child, while a slightly higher percentage of 39.6 do not find that they use relatively less time for childcare.

The qualitative interviews sought to elaborate on and deepen the insight into the effects of having only one child on the lives of urban women. Results from the interviews elucidate the advantages, as well as lack of advantages, inherent in being a one-child mother which the responses to the statements demonstrate. The qualitative interviews compare to the survey results in so far as they also indicate that it is doubtful whether there is necessarily a correlation between being a one-child mother and using less time for housework and childcare. The few women interviewed who use less time for housework and childcare say they do so because they have chosen to give priority to their job. Having only one child has thus made it easier for them to concentrate on their job, but less housework and childcare was not the reason for why they had chosen to do so. On the other hand, the majority of the women interviewed clearly did not feel that having only one child particularly relieved them from housework and childcare. On the contrary, they felt pressured by the time and energy they used in relation to their child, as discussed in the preceding chapter.

Possibly the reason for the discrepancy between the survey responses and the qualitative interviews is that the survey question asks only about the use of time, whereas women feel they use much time and energy on their one child. As many as three-quarters of the women (76.7 per cent) agree that it is best for the health of a woman to give birth to only one child. The high rates of agreement with the positive effects of the policy undoubtedly also reflect verbal compliance with policy norms.

The term 'virtuous wife and good mother' (*xianqi liangmu*) emerged from the interviews as central to women's perception of their roles in both the domestic and the public sphere. The expression 'virtuous wife and good mother' reflects the image of an ideal woman. According to Chen Dongyuan, an early twentieth-century historian who wrote on women in China, the concept of virtuous mother and good wife (*xianmu liangqi*) came to China from Japan in the late nineteenth century. Previously the terms virtuous (*xian*) and good (*liang*) had been used to designate characteristics attributed to women, but the terms had signified a woman who was 'without ability, weak and powerless, as well as gentle and meek'. With the use of the term 'virtuous mother and good wife' the words came to mean a woman of ability – a skilful woman – i.e. a woman who could manage any situation (Chen [1928] 1990: 153).[7]

In the 1980s the traditional value of being a virtuous wife and good mother, which had been attacked during the Cultural Revolution, was revived and reinforced. Set off by a movie in which a woman named Tao Chun blindly obeyed her husband, a debate on the criteria for being a virtuous wife and good mother in the 1980s took place in the magazine *Chinese Women* (*Zhongguo Funü*) in 1984. Tao Chun's motto for her relationship to her husband was 'I will follow you', with the ultimate result that she died. While some urban women viewed Tao Chun as a model worth emulating, most of the debating women opposed Tao Chun's blind obedience to her husband. Nonetheless, what was questioned in the debate was not the ideal of virtuous wife and good mother, but how the ideal was to be interpreted (Honig and Hershatter 1988, Tan 1991a).

The way in which urban women manage consequences of the one-child policy is linked to their cultural perception of themselves as women in relation to the social norm for the appropriate behaviour of an ideal woman. This perception is represented by the concept of virtuous wife and good mother. Being a virtuous wife and good mother means being an ideal woman – being a woman who acts according to the normative prescriptions for correct behaviour. The precise meaning of the concept is not fixed. During the interviews, women used the concept both as being narrowly related to a norm for ideal domestic sphere behaviour and management, and they used it in a more symbolic manner in which it designates a woman who acts according to the norm for a woman's behaviour, not only in the domestic sphere but in all aspects of life.

---

7. The term 'good wife and wise mother' (*ryoosai kenbo*) was coined in 1875 in Japan by Nakumura Masanao in an essay entitled 'Creating Good Mothers' in the *Meiji Six Journal* (Sievers 1983: 22). Before the term arrived in China from Japan, during the Song Dynasty (960–1279) three situations that gave rise to the use of the term 'virtuous wife' (*xianfu*) had been defined. In the first, the husband is weak with a strong wife who is not subordinate to anyone. In the second, the husband gambles away the family fortune, but the wife sustains the family with the help of her son. And in the third case the husband is dead. The wife educates their son very well and she is very industrious so the family prospers. But, according to Chen Dongyuan, this was not the common interpretation of the term (Chen [1928] 1990: 153).

Concurrently with the post-1949 expansion of women's roles, the concept of virtuous wife and good mother has been extended to include the public sphere working role. Thus some women define being a virtuous wife and good mother as first of all concentrating on doing their job well, while others find their domestic role more important. Still others maintained that it was best to be able to manage both their home and their job. One Shenyang woman gave the following example of what it means to her to be a virtuous wife and good mother. She said:

> It means to honour my mother-in-law, which means to treat her as if she were my own mother. To be a good wife, to mind my home and my job and to ensure that my child is healthy, and that his education is coming along well. To support my husband in his work by ensuring a good support base for him.

Of the women surveyed, approximately equal numbers view their job and their home respectively as more important, which is reflected by the survey responses to two questions. In the first question women were asked in which sphere – domestic or public – they place most of their time and energy. In the second question,

Figure 19: One-child mothers' distribution of time and energy (based on answers to the question, 'Where do you place most of your time and energy?')

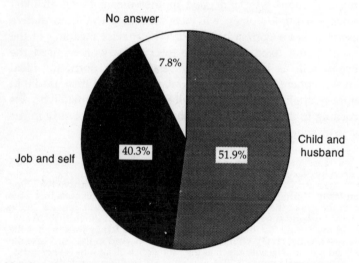

Number of women = 857.

women were asked to indicate where they would prefer to place most of their time and energy (see Figures 19 and 20). While half of the women surveyed use the bulk of their time and energy at work, many prefer to concentrate their efforts at home. The actual distribution of time and energy is very much in accordance with the preferences of these women, as nearly half prefer to place most time and energy at work and about just as many prefer to concentrate their efforts on their child and husband. There is thus only a slightly higher number of women who are using the bulk of their time and energy at work whereas they would prefer to use more time and energy at home.

Figure 20: One-child mothers' preferred use of time and energy (based on answers to the question, 'Where would you prefer to place most of your time and energy?')

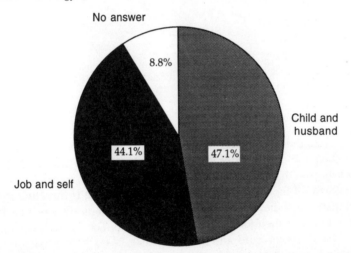

No answer

8.8%

Child and husband

44.1%   47.1%

Job and self

Number of women = 857.

An additional survey question relating to which sphere women would choose to concentrate on if they find themselves in a situation where they have to choose between their job and domestic responsibilities, demonstrates that a majority of 71.8 per cent of one-child mothers would then not choose either, but as far as possible would attend to both (see Figure 21). This response reflects the core conflict of the dual working roles of women with the expectations not only of others, but also of women themselves that they be able to manage both roles.

Figure 21: One-child mothers' solution to conflicting demands between domestic and job responsibilities (based on answers to the question, 'In the case of conflicting demands between your work and family, what would you do?')

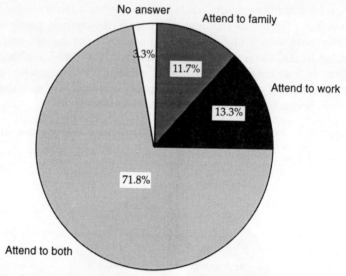

Number of women = 857.

Whether or not women define themselves primarily in relation to their job or their domestic role, the essence of the dual role conflict is that they feel obliged to fulfil both roles. For the majority of the women studied, the central issue is therefore not to distinguish between whether they define themselves primarily in relation to their job or their domestic role. The modern version of the virtuous wife and good mother is no longer narrowly related to the domestic sphere, but has been expanded to encompass the job role. A present-day virtuous wife and good mother is a woman who manages both her domestic and her job responsibilities, corresponding to the role of woman that has been promoted by the CCP. It is obvious from the interviews that women bear the main responsibility for the domestic sphere, with the consequence that they are not able to place as much energy and time in their job role as their husbands do. This does not mean that women feel more attached to their domestic than to their job role. This is illustrated by the survey result where the majority of 71.8 per cent would, to the best of their ability, tend to both domestic and job demands in the situation where a choice between the two arose. The reality of women's attachment to their domestic and job role is for the majority of the women studied not a question of either/or, but of the importance of both roles.

Three properties of women's definition of being a virtuous wife and good mother specifically related to the domestic sphere are, nonetheless, important in relation to cultivation of the perfect only child as a management strategy. These are, first, that most women define themselves, and are aware that they are in any case defined by others, according to how they manage their domestic role. This does not, however, exclude the possibility that women also define themselves in relation to their job role. Second, that women are responsible not only for practical household chores: it is also the responsibility of the wife that her husband does well at his job. And third, that women bear the main responsibility for child-care and -rearing. The implication is that women are prepared and expected to set aside their own interests for those of their husband and child.

A virtuous wife and good mother in the symbolic meaning of the term that also encompasses the job role, is nonetheless first of all defined in relation to how a woman minds her home, her husband and her child. Although men take part in household chores, women view the participation of their husband as help offered to the wife who still holds the main responsibility for household chores.

The low status of the so-called 'old maids' (*da guniang*) serves to illustrate that the significance of the association that 'woman' equals 'wife and mother' sustains. The 'old maids' are usually academically-educated women who have not married, but have passed the age which is usually conceived of as appropriate for marriage. They are typically women in their late thirties or early forties. The reason that they have not married is mainly that very few men are willing to marry a woman whose educational level is as high or higher than their own (Xu 1992: 105). Regardless of their relatively high educational level and the high-level positions they therefore often hold in society, these women generally have a low status, related to the fact that they do not comply with the role of a woman as wife and mother (Tan 1991a).

Another deviation from the norm of marriage and the related roles of women is represented by the so-called 'strong women' (*nüqiangren*). In contrast to the virtuous wife and good mother, *nüqiangren* are first of all viewed as women who are strongly career-minded. One Beijing woman quite logically remarked that there are limits to what one person can overcome. If a woman chooses to concentrate her time and energy on her career, there will not be much time and energy left for her domestic sphere. This woman on the one hand admires *nüqiangren* and she says that she herself is not able to live up to being a *nüqiangren*. On the other hand, she mentions that her sister-in-law is a *nüqiangren*, but that she lacks the quality of being feminine (*nürenwei*).

Part of the quality of being feminine is that women feel that it is their responsibility to bear the bulk of household chores so as to enable their husband to concentrate on doing his job well. As one Beijing woman remarked:

> If the husband is relatively strong, if he is career-minded, then it is most likely that the woman will take more care of the home, so that he will be able to concentrate on his work. If both were career-minded, there would be no-one to take care of the home.

Linked to the way in which women expressed the opinion that their husband's job is more important than their own as an explanation of why they bear the main housework burden is the understanding that caring for the child is also the responsibility of women. This, for instance, is illustrated by the young Beijing woman who does housework during the day, as she works in the evenings. In the evenings, although her husband is at home, her mother-in-law takes care of the child. Another woman explained that both she and her husband originally worked at the same factory. While her husband was able to change to a more challenging and inspiring job, she herself could not change jobs as she had to care for their child which meant that she did not have time for a more demanding job. She also said that she felt that as long as her husband was doing well, the situation was acceptable to her.

Several women stressed that even if a woman is not a virtuous wife, either because she gives priority to her job rather than to her domestic role, or because she and her husband share household tasks, it was important that she be a good mother. Both parents should care for the child but, most of all, it is the mother who should actually care for the child. One woman thought that she herself was a good mother though she would not define herself as a virtuous wife. Using the concept of virtuous wife in the specific meaning related to the domestic sphere, she said that she did not think it was necessary to be a virtuous wife now that she and her husband had known each other for many years and now that they shared many household chores. However, childcare was mainly her domain. Her husband did not take much part in childcare since he was busy with his job and was good at it. Whereas she thought it important to concentrate on her daughter's education from her early years, her husband did not find this as important as she did. According to her, in his opinion she spent too much energy on educating the child. But, she said, she had more time to spend with the child than her husband had, and she had become accustomed to the education of the child being her responsibility.

The ideal of virtuous wife and good mother was not only revived and reinforced in the early 1980s, it was furthermore adapted to the reform period and the one-child family policy. Although the literature on how to educate the only child was ostensibly directed at both parents, it appeared primarily in women's magazines, with articles exalting the virtues of the mother especially in educating the only child (Honig and Hershatter 1988: 180). Of the women surveyed, 80.3 per cent said they read books and periodicals on child education and, according to the women, so did 60.6 per cent of their husbands. Nonetheless, being a good mother in the perception of the women interviewed is primarily related to ensuring that the child receives a good education. 'The mother is the child's first teacher,' says one woman and adds: 'It is the responsibility of the mother that the child does not become a little emperor.' According to another woman, to be a good mother is

> ... mostly to care for your child. In most families women care for their children. Men are more concerned with their jobs and women take care of the child. The child is her responsibility, while husband and wife share other household chores.

Just as women give priority to their husbands' job, they also, as one woman says, 'sacrifice their own time to support their child'.

Women's experience of limits of energy is not only related to the amount of practical work they are responsible for, but even more so to an experience of being pressured by carrying the main responsibility for the education of the child. One mother mentions that she finds it problematic that her own education has been disrupted by the Cultural Revolution, because her ability to assist her child is limited, while another mother says she has contemplated taking classes herself, in order to be able to assist her child in his studies. Another mother of a 3-year-old is already teaching the child to read. And another Shenyang woman, who postponed childbearing in order to go to school, says she did so both because a higher educational level would be an advantage in relation to her job, and also because her higher educational level would benefit her coming child.[8]

The women care for their home, their husband and their child, and they sacrifice themselves for the sake of their husbands' job and their child's education. Above all, women provide harmony in the family by assuming responsibility for the bulk of practical domestic chores. Family harmony is created and maintained when women set aside their own interests and needs to enable their husband to concentrate on his job and to spend time and energy to educate the child. As one woman said, her husband helps her do the washing, but as his job is very tiring, she provides relaxation at home for him. Another woman said that just as she expects her husband to be career-minded, she herself is responsible for maintaining a harmonious home. Responses to two survey questions illustrate the relative importance of harmony between husband and wife. The survey results illustrate that the majority of the women feel that a form of harmony between husband and wife – one that is not necessarily related to love between husband and wife – is important in order to maintain a harmonious family. While 351 women (40.9 per cent) thought that romantic love between spouses was important to maintain a happy family, a significantly higher number of women, 788 of 857 (91.9 per cent), found that harmony between husband and wife was important to maintain a happy family.

A total of 628 women (corresponding to 73.3 per cent) agree that it is important that husband and wife do not have conflicts in regard to sharing housework. Only 154 women (18 per cent) do not find the issue of sharing household chores important in

---

8. In Japan where the virtuous wife and good mother ideal is also employed, a decline in the number of children per woman has not given women time away from domestic responsibilities to engage in other activities. On the contrary, resources have been concentrated on the fewer children. In Japan the 'education mama' syndrome designates that the mother focuses her total time and energy on her children's education. See Refsing 1992.

relation to maintaining a perfect family. The qualitative interviews further illustrate that women perceive that it is their responsibility to maintain harmony by being virtuous wives and good mothers, i.e. by uncomplainingly carrying the bulk of household chores and childcare and by assuming responsibility for avoiding conflicts in the domestic sphere. A Beijing woman, describing how she perceives of herself as a virtuous wife and good mother and how her husband is very satisfied with her, said:

> He always boasts about me to other people. I show my parents-in-law filial obedience. I have never had an argument with them. I also take care of my parents. I am quite busy running back and forth between three homes.

Another woman says that she and her husband have never quarrelled in the fourteen years they have been married. Implicit in her remark is that credit for the avoidance of quarrels should be ascribed to her fulfilment of her role as virtuous wife.[9] She says: 'I attach much importance to his opinion.' She defines their relationship as harmonious and perfectly happy and satisfactory. There are women who do question the lack of sharing of household chores between husband and wife, but not to such a degree that they actually require their husband to take a full share. As one woman said, she thinks her husband's job is more important than her own, and as he has a long distance to travel to work he is tired when he gets home, so she does all their housework. She admits that she does sometimes get angry, because both should take part in housework and she has a job too and she gets tired of doing all the housework, but apart from getting angry, she does not do anything to change the situation.

Limited Self-Determination
Women's attachment to their job role is limited by their practical dual domestic and working roles, as well as by cultural assumptions of gender relations through which women, in spite of structural expansion of their roles to include a job role, are still primarily evaluated according to how they fulfil their normative role as women. In so far as the majority of women identify with the

---

9. The *Marriage and Family Dictionary* defines virtuous wife (*xianqi*) as 'A laudatory title used by a husband to designate his wife' (Chen 1989: 330).

extended meaning of being a virtuous wife and good mother, i.e. fulfilling both their domestic and job role, this implies that it is the responsibility of a woman not only to carry out both roles satisfactorily, but also to maintain family harmony. Once a woman has married and had a child, her role as virtuous wife and good mother is reflected in the limited scope of her expectations in relation to fulfilling her own interests and needs. The majority of the women studied tend to sacrifice or set aside their own needs and interests for those of their husband and their child in order to maintain family harmony. Responding to the survey statements on the lives of women as the mothers of only one child, a high percentage of women felt that they had better job and educational possibilities as the mothers of one child (see Figure 18). However, the picture becomes a great deal more nuanced through the qualitative interviews. Although responses in the interviews tended to coincide with survey responses at first glance, during the interviews it became clear that improvements in employment and education were not perceived as being related to the fact that women have one child.

In the following the aim is, first, to describe the limited scope of possibilities based on their own needs and interests which women perceive of having. Second, the aim is to analyse how the limited scope of expectations relate to the strategy of cultivation of the perfect only child which women employ in order to manage consequences of the one-child family policy.

In the survey, women were asked how satisfied they were with their job. Approximately two-thirds of the women (65.8 per cent) were satisfied with their present jobs, while about one-third (32.7 per cent) were not. Even though one-third of the women were dissatisfied with their present jobs, about half of the women (419 or 48.9 per cent) said they would like to change jobs. However, an additional 66 women answered the subsequent question on why they would want to change jobs,[10] the total number of women responding to this question therefore being 485. Of these 485 women, one third (31.5 per cent), wished to change to a more interesting job, another third (32 per cent) wished to change jobs

---

10. The questionnaire indicated that only if the question on whether or not the respondent wanted to change jobs had been affirmatively answered should the subsequent question on reasons for wanting to change jobs be answered.

in order to be nearer to their home, and the last third (36.5 per cent) wanted to change in order to earn more.

The responses to the three questions – on whether women were satisfied with their present job, on whether they wished to change jobs and on the reasons why they wanted to change jobs – indicate, first, that there is a 50-per-cent degree of job satisfaction and dissatisfaction respectively. Although two-thirds of women responded that they were satisfied with their jobs, nearly half (48.9 per cent) of the respondents would in fact prefer to change jobs. Second, when they were asked in the questionnaire about a change of job in order to hold a more interesting one, to be nearer home or to earn more, a slightly higher percentage (56% or 485) of the women surveyed wished to change jobs. However, although there is thus quite a high per centage of job dissatisfaction, the women interviewed did not consider a change of job to be a realistic possibility.

Women's perception of the possibility of changing jobs should be viewed in the wider context of the reform process since the 1980s. Although new employment opportunities have arisen for men as well as for women during the reform period, as previously mentioned, generally opportunities for women in employment and education have been restricted by the reforms. The focus here is, however, on the fact that in addition to the limited possibilities to change jobs set by the structural framework of the overall reform employment situation, the scope of expectations of the majority of women in regard to education as well as to employment is limited once they have married. Interviews revealed, first, that most women did not have great expectations in regard to their jobs and, second, that whatever hopes and dreams they did have in relation to education and jobs were set aside once they married.

Once they got married, women tended to evaluate their job situation primarily in relation to whether or not they were able to combine their job responsibilities with their domestic responsibilities. One 35-year-old Beijing woman, who was not satisfied with her job because the salary was too low, had not attempted to change to better job because she did not think it would be possible for a woman of her age to find one. Another reason was because her working hours were relatively flexible, something she thought was practical as her husband worked far from home, and she herself bore the main responsibility for caring for their child. Another Beijing woman had recently changed jobs after having worked at one place for ten years. She was relatively satisfied with her new job, mainly because she worked in the evening and was able to do household chores all day as well as care for her child. She did, however, have a dream that she might one day be able to work at a hotel. Working at a hotel would require that she learned to speak English, but she said it was not possible for her to take time off to study. Although she worked in the evenings and her mother-in-law had retired to help her take care of the child, her wish to learn English was apparently not important enough for her to be able to find the time to study for some hours during the day while leaving the child to her mother-in-law. In the evenings, as already mentioned, although her husband was home from work, her mother-in-law minded the child. Although half of the women surveyed said they would prefer to change jobs, during the qualitative interviews it became evident that several women might well have been dissatisfied with their jobs but their expectations that it was at all possible to change their situation were very limited.

This is the aspect that is important in the context of women's employment of cultivation of the perfect only child as a management strategy. The point here is not to measure the degree to which it is in fact possible for women to change jobs within the reform period employment structure. The important aspect is rather women's perception of possibilities for change and their expectations in relation to their defined wishes. Both women's perception of possibilities and their expectations are limited. Yet while women themselves perceive of their limited scope of possibilities for change as structural, I will argue that the limited scope of possibilities is also cultural. The one-child mothers who do spend less time on childcare and housework than they would have as the mothers of two or more children, do so not because they have only one child but because they do not primarily define themselves in relation to the virtuous wife and good mother ideal, but have chosen to concentrate more on their job role, even though they are then not able to fulfil their domestic role according to the prescribed norm. For most women, however, virtuous wife and good mother means fulfilling both their job and their domestic roles. Therefore, although they do possibly spend less time on housework and childcare, they still perceive of this work as being too extensive to allow for other activities, as for instance time off for taking English classes in order to realize a dream of working at a hotel, or for taking time for leisure. The survey response of two-thirds of the women who said they had more time for rest and leisure being the mothers of only one child was not unambiguously supported by the interviews: there seemed to be a divergence between on the one hand the younger women feeling that they were free to amuse themselves and, on the other, the older women, who were teenagers during the Cultural Revolution, who tended not to find that their position as mothers of only one child left much room for amusement.

One woman explains that she felt especially pressured by her double workload when her child was quite small. She is an exception to the majority of the women interviewed in so far as she continued her education following the birth of her child. When her son was only one year old, she attended evening classes. She could do so because her own parents helped out and took care of her child in the evenings. This was necessary, she says, as her husband did not have time; he needed to concentrate 100 per cent on his job. In response to a question of whether she herself would like to be able to concentrate 100 per cent on her job, she answers:

> Of course, but I have only eight hours at work. Then I have to concentrate on my child, whereas my husband can continue his work at home. If I don't pick up our child at a certain time, the kindergarten will close.

However, although this woman, just as other women, is well aware that she has a double working load, she does not expect her situation to be otherwise. Asked directly why her husband and she did not divide domestic responsibilities more equally, she responded that: 'It seems it is just naturally so.' Then she added that she has indicated in the questionnaire that she found women's double burden much too heavy. She mentioned that women had already been liberated, meaning that women had 'entered society,' and that it was not likely that women would return to their homes, therefore she did not think the problem of women's dual roles could be resolved. She perceived of herself as a virtuous wife and good mother and was aware that her colleagues also viewed her as such.

The women take their dual role for granted and do not expect their situation to be otherwise. Moreover, women manage to cope within the framework of their dual roles. This, for instance, is reflected by the one-third of women who wished to change jobs in order to be closer to their home. One woman, who had changed jobs for this reason, explained that her new work place was near to the home of her parents-in-law. She went to their home every day to prepare lunch for them and she went again in the evenings to help them as they were weak and ill.

That women take their dual role for granted is also illustrated by the case of a Beijing woman who had worked hard to get her present job, which she was very satisfied with. She graduated from high school in 1979 when she was 20 years old and immediately started as a worker at a Beijing factory. However, at the same time she financed her evening studies at university aiming to become an accountant. Her motive was to be promoted from worker to cadre status. When she had completed her studies she was, as planned, promoted at the factory. When she was interviewed in 1992, her child was 4 years old and she said that now it would be impossible for her to study, as she had her child to care for.

One survey question required women to state their attitude to the way in which a woman had chosen to continue her studies in order to obtain a university diploma. The woman, Zhang Huiqin, who lived in the suburbs of Beijing, decided to study even though she had two children. Her case has been the focus of a debate on the dual role of women in the magazine, *Chinese Women*. The majority (73.6 per cent) agreed that Zhang Huiqin had done right in studying, while 18.1 per cent thought she should have stayed at home. Responses illustrate a distinction between an equality ideal, corresponding to the official equality rhetoric and reflecting that Zhang Huiqin should study, and the everyday practice illustrated by the cases revealed in the qualitative interviews; here, women do not continue their studies nor do they expect to be able to change to better jobs if they are not satisfied with their present job. Once they have married and especially once they have a child, they do not expect any change for the better as they concentrate on fulfilling, as well as possible, their dual working roles. The responses to the survey question on Zhang Huiqin also illustrate that there is somehow, nonetheless, a contrast between women's everyday practice and their wishes. In responding that they support the choice made by Zhang Huiqin, they may be saying that they wished they too were able to make such a decision.

The solutions women do see to their dual working role are devised within the framework of an acceptance that the burden of the dual roles cannot in principle be changed. One 35-year-old mother of a 3-year-old daughter says she is very busy and that the hours of the day are not sufficient. She solves the problem by cutting down on sleep. Asked whether they would view a shorter working week or shorter working hours as a solution that would enable them to cope better with both their job and their domestic chores, several women said they would appreciate a shorter working time, which would provide them with more time at home to take care of their husband, child and housework, provided they did not become financially dependent on their husband. Even though women feel pressured by their dual role, the majority would not choose to leave their jobs to become housewives. Asked whether they would prefer to keep their job or not if their husband were able to support the family comfortably, a majority (75.7 per cent) of the women responded that they would prefer to keep their job. This was not only because they did not want to be financially dependent on their husband but also because they thought it would be uninteresting and lonely not to have contact with their colleagues at work, and that their way of thinking would become backward. The number of women who would prefer to leave their job to become housewives was 169 (19.7 per cent).[11] They said that they would prefer not to work outside the home at all, if their husband were able to support the family adequately.[12]

One 35-year-old Beijing woman said she would prefer to be a housewife, were it possible, because she felt her double workload was too heavy. She said she would stay at home if her husband could receive her 300-yuan salary or if her salary was only 100 yuan. Her 7-year-old son goes to her mother's home every day after school because there is no one at home. As long as she does have her job, she says, she will of course do her best, but if her

11. An even smaller number of women willing to leave their jobs was found by Margery Wolf 1985: 57, although the women she interviewed were clearly burdened by their dual roles.

12. A 1988 survey of 2,000 men and women in ten cities reported that more than half supported the idea that women could have part-time work to provide them with more time to complete their domestic chores; 81.2 per cent felt that women should not leave their jobs completely (see Jacka 1990: 18).

husband's income were sufficient to support the family, she would really like to stay at home. She believes that many women would choose to do so because they are exhausted. She is aware that the Women's Federation would not agree to women leaving their jobs to become housewives, their position being that women have been liberated by leaving the confines of their home. And she remarks rather angrily:

> Liberation or not is not a question of employment. Women's burden is too heavy. When a man gets home from work he can continue his work. But even if you asked me to continue my work at home, I wouldn't have the energy to do so.[13]

A possible parallel to the way in which women take their dual working role for granted (even though they are far from satisfied with their working load, which they find is far too heavy), and to the way in which women perceive of their scope for achieving change or improvement in their lives (based on needs and interests defined by themselves as limited), might be the pattern of mate choice. There are still marriages that are arranged by parents, although with the consent of the woman and man, as for example the case of the Beijing woman, born in 1953, who married the son of her parents' friends on the suggestion of the two sets of parents. They had planned the marriage since the birth of their children. There are also examples of women whose parents have rejected the spouse that the women themselves had chosen.

The aim in drawing forth this comparison is not to discuss the degree to which whatever self-determination there is in mate choice is still influenced by traditional mate selection patterns such as introduction procedures,[14] but rather to point to the fact that, when asked about their hopes, aspirations and expectations in relation to mate choice and marriage, many women would answer, much as one Beijing worker did, that they did 'not have any special hopes'. The same woman said that she did not have any expectations in particular, she just wanted a job and wanted to do well. Another woman said that getting married was 'an obligatory path', not something she had particularly thought about. Women did not

---

13. The question of employment as liberation or not was debated in relation to the case of the village of Daqiu, where the majority of women left or were forced to leave their jobs in the early 1980s. For an overview of the discussion that originally took place in *Chinese Women* in 1988, see Li 1989:13–18.

14. For the results of a study on the pattern of change in mate choice in the PRC, see Whyte 1992a.

seem to see themselves as major agents in determining their own lives.

The Scope of Self-Determination

The period of reform has clearly shown that, basically, cultural assumptions of gender relations have not changed in the PRC. Women's participation in the public sphere has increased and the position of women has without doubt been impressively improved since 1949. As long as the position of women is measured according to employment and education levels and wage differentials, the Chinese statistics come out quite well. However, if other measures are applied, such as for instance the welfare benefits men and women receive at their work place, the picture that emerges is more nuanced. Not only has the stated equality ideal in the public sphere not been realized; in addition, women alone have been expected to shoulder the domestic sphere's workload. And as soon as privatization and rationalization processes were initiated following reforms, women were the first to be affected, because the work women do in the public sphere is considered secondary to the work they do in the domestic sphere. The discrimination against female employees during the reform period reflects a historical pattern in which women have been pressured to withdraw from the labour force in times of excess labour supply (Andors 1983). Furthermore, the media and CCP statements have simultaneously constructed an image of the ideal woman as primarily a mother and housewife, rather than, as at other times, a good industrial worker (Jacka 1990: 22).

'Because urban women now are employed and therefore manage all aspects of their own lives, their concept of fertility has changed.' This was the remark by a birth planning cadre quoted at the beginning of this chapter. Chinese urban women in the 1980s and 1990s do manage many aspects of their lives in the sense that they have a say in making the educational, employment and marriage arrangements that concern their lives. The legal, economic and social programs promoted by the CCP have made a difference and have led to substantial change. The women of this study and their age cohorts have a degree of self-determination which their mothers and grandmothers did not have.

However, women's management of their lives is not primarily based on their own needs and interests. The scope of self-determination is wide (compared to times prior to the CCP's promotion of women's liberation) but nonetheless narrow because cultural assumptions pertaining to the proper conduct of a woman are still defined within the context of the concept of her being a virtuous wife and good mother. Women manage their dual working roles in the sense that they cope with them. The significance of the lack of fundamental change of gender relations is not only that women's roles have been expanded rather than actually changed, but also that women are still fundamentally considered minders of the domestic sphere. In a way women remain '*neiren*'. The word is an old form for wife, but the literal meaning is 'inside person'. The inside person was subject to other people managing all aspects of her life, the norm for the appropriate behaviour of the traditional *neiren* was the submissive daughter, wife and mother. When women entered society, they were no longer inside people. The degree of self-determination women have over their lives has been drastically extended, but women do not question the structural framework of their dual working roles. On the contrary, they cope as best as they can within this framework.

In spite of their dual working role, the majority of women would not choose to become housewives. While survey results illustrated that an equal number of women preferred to use most of their time and energy in the domestic and public sphere respectively, a majority of the women interviewed would seem to identify primarily with their domestic role in so far as this was obviously the role to which they gave priority in the everyday dual-role conflict. The survey response that a majority of 71.8 per cent would not choose between either role in a conflict situation, but would try their best to manage both, demonstrates that to women both roles have become a part of their lives which they take for granted. However, two parallel and incompatible sets of attitudes to equality in the public sphere and the domestic sphere coexist in the perspective of women. They obviously view entering society as liberation. Therefore, although women are certainly not satisfied with having a dual and quite pressured working role, they try as best as they can to cope with both roles. Coping is exactly what they also do when they employ cultivation of the perfect only child as a management strategy. Within the framework of the structures of society and the cultural assumptions of the virtuous wife and good mother, women attempt to make the best of the situation and cope with the consequences. While being a virtuous wife is viewed as less important by some women, the good mother aspect was important for most of the women interviewed. This is the aspect that one-child mothers reinforce in their strategy to manage the consequence of the one-child family policy which their prospect of fulfilling a cultural obligation of securing care has weakened. Cultivation of the perfect only child is a management or coping strategy that does not question the policy that has led to the consequence towards which women are reacting.

Attitudes to the dual role of working women are changing, as there is an initial recognition of the pressure and the burden of the dual roles as well as of the consequences. In 1984, the problem of a woman sacrificing her own career, in order to guarantee her husband's career by assuming responsibility for housekeeping and thereby guaranteeing that the husband would be able to devote all attention to his job, was discussed in the Shanghai magazine *Society*. One of the suggestions put forward was that the husband take his share of housework, and it was acknowledged that this would involve a change in social values (Tan 1991a: 27). One of the arguments put forward to justify laying off women as well as the lack of willingness to employ women is that women are too busy. 'What then is it we are so busy doing', asked Liang Jun of the Zhengzhou Women's Studies Centre in a 1989 radio programme. 'Minding our homes', was her answer. The solution that she pointed to was that as women bear the bulk of domestic chores, they should not be expected to contribute equally to men in the employment sphere (Liang 1989). During the 1980s some women, mainly intellectuals, started defining the problems that face them and pointing to solutions. But the women in this study generally do not view their situation as changeable. Some of the women expressed this in their satisfaction that their child was a boy. Their satisfaction did not relate to carrying on the family line nor to their own status in the family as the mother of a son, but to unequal gender relations in society. One Beijing mother of a 7-year-old son said:

> I am really glad I have a son, not because I find it important to carry on the family line or because giving birth to a son is honourable, but because I feel that the suffering of women is too extensive. The lives of men are better than the lives of women.

Another Beijing woman remarked that she was encouraging her son to be brave and independent because men have more influence in society than women. Yet another woman commented on the *nüqiangren* phenomenon and said:

> Even though it is said that 'women hold up half of heaven', in reality this in not the case. There is not equality between men and women.

Conscientious Acceptance

> In practical terms, people know that both the family
> and the government may do harm as well as good, and
> both may be resented, but in terms of ideals and
> morality, respect for these institutions is a fundamental
> quality of the social order.
>
> *Sulamith Heins Potter and Jack Potter 1990: 226*

Several studies have shown that there is a disparity between the
fertility preferences of Chinese citizens and the one-child limit
mandated by the population policy. However, knowledge of the
consequences, other than demographic, of imposing a fertility
limit by way of population control contrary to family size preferences is limited. The objective of this study has been to contribute
to the knowledge of population control as a means of limiting
population increase by studying the demographically successful
urban city district one-child family policy in terms of one-child
mothers' experience and management of non-demographic
consequences of the policy. The aim of the analysis, based on the
grounded theory mode of theoretical generalization, has been to
account for much of relevant behaviour within the area studied.
The study provides an inductively derived insight into and understanding of city district women's cultural management of the
one-child family policy.

Other studies imply that a discrepancy between fertility
preferences and the one-child limit imposed by the policy signifies

a lack of policy acceptance on the part of citizens of the PRC. This study has found that city district Chinese women are able to accept a policy that does not necessarily correspond to their own fertility preferences. However, there are also examples of distinct opposition to policy implementation among city district women.

Owing to a rigorous control system, it is practically impossible for city district women to have more than one child. Structurally the control system is coercive. City district women are forced to comply with the policy limit of only one child. However, even when there is a discrepancy between the preferred number of children and the one child, the one-child family policy ideology and implementation are generally accepted. The preferred number of children may be used as a measure of urban population control, in so far as a higher preference than one child indicates that the population policy has been a decisive fertility determinant for many of the families who have only one child. However, a preference for more than one child cannot be applied as a measure of non-acceptance of the policy. On the contrary, acceptance can transcend individual and family fertility preferences when these are in conflict with the policy requirement. Urban one-child mothers view the policy as necessary, given the present demographic and economic situation. Women expressed their knowledge of and support for the leadership's interpretation of rapid population increase as a main cause of socio-economic problems. For some women there is in any case a consistency between the one-child requirement and the number of children the women felt they and their families were able to support. Other women were definitely complying with the policy because they had no other choice. However, they did not define compliance as something negative. This is the main reason why their attitude has been termed 'acceptance' in this study.

Cultural Bias and Cross-Cultural Images of Acceptance

Sometimes previously unknown concepts from other worlds have a conceptual name which we incorporate into our language. These new concepts can then be distinguished from any already known concepts; they are not confused with something we already know. When this is the case, it may be relatively uncomplicated for us to incorporate the new concept into our world. When we have incorporated words such as 'taboo' and 'healing' into

European languages, we have been conceptually enriched. And we have at the same time acknowledged that there are people in other parts of the world who think in ways other than we do (Hastrup 1992: 40). In this study the objective has been to undertake a cultural translation – to see others as they see themselves, and not just as we are able to understand them when using our concepts. The cultural translation communicates a quite different way of understanding. It elucidates the meaning of verbal expressions and actions which take place within a different mode of reasoning (ibid.: 47). The aim of the cultural translation is, furthermore, to maintain the difference between cultures rather than to re-establish the other culture in terms of our concepts (ibid.: 48–49).

Non-Chinese interpretation of fertility limits and implementation of the population policy has been complicated by the Chinese tendency to send conflicting messages concerning the development and practice of the policy, depending on whether the receiver is the foreign observer and/or scholar or the Chinese public. Difficulties in distinguishing rhetoric from reality have been and are being resolved by the practice of conducting local-level, first-hand studies in combination with documentary studies. However, there are further complications. Whether the study approach is based mainly on official documents, or on local-level first-hand studies or on a combination of the two, the implications of culturally based normative value judgements – which are implied in the study approach but seldom elucidated – complicate the scholarly appraisal of policy implementation. For instance, one scholar notes that: 'Even after a distinct national escalation of compulsory fertility control in the beginning of 1983, Chinese government representatives continued to maintain that the program is voluntary' (Banister 1987: 193). I would argue that the core to understanding the incompatibility of views between the Western scholar and official China, on whether or not the policy is in fact voluntary, lies in the culturally contradictory use and understanding of the concept of 'voluntary'. It is nice to see that there exist China scholars who are willing to criticize the Chinese population control policy and state their position as frankly as Judith Banister. The critical standpoint may, nonetheless, become counterproductive to a better understanding of Chinese local-level reality because it is based on an insistence on a Western interpretation of individual human rights. My position in the present study has been that a certain amount of cultural relativism should necessarily be included as a tool for an analysis that has cross-cultural understanding as its aim.[1]

During the process of interviewing one-child women in Beijing and Shenyang, I gradually came to realize that my assumption of a violation of human rights being inherent in the one-child family policy was not shared by the women I was interviewing. It was obvious that their perceptions did not fall within the framework of family planning as a human right. I also realized that my personal opinions on human rights as well as on reproductive self-determination were apparent and prominent in my whole attitude and therefore would also be reflected in the analysis of the interview data. A condemnatory approach to the study of the Chinese population policy is under no circumstances conducive to a better understanding of Chinese local-level reality. Therefore, it became necessary and appropriate to state explicitly my attitude in order to bracket[2] my presuppositions and culturally based perspective or cultural bias on human rights and reproductive self-determination. As well as introducing the problem area, the purpose of Chapter 1 was to state my subscription to the view of family planning as a human right as well as to the broader concept of reproductive rights. The purpose of then setting aside the human rights definition in the analysis of the following chapters should definitely not be seen as an attempt to justify the Chinese leadership's view on human rights, nor as an attempt to avoid a critical stance. On the contrary, the purpose is to adopt a stance without presuppositions in order to grasp the meaning of what women themselves are expressing across cultures.

There can be no doubt that the Chinese population policy is contrary to human rights as defined internationally. However, at the same time it must be acknowledged that, although the Universal Declaration of Human Rights as well as other documents on human rights are in fact termed universal, they have been defined on the basis of, and are the product of, a specific Euro-American cultural and historical development. Here again, the aim is not to justify the way in which Asian political leaders have

---

1. For a discussion of the application of cultural relativism in studying a culture other than the scholar's own, see Helgesen 1994.
2. The term 'bracketing' was first used by E. Husserl to describe how one must take hold of a phenomenon and then place it outside one's knowledge about the phenomenon (see Van Manen 1990: 47).

coopted the anti-colonial analysis of feminists in Asia towards western market-oriented economic development models. They have also warned them against the dangers of Westernization and have argued that feminism and reproductive rights are mere importations by upper-class Asian women, thus alien to the traditional Confucian ideal of a docile, quiet and all-sacrificing woman (Estrada-Claudio 1993). The aim of this study is to understand Chinese reality at the micro level of society based on the perspective of city district one-child women. As far as possible my aim has been to set aside my image of the reality of the women being studied in order to grasp their image.

Teaching Acceptance

According to birth planning workers, due to effective 'thought work' and ideological education on their part, the city district population has come to accept (*jieshou*) the policy. What exactly is thought work and ideological education in terms of the population policy? And what is the cultural meaning of acceptance at the implementation level of the policy? The following examples illustrate how birth planning workers and the interviewed women define population policy thought work. One woman mentions that thought work is carried out because people have 'feudal thoughts'. Feudal thoughts are expressed, for instance, when someone prefers a son to a daughter. Thought work is also carried out to counteract the cases when someone's 'thoughts have been influenced' (*shou sixiang yingxiang*). An example of this was the case of a woman who was extremely unhappy when she gave birth to a daughter.

When they carry out thought work, birth planning workers 'raise the knowledge and understanding of people' and 'make clear to people' what the policy is about. Using calculations that illustrate the balance between resources and people and the necessity of the policy of limiting population growth, birth planning workers teach the correct ideological attitude concerning the population policy to the people. Using role models – as for instance the woman Liu Huifang from the TV series *Kewang*, who accepted an orphan as her own child – birth planning workers teach new values and suppress old ways of thinking, such as son-preference, that restrict policy implementation. When population policy thought work succeeds, the result, as expressed by a birth planning cadre, is that 'people really comprehend' the context and necessity of the policy so that 'in the minds of people the concept of one child being good is established'.

How then do 'raised knowledge' and 'real comprehension' – in other words correct thoughts in terms of the population policy – relate to acceptance? The women who would prefer two children are complying with the policy. They are complying in the sense that thay are setting aside individual and/or family preferences because it would not be possible for them to do otherwise owing to the tight control system. However, *compliance is not necessarily perceived as something negative.*

The aim of using ideological education, thought work and persuasion is to educate people to set aside their innermost and selfish preferences which are based on the interests of the individual or family. Instead they should acquire the correct thought or attitude based on the perspective of the good of the nation and act accordingly. This form of educating people to act appropriately according to the norms of a given policy is rooted in two characteristics of Chinese culture. One is the assumption that education can change human behaviour and that educational reform is the key to solving urgent political and social problems. In classical Confucian thought, education contained the notion of moral training in which people learned through the emulation of models (Munro 1969: Ch. 8). This traditional conception of education is reflected in the CCP conception of thought (*sixiang*), in which it is implied that thought can be changed so that in principle every individual can achieve the correct thought (Schurmann [1966] 1968: 24–33). One of the ways of arriving at the correct thought is to emulate a model. In the PRC, the basic assumptions of the word to study include 'to analyse the merits of a meritorious person, and model your behavior after his' (Schoenhals 1993: 25). The other characteristic is 'the collectivist logic of East Asian culture' in which there is 'a tendency to define the individual in relation to 'significant others', and to inculcate in the former a sense of deficit on the social balance-sheet' (Sun 1991: 34–35). As expressed by Lucian Pye:

> In place of a divine source of authority, the Chinese, with their Confucianism, created an elaborate intellectual structure of *an ethical order which all enlightened peoples were expected to acknowledge and respect*. The political order was seen as essentially coterminous with the social order, and *everything depended upon correct conduct in*

fulfilling personal roles, especially in seeking a harmonious family life. (Pye 1985: 42, emphasis added)

Ideological education, thought work and the procedures of persuasion are aimed at establishing self-control and self-sacrifice in order to incorporate the 'selfish' individual into the collective. The individual is encouraged to put aside selfish feelings and to exert self-control for the sake of the collective (Sun 1991: 34–35).

Women do not question the ideology of the population policy, nor the demographic targets. Their support of these two levels of population policy can probably be interpreted as an expression of the following statement which derives from a set of ideological education materials: 'Giving birth to children is a family matter. It is even more a national matter.' The statement is rooted in the cultural tradition also expressed by a Shenyang woman that 'family is the small issue, society is the big issue' (*jiating shi xiao wenti, shehui shi da wenti*). A dominant feature of Confucian tradition which has been continued by the CCP is that the individual is taught to be selfless and to defer to communitarian values (Pye 1991). In the cultural context of this relationship between the collective and the individual, the slogan 'Sacrifice the little me to complete the big me (*xisheng xiaowo, wancheng dawo*)' is resorted to 'when there is a need to urge an individual to die for the country or to sacrifice for the group interest' (Sun 1991: 30). In accordance with this relationship between the individual and the collective, women accept the policy and the cultural obligation of sacrificing the 'little me' for the good of the nation. As one Shenyang woman said, 'Because the national call is one couple one child, I do not have any opinion. I just want one child in response to the call.'

Suzanne Ogden cites a dissident leader who is critically aware of the system of unifying the thought of the people of China from cradle to grave, and she writes:

Thought reform serves both as a preventive control measure and a corrective to crime and deviance. The entire ideological educational machine produces a uniform normative framework in an effort to create a unified national will and objective. (Ogden 1989: 222)

In its ideal form, following the successful establishment of such a normative framework through ideological education and thought work, the political consciousness of people reaches a stage at which they will conscientiously (*zijue*) act according to the prescribed norm. The core to understanding the incompatibility of the human rights view and the official Chinese view on whether the Chinese population policy is voluntary, lies in the culturally incompatible use and understanding of the concept of 'voluntary'. Often *zijue* is mistakenly translated as 'voluntary'. A more precise translation that would indicate the Chinese cultural meaning of the concept would therefore be *conscientious acceptance*. The word *zijue*, which denotes political consciousness, was used for instance by a birth planning worker who explained how women would conscientiously have an abortion if their contraceptives failed without her having to convince them. *Zijue* is also the word that the head of the State Family Planning Group,[3] Vice-Premier Chen Muhua, used when in 1979 she explained how population policy implementation was intended to work. She wrote that, if there was a conflict between the interests of the state and the interests of the individual, the latter was expected to 'conscientiously (*zijue*) subordinate' individual interest to those of the state (Chen [1979] 1981: 11). The term *zijue* connotes the exercise of self-control and is related to political consciousness in terms of acting according to the prescribed norm without having to be persuaded. The following extract from a speech at the opening of the Third National Conference on Population Science on 21 February 1981 further illustrates the use of the concept:

> Here, we must point out that population control under the socialist system has the following two characteristics: the first is that it is carried out according to plan and the second is that it is carried out *conscientiously* (*zijue*). Under the capitalist system, limiting population is carried out individually and in circumstances of anarchy which can certainly not be called planned. In our country, the control of blind population increase is carried out according to the overall national plan. This is an outstanding difference between our control of blind population increase and that of capitalist countries. *Moreover, socialist control of population is based on the conscientious behavior (zijue xingwei) of people in regard to their reproduction. Of course, this form of conscientious behavior does not materialize automatically.* This means that to achieve population control it is not only necessary continuously to make an effort in terms of social security and safe pregnancy, it is also necessary for us to do meticulous and long-term ideological education work among the people. This form of meticulous and long-term ideological education work can cause the broad masses to change from a non-

---

3. Since 1981 the State Family Planning Commission.

conscientious (*bu zijue*) to a conscientious (*zijue*) attitude to birth control. (Xu Dixin 1981: 5, emphasis added)

Obtaining a one-child certificate is a demonstration of correct thought. As birth planning workers noted, during the early years of the one-child policy they had to do thought work to encourage women to apply for a certificate. Since then, again according to birth planning workers, women's attitudes have improved and it has become a matter of course for them to apply for a certificate. Applying for a certificate is a demonstration of policy acceptance. It is a demonstration of having set aside individual and/or family desires and acting according to the policy norm. The one-child certificates illustrate that acceptance does not necessarily imply agreement but reflects adhering to the correct thoughts or attitude regardless of heartfelt preferences and therefore acting according to the normative prescriptions of the policy.[4]

The distinction between attitude or thought (*sixiang*) and heartfelt (*xinli*), literally 'in-the-heart' preferences, was expressed for example by the woman who said that her parents-in-law did not have a feudal son-preference attitude (*sixiang*) but that anyhow she believed that in their hearts (*xinli*) they would probably have preferred a grandson to a granddaughter. When she said that although in her heart she might prefer two children but she did not dare to have more than one for fear of losing her job, the woman cited in Chapter 5 also used the words *xinli*. Accepting means doing the correct thing, acting in accordance with the politically correct attitude regardless of heartfelt preferences. As such, the one-child certificate is a measure of acceptance. It does not measure the degree to which there is a correspondence between the preferred number of children and the policy requirement. In its ideal form, the one-child certificate rate is a measure of the degree to which parents ascribe to the politically correct attitude. It is a measure of the degree to which they self-consciously determine to set aside heartfelt preferences in order to act correctly. Would it then be possible to prefer one child and definitely not to want more than one child, but at the same time

---

4. Honig and Hershatter cite a case in which a young couple had decided to postpone childbearing. At a meeting the husband, who was a CCP member, was criticized and a colleague said: 'If you don't have any children you are guilty of bourgeois thinking; if you have too many children you are guilty of feudal thinking; only by having one child can you demonstrate true proletarian thinking' (Honig and Hershatter 1988: 188).

not to apply for a one-child certificate? Responding to this question a Beijing woman said:

> That would not do, they [birth planning workers] would say you were not responding to the call [of the nation to have only one child]. They would say that you in your heart [*xinli*] wanted a second child.

In practice, city district residents do not always apply for a certificate of their own free will. Sometimes people are forced to take out a certificate under the threat of penalties. This means that the certificate rate does not actually, as it is intended to, reflect acceptance.

However, the central issue is not whether thought can be changed or is in fact being changed. More important is whether people are willing to accept that, according to the cultural norms, their own preferences ought to take second place whether or not they in fact do so. While the women of this study are aware of the leadership's system of teaching the correct attitude to the population policy, they are not critical of the system. On the contrary, they take it for granted at a level of cultural assumption. The ideal is part of the cultural assumptions from which the women studied operate.

When women control their heartfelt fertility preferences and when they sacrifice their own preferences, their action is morally and politically appropriate. This is precisely what they have been taught to do. The action in its ideal form contains self-control and self-sacrifice as selfish individual interests are set aside for the sake of the collective, be it the family or the nation. The action which aims at making the collective function is appropriate in the cultural and political context, even though in practice women might not adhere to the ideal. When directly asked, women would laughingly deny that their decision to have only one child had anything to do with sacrifice, whereas they specifically applied the term sacrifice in relation to their domestic sphere actions related to their child and husband. In Euro-American scholarship on China, the mode of teaching one correct political truth and the action that corresponds to the norm gives rise to connotations such as propaganda, indoctrination and coercion. However, within the framework of the cultural assumptions of an ideal in which the interests of the collective take precedence over those of the individual, self-control and self-sacrifice do not have these negative connotations.

Most of the city district one-child mothers interviewed make acceptance of the policy an active choice in terms of their perception of *control as care*. Within the framework of accepting the ideological level of the population policy, the way in which the policy is implemented is perceived of as care. As described in Chapter 5, the majority of the women studied regard the control that birth planning workers exercise – when, for instance, they insist that women use an IUD under the threat of penalty – as an expression of care, because in any case they would be pressured or forced to have an abortion if they did become pregnant. It is thus obvious that a considerable amount of control is exerted. The majority of women do not agree with the one-child fertility limit – they would prefer two children. Nonetheless, they only give birth to one child and they accept the implementation measures. There are, however, some exceptions. One woman at whose work unit IUD insertion was compulsory after the birth of one child was explicitly resentful that she could not herself decide what kind of contraceptive method she wished to use. In her opinion, it should be up to her to decide as long as she did not give birth to a second child, which, she said, she had absolutely no intention of doing. At another work unit women had been required to take a test on their knowledge of the one-child family policy, and they had been required once again, as they had already signed a one-child certificate, to sign a declaration stating that they would not give birth to a second child.

These women do not question the one-child policy ideology or policy targets. They do question, however, the way in which the policy is being implemented at their particular workplace. They express resentment and indignation that they are being controlled, as they have already pledged to have only one child. They feel capable of keeping the pledge themselves, and perceive of the control in the form of compulsory IUDs, tests and additional pledges as unnecessary. The women at whose unit IUDs are compulsory had no means of avoiding the requirement. Just as the women who were given a test did not have the option of not handing in completed forms. They had protested against the test by letting one woman in their office fill in the test forms of all eight women.

An identical form of silent protest represented by non-action is practised by a woman who deliberately has avoided taking part in the annual gynaecological check-ups for two years. She does so simply by ignoring the request of the birth planning worker that she take part. She does not openly say that she is unable to take part or that she does not intend to; on the contrary, she assures the birth planning worker that she will attend. Not only does she not take part in the annual check-ups, she is not using an IUD, although birth planning workers have tried to make her use one and have reprimanded her. In her present job, she is not often present at the work unit, so as she remarks: 'Nobody keeps an eye on me. I have not taken part in the check-ups these past two years because I don't feel I have any health problems. Also sometimes I am busy working, so who cares.' The two years she has not taken part in the check-ups correspond to the two years she has had her present job in which her work does not take place at the unit itself. She has thus been out of the reach of the daily work unit birth planning control system.

There is only an extremely narrow margin for evading the control system. One of them is to be, as for this Beijing woman, physically out of sight and reach of daily work unit control; another is to evade the annual check-ups. Other women who did not themselves articulate their antipathy as precisely as this woman were probably also evading control when they were not attending the check-ups, just as physiological reasons were certainly used as an excuse for not using an IUD, in the context that no other reasons were approved by birth planning workers. One young Beijing woman, who was not using an IUD though her child was one-and-a-half years old, remarked about the efforts of birth planning workers:

> They told me to have an IUD inserted, but I did not want one, because I am not healthy as I lost a lot of blood when I gave birth. I am waiting for my health to improve and for my child to be a bit older, about three years, then I will have an IUD inserted.

This woman had, however, only recently changed jobs and was therefore in-between birth control systems. It is not unlikely that this was the reason she had been able to avoid IUD insertion.

In these examples of resentment and anger aimed at compulsory IUD use, of protesting the population policy knowledge test, of avoiding having an IUD inserted and of avoiding the gynaecological check-up, women are silently protesting against being controlled and are applying a strategy of avoidance or non-action. It is, however, neither the policy itself nor the policy requirement of one child that is being contested. Just as the leadership has criticized coercive practices that take place locally and periodically in implementing the policy, women are criticizing not the policy itself but local-level implementation practice. In these examples, however, contrary to the experience of the majority of women, control is viewed as control and not as care.

Not only do women accept the demographic rationale under-lying the one-child policy, most also accept the control with which the policy measure of only one child per couple is implemented. And on condition that the policy applies unequivocally to all city district citizens, they are willing to adhere to the policy require-ment of only one child, at least in so far as policy evasion is made impossible by strict control measures. However, regardless of women's acceptance of the call of the leadership to have only one child, the one-child family is a radical break with tradition. The consequence that emerged as most prominent from the data of this study was that parents' prospect is weakened of establishing an intergenerational contract as the basis for their own support in later life. The intergenerational contract is established as a recip-rocal relationship and is an important aspect of the objective of childbearing.

Urban women's management strategy of *cultivating the perfect only child* is also a property of acceptance because women do not question the policy that has led to the situation with which they are coping. Women's choice of management strategy takes place within the framework of their overall acceptance of the policy. Another feature which might further explain the phenomenon of cultivation of the perfect only child is related to conscientious acceptance. This is the combination of the idealization of self-sacrifice with recognition through achievement which is part of the learning of selflessness in Chinese culture. On the one hand, the individual is expected to be selfless, while on the other hand, the individual is expected to gain recognition through achievement (Pye 1991: 448–449). Mothers are expected to sacrifice themselves for the sake of their child while at the same time they gain recognition through their achievements in cultivating the perfect child. Martin Schoenhals mentions the example of a mother who gained recognition when her son won an inter-national maths award. When her son's school established a class for parents devoted to how parents could raise a talented child, this mother was invited to give lectures to the class (Schoenhals 1993: 146).

Traditionally, women's status has been tied to giving birth to the sons the family needed to ensure continuity as well as to secure the welfare of the older generation. As discussed in Chapter 6, the traditional son-requirement has been transformed to an actual son-preference, with a decidedly weaker pressure being placed on urban women to give birth to a son. An urban, city-district woman's status in the family and in society is no longer closely linked to the number of sons she gives birth to. However, the education of the child is primarily the responsibility of the mother. The long-term objective of educating the child is two-fold. The aim is to ensure the future of the child and to secure support of parents. As described in Chapter 7, a woman is evaluated according to how well she manages her family, which includes bringing up and educating the child to do well in school as well as building a reciprocal relationship between the child and parents. Although the economic and practical realities of urban families have changed so that parents are no longer as financially and practically dependent on their children as rural parents are, the cultural reality of ensuring care in old age is no less strong.

Women feel that they bear the brunt of policy consequences both in terms of contraceptive use and the control linked to contraceptive use and in terms of their role as the mother of an only child. The break with tradition imposed upon urban families by the population policy requirement that they have only one child has had the consequence that the potential for fulfilling the moral obligation of securing care has been weakened. In a context where a woman's role and status are linked to marriage and childbearing, and in which a woman is evaluated according to the ideal of the virtuous wife and especially the good mother, the moral obligation is mainly the responsibility of women. By cultivating the perfect only child, the mother strengthens the tie between the child and the parents, thereby ensuring that the child will provide care at a later stage. In so doing, the mother fulfils her moral and cultural obligation of ensuring care.

The One-Child Family as a Population Control Model

This study has underscored that the one-child family policy does not operate as a form of 'feminism from above' breaking down unequal gender relations. This is quite apparent in the areas that have been designated as priority areas in birth planning work.

These are 'the importance of contraceptives', 'the importance of ideological education' and 'the importance of regular work,' whereas women's reproductive, employment and educational interests are not deemed priority areas. As such, the policy and the practice of birth planning workers in implementing the policy rather than providing the basis for a change of gender relations are, on the contrary, built upon and maintain a traditional socialization of women to a self-sacrificing role in which they hold a special position in relation to sustaining social morality in society (see Evans 1992).

The policy requirement of only one child may serve to support individual women who would otherwise be pressured by their family to have several children. And, in the long run, the policy may lead to a transformation of gender relations resulting from the new position daughters may have in the one-child family. But it is most unlikely that the one-child family policy in general will bring positive change for the generation of mandatory one-child mothers. The reason is that the policy is based on a perpetuation of assumptions of unequal gender relations; moreover, it reinforces gender relations that are contradictory to change in terms of self-determination for women. Nonetheless, neither the women themselves nor birth planning workers seem to see a contradiction between the degree of self-determination women have gained in the PRC, especially in the fields of education and employment, and the lack of reproductive self-determination due to the population policy.

In applying the qualitative mode of theoretical sampling in this study, the aim has been to reach a plausible interpretation of the ways in which urban women react to and manage consequences of the one-child family policy. During the process of interviewing, it became evident that, although women did not share the interviewer's assumptions about reproductive rights, there were some women who did experience a form of reproductive self-determination in regard to implementation of the one-child policy. The exposure of a form of reproductive self-determination is an example of how the qualitative interview is able to grasp meanings that would not enter the study if it relied solely on the preset limits of a survey or a more closed form of interview. Acceptance implies agreement at the ideological level of the population policy, but not necessarily agreement at the level of implementation. When a criticism of the policy is voiced, it is aimed at the implementation level of the policy. This is also the level that is criticized by the leadership itself. While the majority of women accept control measures as care, the criticism that a minority of the women studied do express, although in a silent form of avoidance, is aimed at the implementation level in a non-conceptionalized experience of reproductive self-determination. These few women do not have a concept that will adequately identify their experience nor their action of silent protest and avoidance. A minority of urban women experience a violation of their reproductive self-determination but they do not have a concept with which to label the experience.

One of the reasons why it is important to be aware of the consequences of the demographically successful urban Chinese population policy is that the policy is held up as a model for other nations to emulate. The case of the urban Chinese population policy may be a demographic success but, according to international definitions of human rights, it is obviously based on elements of control and coercion. The main reason for other countries not to model their population policies on the Chinese example is that the policy is not in accordance with international human rights standards. In any case it is arguable that the success of the Chinese example relies on a culturally-based acceptance of the policy. The cultural underpinnings of such acceptance may not be found elsewhere.

Nonetheless, provocatively, it could be argued that the world, when seeking to solve the global 'population problem', should adopt the approach of many of the Chinese women studied – that the individual sacrifice herself to the collective interest. Highly industrialized and overconsuming nations of the North might choose a strategy that is not based on the rights of individuals and couples to have as many children as they want and to consume as much as they want. Instead we might turn our perception of the world upside down. Opponents to population control have stressed the need to maintain the rights of individuals to plan the size of their family. Perhaps we should contemplate an alternative approach to solving the global 'population problem'. This approach would not be narrowly focused on the populations of the countries of the South. Inspired by the Chinese mode of conscientious sacrifice of individual wishes and needs, we might choose a strategy where the individual in the North must sacrifice individual rights to ensure global survival.

The cultural meaning of *acceptance*, from which the majority of the urban women studied perceive policy implementation, differs fundamentally from the human rights definition of family planning as an individual right. However, although the protest that a minority of the women studied do express, via a silent form of avoidance, is aimed at the implementation level of population policy rather than at the ideology of the policy itself, the reactions of these few women, for whom control is not viewed as care, suggest that a change might be taking place in the cultural assumptions within which women perceive of control. The non-conceptionalised experience of reproductive self-determination of a minority of women might be an indication of the cracks that, according to Lucian Pye are appearing both in the public's awe of state authority and in the general hostility toward individualism following the economic reforms and the initial stages of the establishment of civil society (Pye 1991). This is one possible future development, which would then probably influence the future demographic success of urban population policy negatively.

Methodology

> Certain foreign colleagues are even more ingenious: if
> only they can get hold of a floppy disk of data, they
> can stuff China's numbers into a theoretical frame-
> work, and thus complete a 'sinological' treatise.
>
> *Chen Yiyun 1994: 70*

With the studies of everyday life and an understanding of culture
as human praxis as its point of departure, this 'sinological treatise'
has drawn heavily on both the theory and the practical techniques
of the grounded theory approach. Based on the objective of
explicating the meaning of the human phenomena of consequences
of population control and of understanding the everyday experience of one-child mothers from their perspective, the study
was designed as a multiple case study with each of the four cases
corresponding to an urban city district location. Furthermore,
the study was based on a combination of quantitative and
qualitative data supported by documentary research.

Although inspired by the studies of everyday life with their
intention of including both the local, the national and the international levels, this study has primarily focused on the local
level. The local, national and international levels involved in the
present study at various degrees of depth pertain first of all to the
urban one-child family, specifically the one-child mothers. At the
local level, the study is concerned with implementation in work
units where the one-child women work and in the residential areas
where they live. Above the local level of policy implementation

is the national level of 'population problem' interpretation, policy formulation and policy implementation, described mainly in Chapters 3 and 5. And at the international level are the various population policy ideologies, i.e. interpretations of the 'population problem' and formulations of policies and remedial measures. Some of these were briefly outlined in Chapter 1.

Feminists have criticized existing theories for omitting the experiences of women and have suggested alternative approaches based on the experience of women. As long as women's experiences do not provide the grounding for the theories, and as long as theories are formulated by the Western discourse, aspects of women's lives will remain invisible (Harding 1989, Smith 1988). In the grounded theory approach developed by Barney G. Glaser and Anselm L. Strauss, a method was found that would in practice grasp the experienced everyday life of the women being studied (Glaser and Strauss 1967, Strauss [1987] 1991 and Strauss and Corbin 1990). 'The grounded theory approach is a qualitative research *method* that uses a *systematic* set of procedures to *develop* an inductively derived grounded *theory* about a *phenomenon*' (Strauss and Corbin 1990: 24).

The grounded theory method is a mode of qualitative analysis. The aim is inductively to build a substantive theory – i.e. a theory that evolves from the study of a phenomenon situated in one particular situational context. The substantive area of this study is the management of consequences of low fertility achieved by way of population control. Basically, grounded theory is a process of generating core categories and their properties and formulating a theory for the substantive area on which the research has been done that fits and works, i.e. a theory that is indicated by data or grounded in the empirical data and which explains, predicts and interprets the phenomenon being studied.

The study was furthermore designed as a multiple case study. A case study is defined by Robert K. Yin as 'An empirical enquiry that: investigates a contemporary phenomenon within its real-life context; when the boundaries between phenomenon and context are not clearly evident; and in which multiple sources of evidence are used.' (Yin 1989: 23). The case study approach was chosen as a practical approach to implementation of the present study due to its applicability when the following three conditions exist:

1. when descriptive (*how*) or interpretative (*why*) questions are being posed;

2.   when the investigator has little control over events; and

3.   when the focus is on contemporary phenomena within some real-life context. (Yin 1989: 13)

These three conditions fit the present research project quite well. Briefly summarized, the research objective is: to describe *how* urban Chinese women perceive the one-child family policy and *how* they manage consequences of the policy; *how* interaction between women and birth planning institutions evolves; as well as to understand *why* women perceive and manage consequences of the one-child family policy as they do, and *why* women interact with the birth planning institution as they do.

When studying a phenomenon in China within its real-life context, the aspect of not having 'control over events' takes on an extra meaning as many restrictions are placed on the scope of data collection by foreign scholars in the People's Republic of China, especially when data collection is based on surveys and interviews. Foreign social science scholars who since the late 1970s have been permitted to do research in China have encountered many problems and restrictions in their work. Access to certain localities may be out of bounds and certain topics may not be approved by Chinese officials just as prolonged negotiation concerning these matters often impedes the research practice (see Bruun *et al.* 1991, Lunddahl 1988, Pieke 1986–87, Wolf 1985). Subsequent to the 1989 student and worker protests, further restrictions were imposed with the issuance in 1990 of Document 598, 'Notice on Issues Relating to Cooperation with Foreigners Doing Social Science Investigation in Our Country'. This prohibited social science data collection in the form of public opinion polls or written questionnaires being undertaken by members of foreign academic institutions and research institutes (see Meizhong 1991: 2).

An additional reason for the choice of a multiple case study was that the approach could be applied flexibly. Based on the often frustrated experiences of scholars who have done fieldwork in China even before the post-1989 restrictions and their conclusion that flexibility is crucial to successful data collection (see Pieke 1991 and Wolf 1985), flexibility was built into the basic research design with the multiple case study method. Due to the difficulties in collecting data in China, Elisabeth Croll has recommended that empirical data be limited to the 'icing on the cake' with the main study being based on documentary studies (Croll 1987).

Notwithstanding this being excellent advice in the light of the restrictions, it was a prerequisite for the implementation of this study, with its point of departure placed on *the perspective of women*, that a survey and interviews be carried out in China and that this data form the basis of the analysis. Data collection was therefore divided over four locations, the rationale being that should data collection from one or several of the locations turn out to be restricted or infeasible, the study as a whole would still be able to continue although with a smaller sample. As it turned out, data collection was carried out at all four locations. Nonetheless, the appropriateness of this flexible multiple case study design was demonstrated in relation to the arrangement of interviews with birth planning personnel at the four sites. Although it was not possible to interview birth planning personnel at the Beijing residential area, the overall study was not affected.

A third reason for choosing the case study approach was the aim of studying interaction between women and the birth planning institution and personnel at the local level. An optimal research design for studying the interaction between women and the birth planning institution would have been based on fieldwork including participant observation over a period of several months. However, the overall climate for research by foreigners in China and the high sensitivity of the studying of any aspect of the population policy precluded any attempt to make such arrangements.

In spite of the difficulties in gaining access to research in the PRC, several Danish sinologists and anthropologists during recent years have carried out extensive social science data collection and fieldwork in China. A main problem is that Danish universities do not have a tradition of large-scale collaborative research projects with universities in China in which the research of graduate students is included. However, based on personal contacts and connections (*guanxi*) in China, individual scholars have been able to carry out their research (see Bruun *et al.* and Delman 1991). Due to the difficulties in making research arrangements that in part are related to the limits imposed upon Chinese scholars by their institutions and due to difficulties in getting through and receiving answers to correspondence, it is certainly an advantage – if not essential – to travel to China and personally make contact with Chinese institutions and scholars. The result of my negotiations during a two-month stay in Beijing in 1991 with several institutions in the capital, as well as with institutions in several other localities, was that in Beijing the study was carried out in collaboration with the Division of Social Development, the National Research Centre for Science and Technology for Development (NRCSTD). And in Shenyang, an arrangement was made with the Institute of Sociology at the Liaoning Academy of Social Sciences (LASS). These two institutions handled the official arrangements concerning the survey and interviews, as well as appointments for interviews with officials at, for instance, branches of the Women's Federation and at various levels of the birth planning institution.

The reason for expanding the study to include a setting other than Beijing was first of all motivated by the built-in flexibility of the research strategy, as both non-Chinese and Chinese scholars advised against attempting to carry out data collection in Beijing, where official control and caution is more intense than in the provinces, the advice generally being to get as far away from the capital as possible. Should data collection in Beijing have turned out to be infeasible, the study would then have been based solely on data from Shenyang. The choice of Shenyang was based on what was practically and economically feasible in terms of obtaining official research authorization and on the amount of project finances. Contacts were made with Social Science Academies in several provinces of which LASS provided the best conditions for the realization of the study. An additional reason for choosing Shenyang as a supplement to Beijing was the affinity of the language spoken in Shenyang to the standard Chinese language (*putonghua*) used in the interviews.

Data Collection and Analysis

The study is based on a combination of a questionnaire survey followed by in-depth interviews supported by documentary sources and statistical data. In addition to interviews with urban women, interviews were also conducted with representatives of the family planning institution at various levels and with scholars and officials. The data was collected during periods totalling seven months in China, first a two month stay in July and August 1991 and then five months from February to July 1992.

The aim of the survey was to enumerate the behaviour and attitudes of women in relation to consequences of the one-child family policy, the focus being on the occurrence and frequency of these consequences as well as the women's reactions to and management of them in the context of their family and working life in general. Analysis of the survey was combined with analysis of the qualitative interviews, which were concerned with an interpretation of the cultural context of women's perception and management of the policy's consequences. In the combined use of quantitative and qualitative data, the statistical survey data is often used to provide a summary of major patterns while qualitative interview data support these patterns by providing depth, detail and meaning. In this study, the relationship between the survey and the qualitative interviews has a somewhat different quality as the interview data provides the basis for the building of a pattern of interpretation while the survey data plays a more secondary and supportive role.

The survey and the qualitative interviews were developed and applied simultaneously following the grounded theory approach. As grounded theory is an inductive mode of formulating theoretical interpretations of data grounded in reality, the mode of grounded theory analysis does not start when data have been collected but with data collection itself. The analysis is integrated into data collection itself in the manner that, as categories emerge from the data, further interviews and additional data collection concentrate on these.

In the summer of 1991, a pre-test of the questionnaire survey was carried out in Beijing. The draft questionnaire for the pre-test was formulated on the basis of literature on the subject as well as on five exploratory interviews carried out in February 1991 with urban city district women from the PRC temporarily living in Copenhagen. Based on the pre-test of the questionnaire and further interviews in Beijing in 1991, the final questionnaire was formulated and the survey was carried out in the spring and summer of 1992.

The questionnaire survey is based on a sample of 857 urban one-child women, 400 from Shenyang and 457 from Beijing. Qualitative interviews were carried out with 40 of these women. Due to problems with official authorization procedures in Shenyang, interviews took place prior to the survey, while in Beijing interviews followed the survey. In Beijing ten women employed at the Beijing factory and nine women living in the Beijing residential area were interviewed. Of the twenty-one women interviewed in

Shenyang, nine were women living in the Shenyang residential area, four were women employed at the Shenyang factory and nine were women outside the cases. As these latter nine women were the first to be interviewed, although outside the cases, the interviews have been included in the analysis because central themes that were to evolve and become more accentuated in the later interviews – such as for instance the relevance of 'the virtuous wife and good mother ideal', which is important as an aspect of women's self-perception – became apparent at this early stage of interviewing.

In addition to the requirement that the women included in the survey be registered city district residents, the sampling criteria for the women were that they were one-child mothers and had been born between 1953 and 1967 (because this is the generation of women that has been most influenced by the one-child family policy since its implementation). The youngest women were thus 12 years old in 1979 when the one-child family policy was put into practice while the oldest were 26 years old (for a list of the main characteristics of the women surveyed, see Table 2).

In Beijing 500 survey questionnaires were distributed (250 at each of the two sites) with 457 questionnaires returned (corresponding to a response rate of 91.4 per cent). Questionnaires were handed out both at the factory and in the residential area by sociology students, who then collected them again a few days later. In Shenyang questionnaires were distributed through face-to-face interviews at the residential area by LASS personnel. At the factory, questionnaires were handed out and collected by factory administrative personnel. Due to the mode of question-naire distribution, all 400 questionnaires distributed in Shenyang were returned. Within the case areas, the women in the two residential areas were selected for the survey based on a total listing of all households obtained from the local police stations. As the number of female employees fulfilling the selection criteria at the factories did not exceed the 250 required for the study by more than a small number, no specific selection procedures were employed.

The title of the questionnaire reflected the problems of obtaining permission to carry out a study on a topic related to the population policy, even in the demographically successful city districts. Following advice during my 1991 stay in Beijing from Chinese scholars that a precondition for permission to carry out the survey would be to obscure the topic of the study by changing the title of the research proposal as well as that of the question-naire, the latter's title became: 'Changes in the social status and role of Chinese urban women in education, employment and family life' (*Zhongguo chengshi funü zai jiaoyu, jiuye yiji jiating shenghuozhong de shehui diwei he zuoyong de bianhua*). The questionnaire was divided into four sections of which the family section (section four), con-taining the questions directly related to the population policy, was the most extensive. Responses to the open-ended question at the end of the questionnaire reflect that, regardless of the title, respondents were well aware of what the main topic of the questionnaire was.

Chinese scholars have pointed to the problem of transferring application of the Western survey questionnaire to China due to Chinese not being used to expressing their personal opinion in this way and tending to convey opinions in accordance with the social norm (Chen 1994: 70–71, Tan 1991a: 39–40). Non-Chinese scholars have also pointed out that caution should be applied in accepting the validity of responses to policy sensitive issues such as questions on family size preferences in China, as fertility prefer-ences are likely to be under-reported in view of the government population policy (Hermalin and Liu 1990: 338, Whyte and Gu 1987). Reluctance to respond to a question on fertility preferences was obvious in a study in Anhui in which 14 per cent of parents holding one-child certificates did not answer the question of how many children they would prefer, while as many as 56 per cent of the parents without a certificate did not answer (Anhui 1988).

In comparing results from the In-Depth Fertility Survey (IDFS) with results from the Shanghai Survey of Desired Family Size (SSDFS), Albert I. Hermalin and Xian Liu found that under-reporting of fertility preferences does take place and pointed to the mode of questionnaire administration as a factor that could explain under-reporting of fertility preferences. The IDFS was carried out in the form of face-to-face interviews, while in the SSDFS questionnaires were distributed in person and the respondent was asked to fill out the questionnaire and return the completed forms by mail. In the IDFS, only a tiny percentage of women with two or fewer children expressed a desire for more children. By contrast, in the SSDFS, more than one-third of the women who currently had two children expressed a desire for three or more children. Hermalin and Liu conclude that these contrasts are perhaps the strongest evidence that the method of eliciting responses on family size preference can strongly influence the results and that there is good reason to presume that women in Shanghai under-reported their desired family size in face-to-face interviews (Hermalin and Liu 1990). However, Hermalin and Liu also note that the largest differences between the two surveys exist among rural women. In suburban areas and the city, the differences were smaller. Although based on different modes of questionnaire distribution, results from Shenyang and Beijing in this study were similar with regard to fertility preferences.

The Interviews

Based on the requirement that the interview method must enable women to express their experience of their everyday lives, the interviews were carried out using the qualitative research interview method as defined by Steinar Kvale (Kvale 1979, 1983). This method attempts to grasp opinions, feelings, attitudes and the meanings that are implicit in the actions of people from their own viewpoint. This is done by obtaining as many nuanced descriptions from the different qualitative aspects of the informant's everyday life as possible. Descriptions of the life experience of the informant are collected with a view to interpreting the meaning of the described phenomena. Technically, the qualitative research interview is semi-structured and carried through following an interview guide which does not contain exact questions, but instead focuses on certain themes.

The object of the qualitative research interview is the life experience of the informant and the meanings she ascribes to this – in this study specifically we are interested in the experience of urban women as it relates to the one-child family policy. The objective of the interview is to describe and understand central themes in this experience as they are experienced by the informant and as she acts in relation to them. The interview seeks to elicit descriptions of specific situations as opposed to general opinions. To know the general opinions of the informant on the theme is subordinated to obtaining concrete descriptions of what the informant has experienced and how she has acted. In this study, the central theme is the one-child policy. How do the informants think, act and relate to the policy? Do they experience the one-child policy as a restriction on their lives or as a positive change?

The mode of understanding in the interview implies that the meanings, attitudes in the interview are defined by the informant. The purpose is, through the informant, to obtain knowledge and understanding of phenomena in her experience. The most important element of the interview is for the interviewer to understand the meanings that underlie what the informant is saying, including the manner of speaking, intonation and so on.

In order to capture these meanings, each interview was taped and transcribed verbatim. The written version of the interviews (about one thousand handwritten pages in Chinese) together with the tape constituted the material for the subsequent interpretation of meaning. During the process of interviewing and analysing, each interview was replayed once and preliminary coded notes taken prior to the next interview being conducted. Interviews took between half an hour and one and a half hours, with only a few exceeding this time range (the most lengthy being a four-hour interview). During analysis all tapes were played through a second time, while some have been played three times.

Some writers on qualitative methods advise against the use of a tape recorder (Bogdan and Taylor 1975), but it was necessary to use one in this study. First of all, I would not have been able to remember the essence of the four to six interviews that took place consecutively in one day at the factories. Secondly, analysis depended on the identification and validation of core concepts. As the meaning or very existence of a concept with which I was not familiar often did not occur to me until after several interviews, it was important that the analysis be based on the precise transcripts. And it was important to be able to return to earlier interviews for aspects that had not originally been observed. Interpretation in the qualitative research interview takes place from the very start of the interview. The interviewer must be able to grasp the factual level as well as the level of meaning of what is said. And the interviewer must, as far as possible, try to send her interpretations back to the informant for confirmation. In the phases of description and interpretation, which do not necessarily presuppose each other logically or chrono-logically, the informant first describes her life-story, her experiences, feelings and actions without any interpretation from the interviewer. The interviewer then condenses and interprets the meaning of the provisional categories that emerge during the interview based on what the informant describes and sends the interpreted meaning back to the informant for 'on-the-spot verification' (Kvale 1979).

In accordance with the method of grounded theory, the gathering of data and the analysis were carried out as an interactive process that started with the pilot interviews with expatriate Chinese in Copenhagen in February 1991. Interviewing continued in China in 1991. During the course of the stay in Shenyang and Beijing in 1992, the final interviews were conducted as two short-term investigations within the five-month stay. Interviews in Shenyang took place during a three-week stay in March and April, and interviews in Beijing took place from mid-May to early June. The first interview site was the Shenyang residential area. Here five women had been requested by street committee cadres to attend the interviews, which took place at the street committee office in a formal meeting room. Besides two sociologists from LASS, two street committee cadres attended the interviews. These circumstances were far from conducive to obtaining a sense of ease and confidentiality between each woman and her interviewer.

Following these rather constrained interview circumstances in the residential area office, further interviews with women from the residential area were arranged at LASS, without the participation of the street committee. The LASS sociologists, who were not familiar with the qualitative mode of interviewing and therefore interested to monitor the interview session, attended some of these interviews but most comprised only one informant and the interviewer. As the interviews demanded a great deal of concentration on my part, I was – especially during the early interviews – most comfortable when only one informant and I myself took part. When they did attend interview sessions, the LASS sociologists were quite helpful in explaining aspects of the informants' descriptions which I did not seem to be catching and their presence was mostly conducive to the interview situation. However, a couple of times their help tended to conflict with the interview purpose of eliciting descriptions in the words of the informant. Apart from the attendance of the street committee cadres at the Shenyang residential area, I do not think the attendance of others bothered the women being interviewed. One reason may be that the interview was the first direct contact most of the women had ever had with a foreigner. My impression was that they felt less ill at ease, at least at the initial stage of the interview, with being confronted with a foreigner when supported by a fellow Chinese. During the first interviews at LASS, I was annoyed (because my concentration was negatively influenced) when people kept going in and out of the room; in contrast, informants did not seem to notice or mind.

Interviews with women at the factory sites in both Shenyang and Beijing took place in formal meeting rooms at the factories. As I obtained permission to visit both factories for only a few days, the factory interviews were carried out in rapid succession. At the Shenyang factory, four women were interviewed consecutively in one afternoon. At the Beijing factory, six interviews took place in the course of one day and the remaining four interviews a couple of weeks later, also in one day.

Both the circumstances of selection of women from the Beijing residential area case for interviews and the physical setting of interviews with these women were optimal. These interviews have been especially valuable in the analysis as they were furthermore (although coincidentally) carried out during the latter part of the data collection when categories and their properties were being finally validated in the data. Women from the Beijing residential area were asked by questionnaire administrators whether they would be interested to take part in an interview at the NRCSTD. The women selected in this way were therefore probably more motivated to take part in the interview than the women who were selected for interviews by cadres at the factories and the Shenyang residential area. One of the Beijing residential area informants said she and her husband were woken up at ten o'clock in the evening when they had already gone to bed by two of the young sociology students distributing questionnaires. As the students were very polite, she agreed to complete the questionnaire and later to take part in an interview.

Once they had overcome their anxiety due to being confronted with an unfamiliar interview situation as well as by a foreigner, the women interviewed were very cooperative. The practical arrangements for the Beijing residential area case interviews included a document from the NRCSTD to each woman willing to take part in an interview, confirming that she was taking part in an investigation supported by the NRCSTD. The document was submitted by the women at their work unit in order for them to get permission for a day off. Each of the women in Beijing who took part in an interview received 10 yuan. As in Shenyang, the three Beijing scholars involved all attended at least one interview, both because they were curious about the technique of the interviews and because women had interesting stories to tell.

A few of the interviews were attended by two people together. One woman brought her husband, and twice women from the Beijing residential area who were neighbours arrived for the interview together. This worked quite well. In both cases the two knew and complemented each other in a way that was conducive to the interview situation. An example: I asked one of the women (A) whether she had felt any pressure from her mother-in-law to give birth to a son.

> A: 'No, she is relatively open-minded, but when I did give birth to a son my mother-in-law was quite satisfied. She was very happy and came to fetch me at the hospital. The first month celebration (*manyue*)[1] for my son was quite lively.'

> B: [who has a daughter] 'No matter whether the child is a girl or a boy, we celebrate the passing of the first month. It is important not to give outsiders the impression that [here she paused and laughed uncertainly] not to give other people the impression that [pause] you know.'

> Interviewer: 'No, I do not know.'

> B: [still hesitant] How should I explain this?

> A: The point is not to make a difference between celebrating a boy and a girl, because boys and girls are equal.

Her response revealed that one of the reasons for a girl to be celebrated just as much as a boy is that, if a girl is celebrated less than a boy, outsiders will notice that the family attitude is not up to the official gender equality standard.

Main Characteristics of the Women Surveyed

Half of the women surveyed belonged to the age-group born in the five years from 1953 and 1957, one third of the women were born in the years 1958–62 and 17.2 per cent from 1963–67. Three-quarters of the women had given birth to their child in the period up to 1989, 16.3 per cent had given birth in the years 1989–91 and

---

1. In China a celebration takes place a month after the birth of a child.

Table 2: Characteristics of women surveyed

Characteristic	Number	Per cent
Year of birth of woman		
• 1953–57	423	49.4
• 1958–62	259	30.2
• 1963–67	147	17.2
• unknown	28	3.3
Educational level		
• primary school	18	2.1
• lower middle school	368	42.9
• higher middle school	293	34.2
• university and above	158	18.4
• unknown	20	2.3
Type of workplace		
• state enterprise	505	58.9
• collective enterprise	318	37.1
• private enterprise	6	0.7
• other	18	2.1
• unknown	10	1.2
Family category		
• worker	505	58.9
• intellectual	138	16.1
• cadre	159	18.6
• private entrepreneur	13	1.5
• other	18	2.1
• unknown	24	2.8
Interval between marriage and birth of child		
• 1–2 years	713	82.2
• 3–4 years	78	9.1
• 5 years or more	26	3.0
• unknown	40	4.7
Year of birth of child		
• before 1982	232	27.1
• 1983–85	237	27.7
• 1986–88	172	20.1
• 1989–91	140	16.3
• after 1992	9	1.1
• unknown	67	7.8
Sex of child		
• female	393	45.9
• male	429	50.1
• unknown	35	4.1

Total number of women: 857

nine women had given birth in 1992. About half of the women had a daughter and half had a son (see Table 2).

A majority of the women surveyed (82.2 per cent) had given birth to their child within two years of their marriage. Only 12.1 per cent had given birth three or more years after they had married. Whereas a small percentage (2.1) of the women had only primary level education, nearly half (42.9 per cent) had lower middle school education, while one third (34.2 per cent) had higher middle school level education, and 18.4 per cent had university level education. The majority of the women were employed in state enterprises (58.9 per cent), and 37.1 per cent were employed in collective enterprises, a distribution which corresponds relatively well with the overall urban distribution of workers, while a minority of six women were private entrepreneurs.[2]

In addition to being categorized as either agricultural or non-agricultural (as described in Chapter 2), people in China are furthermore categorized according to an identity system as either peasants (*nongmin*), workers (*gongren*) or cadres (*ganbu*). The three categories differ as to ownership of resources, forms of ownership as well as eligibility for allocation of state subsidies. In the context of this study of people registered in urban households, the two categories of workers and cadres are relevant. Approximately two thirds (58.9 per cent) of the women surveyed classified their families as worker families, while one third (34.7 per cent) classified their families as cadre or intellectual. Intellectuals are also defined as cadres. While workers are the people engaged in productive labour, cadres include people who are employed in all types of state institutions and systems at various levels. They are paid from the state budget but not engaged in productive labour (see Li *et al.* 1991: 29–30). The reason that women were asked not about their personal status but about the family status was that a woman who is herself a worker may very well be married into a cadre family, meaning that her overall everyday environment would be a cadre environment.

---

2. In urban areas, industries can be divided into three sectors: the state sector, the collective sector and the private sector. The state sector employs approximately 70 per cent of all workers, the collective sector about 26 per cent and the private sector about 4 per cent (*Zhongguo tongji* 1991: 95).

Theoretical Sampling

In the following pages, the issue of validity in terms of the qualitative and quantitative data collection and qualitative analysis of the
study is discussed. In the grounded theory approach, theoretical
sampling as opposed to statistical sampling guides the choosing
and handling of the data because generation of theory rather
than verification is the purpose. The study starts with a set of
propositions or a statement posed for investigation. The rule for
the generation of theory is not to have any pre-set or valued
hypothesis, but to maintain a sensitivity to all possible theoretical
relevances. As such, the hypotheses come after the analysis – they
are suggested from the findings, not tested with them (Glaser and
Strauss 1967: 194). The grounded theory approach as a qualitative
mode of data analysis is focused on establishing a general pattern
of one-child management among urban women. Because the aim
is to build a general pattern, the four case areas are combined in
the analysis. The aim of the analysis is not quantitatively to test
the relationship among variables such as the degree to which, for
instance, educational level or type of workplace influences the
experience and management of the policy. The aim is qualitatively to discover relevant categories and the relationship among
them and to put together categories to form a theory (Strauss and
Corbin 1990: 49).

The statements of the informant may sometimes be ambiguous. The task of the interviewer is then to clarify whether such
an ambiguity is due to failure of communication in the interview
or a reflection of real inconsistencies or ambivalence. The aim of
the qualitative research interview is not to end up with un-
equivocal and quantifiable meanings on themes of the interview, but
rather to describe precisely the inherently contradictory meanings
the informant expresses. The contradictions expressed need not
be due to faulty communication but may be adequate reflections
of objective contradictions in the world the informant lives in.

The process of generating a grounded theory is an inductive
process as opposed to a logical-deductive process. The aim of
theoretical sampling is not to provide a perfect description of an
area, but to develop a theory that accounts for much of the
relevant behaviour (Glaser and Strauss 1967: 30). The theory is
conceptualized and formulated as it emerges from the data.
Whereas statistical sampling is done to obtain accurate evidence
on distributions of people among categories to be used in de-

scriptions or verification, theoretical sampling is done in order to discover categories and their properties and to suggest inter-relationships into the theory (Glaser and Strauss 1967: 62). Thus the survey describes and enumerates consequences and the context of management of the one-child policy, while the qualitative interviews form the core of the interpretation of the way women manage consequences of the policy.

Gradually throughout the interviewing process the qualitative interviews were directed more and more towards the categories of the emerging theory. This means that, although both the first and the last group of interviews lasted about one hour, the later interviews were more focused at the evolving categories and their properties than were the early interviews. The interviews played different roles in the generation of theory. While the first inter-views would seem to be more exploratory and did not play as important a role in the final analysis as the later interviews, they were a precondition for the realization of the later interviews. According to the mode of conducting grounded theory, data collection and data analysis are tightly interwoven processes which occur alternately because the analysis of the data directs the sampling. Due to the difficulties in conducting social science studies in China, selection of the four case areas for the interviews did not take place gradually in the process of the data collection but was at an early stage of the process determined by the basic design of the study as a multiple case study.

The case study method as well as the qualitative mode of grounded theory sampling have been criticized for not being scientifically generalizable to larger populations. While the sample is not statistically representative and therefore does not provide evidence of general trends and cannot be generalized to urban China or to other parts of China, the patterns that are established through the analysis provide an insight into and a deepened understanding of the cultural management by urban women of the one-child policy. In the case study approach, the aim is not to enumerate frequencies in the form of statistical generalization but to develop a theoretical pattern in which the case study or sample is generalizable to theoretical propositions (Yin 1989: 21). Rather than to generalize to larger populations, the aim is to specify the conditions under which the phenomena studied exist, the action and interaction that pertain to the phenomena and the associated outcomes of these. The validity of the qualitative analysis is determined in terms of the patterns of understanding established work, i.e. whether they provide a deeper understanding of the phenomenon being studied.

A traditional requirement of scientific method is that the data should be reproducible both inter-subjectively and intra-subjectively. In the qualitative interview and grounded theory process of building theory, no single interview is reproducible. The interviews are not only neither inter- nor intra-subjectively reproducible, but also it would be impossible for an informant to carry through exactly the same interview at a later time, as her consciousness of the topic of the interview has changed during the very process of the interview (Kvale 1983: 177). One example illustrating the change of outlook that can take place for the informant was that of a 32-year-old Beijing woman who was quite astonished when during the interview I asked her why it was a matter of course to her that she and not her husband took leave from work when their child was ill. She had obviously not questioned their sharing of responsibilities in relation to the child. Afterwards she said the interview had provided her with much food for thought. As the criterion of reproducibility in its 'normal' form does not work in terms of the qualitative interview, it must be redefined. Whereas reproduction of each specific interview is not possible, reproducibility of the qualitative study should be defined in terms of reproduction of the overall study, applying an identical theoretical perspective and research procedures (Strauss and Corbin 1990: 251). And as control of data come from the researcher's context and perspective of the data (Giorgi 1975: 96), it is important that the research process is visible throughout the analysis.

In order to understand the meanings informants present, it is furthermore a precondition that the interviewer's knowledge of China is based on reality; that the interviewer has a conception of Chinese society and culture which is rooted in practical experience. The distinction between having *a concept for* something and having *a conception of* something has been elucidated by Jette Fog using the example of the child who has read about passionate love between man and woman. The child has words and a concept for this kind of love. But the concept is detached from reality, from praxis. The child has an experience of love between man and woman from having read about love that is not based in reality, because the very object, love between man and woman, has not been experienced by the child (Fog 1985).

A conception of Chinese reality rooted in praxis is also important in relation to creating sensitivity between interviewer and informant. The qualitative interview is an interpersonal situation, and whether or not it turns out successfully depends to a large degree on the sensitivity of the interviewer. Kvale gives the example that an interviewer who does not have an ear for music will have difficulty in understanding or may be incapable of understanding music experiences. I would compare the state of not having an ear for music with that of not having a conception of Chinese reality. Parts of the knowledge of the research interview are constituted as a result of the dialogue between interviewer and informant. This dialogue is based on the sensitivity of the interviewer and therefore also on her knowledge of the culture and society in which she is working. So the stance of being without presuppositions must rest upon knowledge of the culture in question.

A prerequisite for the cross-cultural study is on the one hand a presuppositionless stance and on the other hand that the interviewer must have a conception of the culture in question in terms of the material conditions of life, the observable actions of people, and the meanings ascribed to the actions. Regardless of the intention of a presuppositionless interpretation that avoids appropriating the experience of informants, the subjectivity of the researcher will influence the final analysis. This is a fact that has led postmodern critics to question the possibility of representing the experience of another culture at all. Feminists who have been grappling with these problems, before postmodernists turned their attention to the problems, point out that as a certain degree of objectification cannot be avoided when speaking of others, the question is how to minimize objectification (Wolf 1992, Caplan 1992, Chow 1993).

Bibliography

Aird, John S. 1963. 'Population Policy in Mainland China'. *Population Studies*. Vol. XVI, 1962–63, 38–57.

—— 1973. 'Population Problems, Theories, and Policies'. In Yuan-li Wu (ed.). *China. A Handbook*. Newton Abbot: David & Charles, 443–466.

—— 1978. 'Fertility Decline and Birth Control in the People's Republic of China'. *Population and Development Review*. Vol. 4. No. 2. (June), 225–252.

—— 1990. *Slaughter of the Innocents*. Washington, DC: The AEI Press.

Akhter, Farida 1990. *Issues of Women's Health and Reproductive Rights*. Paper presented at the 6th International Women and Health Meeting, Quezon City, Philippines, 5 November.

—— 1991. 'Feminist Critique of Population Control Programs and Their Abuse of Women'. In *Women Creating Reproductive Freedom. Challenges and Dilemmas: a Critique of Population Control*. Introductory Presentations Made at a Workshop Organized by Women's Health Interaction and INTER PARES. Ottawa, June 10–14.

Andors, Phyllis 1983. *The Unfinished Liberation of Chinese Women 1949–1980*. Bloomington: Indiana University Press.

Anhui daxue renkou yanjiusuo 1988. *Hefeishi dusheng zinü jiating zhuizong diaocha* [Investigation of One-Child Families in Hefei City]. *Zhongguo renkou kexue* [China Population Science]. No. 1, 43–51, 58.

Arnold, Fred and Liu Zhaoxiang 1986. 'Sex Preference, Fertility and Family Planning in China'. *Population and Development Review*. Vol. 12. No. 2. (June), 221–246.

Baker, Hugh D. 1979. *Chinese Family and Kinship*. London: Macmillan Press.

Bakken, Børge 1993. 'Prejudice and Danger: the Only-Child in China'. *Childhood*. Vol. 1, 46–61.

Banister, Judith 1984. 'Population Policy and Trends in China, 1978–83'. *The China Quarterly*. No. 100 (December), 717–741.

—— 1987. *China's Changing Population*. Stanford: Stanford University Press.

Bauer John, Wang Feng, Nancy E. Riley and Zhao Xiaohua 1992. 'Gender Inequality in Urban China'. *Modern China*. Vol. 18. No. 3 (July), 333–369.

Beijing jingji xueyuan renkou jingji yanjiusuo (ed.) 1981. *Jihua shengyu zhishi jianghua* [Introduction to Birth Planning Knowledge]. Beijing: Beijing jihua shengyu xuanchuan jiaoyu zhongxin.

Beijingshi jihua shengyu tiaoli [Beijing Municipal Birth Planning Regulaions] 15 January 1991. Beijingshi dijiuju renmin daibiao dahui changwu weiyuanhui diershiwuci huiyi tongguo [Passed by the 25th Meeting of the Standing Committee of the Ninth Beijing Municipal People's Congress].

Beijingshi renkou tongji ziliao huibian (1949–87) [Compilation of Beijing Population Statistics (1949–87)] 1988. Beijing: Beijingshi tongjiju, Zhongguo tongji chubanshe.

Beijingshi shehui jingji tongji nianjian (1989) [Beijing Socio-economic Statistical Yearbook 1989] 1990. Beijing: Beijingshi tongjiju, Zhongguo tongjiju chubanshe.

Beijing sishi nian 1949–89 [Beijing Forty Years 1949–89] 1990. Beijing: Beijingshi tongjiju, Zhongguo tongji chubanshe.

Berelson, Bernhard [1975] 1990. 'The Great Debate on Population Policy: an Instructive Entertainment'. *International Family Planning Perspectives*. Vol. 16. No. 4. (December), 126–138.

Berer, Marge 1990a. 'What Would a Feminist Population Policy Be Like?' *Women's Health Journal*. No. 18. (April–May–June), 4–7.

—— 1990b. *Reproductive Rights: a Definition and Perspectives for the Future*. Paper presented at the 6th International Women and Health Meeting, Quezon City, Philippines, 5 November.

—— 1993. 'Population and Family Planning Policies: Women-Centered Perspectives'. *Reproductive Health Matters*. No. 1, 4–12.

Bergström, Staffan 1994. 'Population Control. Controlling the Poor or the Poverty?' In K.S. Lankinen, S. Bergström and M. Peltomaa (eds). *Health and Disease in Developing Countries*. London: Macmillan Press.

Bian Yanjiu 1987. 'A Preliminary Analysis of the Basic Features of the Life Styles of China's Single-Child Families'. *Social Sciences in China*. Vol. 8. No. 3. (September).

Bianco, Lucien and Hua Chang-ming 1988. 'Implementation and Resistance: the Single-Child Family Policy'. In Stephen Feuchtwang, Athar Hussain and Thierry Pairault (eds). *Transforming China's Economy in the Eighties*. Vol. 1: The Rural Sector, Welfare and Employment. Boulder, Colorado: Westview Press; London: Zed Books, 147–169.

'Birth Planning in Sichuan Province, China' 1988. *Population and Development Review*. Vol. 14. No. 2. (June), 369–375.

Bloch, Charlotte and Lis Højgaard (eds) 1986. 'Hverdagsliv under forandring' [Changing Everyday Life]. *Repro-serie*. No. 6. Department of Cultural Sociology, University of Copenhagen.

Bloch, Charlotte, Lis Højgaard, Birte Bech Jørgensen and Birthe Lindeskov Nautrup 1988. *Hverdagsliv, Kultur og Subjektivitet* [Everyday Life, Culture and Subjectivity]. Copenhagen: Akademisk Forlag.

Bogdan, Robert and Steven J. Taylor 1975. *Introduction to Qualitative Research Methods*. New York: John Wiley & Sons.

Bondestam, Lars 1983. 'The Political Ideology of Population Control'. In Hamza Alavi and Teodor Shanin (eds). *Introduction to the Sociology of 'Developing Societies'*. London: Academic Press, 252–259.

Bongaarts, John and Susan Greenhalgh 1985. 'An Alternative to the One-Child Policy in China'. *Population and Development Review*. Vol. 11. No. 4. (December), 585–617.

Borum, Finn and Harald Enderud 1980. 'Organisationsforskeren som Reporter' [The Organization Researcher as Reporter]. *Tidsskrift for Samfunnsforskning*. Vol. 21, 359–382.

Bose, Ashish 1993. 'Indiens familieplanlægningsprogrammer – søgen efter nye strategier' [India's Family Planning Programmes – in Search of New Strategies]. In Bertil Egerö *et al.* (eds). *Den Ny Verden*. Vol. 26. No. 3, 60–70.

Bruun, Ole 1991. 'Anthropological Fieldwork and Social Theory'. In Ole Bruun, Søren Poulsen and Hatla Thelle (eds). *Modern China Research: Danish Experiences. Copenhagen Discussion Papers Special Issue*. Copenhagen: Centre for East and Southeast Asian Studies, University of Copenhagen. (September), 67–87.

Bruun, Ole, Søren Poulsen and Hatla Thelle (eds) 1991. *Modern China Research: Danish Experiences. Copenhagen Discussion Papers Special Issue*. Centre for East and Southeast Asian Studies, University of Copenhagen. (September).

Cai Wenmei 1989. 'Ruhe jiejue Zhongguo renkou wenti' [Solutions to China's Population Problem]. *Zhongguo keji daobao* [China Science and Technology Review]. No. 4, 3–5.

Cai Wenmei, Zhou Xiou-zheng (Zhou Xiaozheng) and Li Qiang 1991. 'An Analysis of Social Factors Affecting Abortion in China'. In

Fertility in China. International Statistical Institute Voorburg, the Netherlands, 315–320.

Cao Jingchun (ed.) 1990. *Renkou jichu zhishi duben* [Basic Population Knowledge]. Guojia jihua shengyu weiyuanhui xuanchuan jiaoyu si [Ideological Education Department of the State Family Planning Commission]. Shenyang: Liaoning daxue chubanshi.

Caplan, Pat 1992. 'Engendering Knowledge: The Politics of Ethnography'. In Shirley Ardener (ed.). *Persons and Powers of Women in Diverse Cultures*. New York/Oxford: Berg, 65–89.

Chao Yü-shen 1980. 'Population Pressure on Chinese Mainland'. *Issues and Studies*. Vol. 16. No. 4, 10–13.

Chen, Charles and Carl W. Tyler 1982. 'Demographic Implications of Family Size Alternatives in the PRC'. *The China Quarterly*. No. 89. (March), 65–73.

Chen Dongyuan [1928] 1990. *Zhongguo funü shenghuoshi* [A History of the Lives of Chinese Women]. Taiwan: Taiwan shangwu yinshuguan. Shanghai: Shangwu yinshuguan.

Chen Kejin (ed.) 1989. *Hunyin jiating cidian* [Marriage and Family Dictionary]. Beijing: Zhongguo guoji quangbo chubanshe 1989.

Chen Muhua [1979] 1981. 'Shixian sige xiandaihua, bixu you jihua de kongzhi renkou zengzhang' [Planned Control of Population Increase is Necessary for Realization of the Four Modernizations]. Originally published in *Renmin ribao*. 11 August 1979. Reprinted in Deng Xingying (ed.) 1981. *Renkou wenti yu sihua* [Population Issues and the Four Modernizations]. Chengdu: Sichuan renmin chubanshe. Also translated with an introductory note and commentary by Pi-chao Chen 1979. Birth Planning in China. *International Family Planning Perspectives*. Vol. 5. No. 3. (September), 92–100.

Chen, Pi Chao 1979. 'The Chinese Experience'. *People*. Vol. 6. No. 2, 19.

——1980. 'Three in 10 Chinese Couples with One Child Apply for Certificate Pledging They Will Have No More'. *International Family Planning Perspectives*. Vol. 6. No. 2. (June), 70.

Chen, Pi Chao and Adrienne Kols 1982. Population and Birth Planning in the People's Republic of China. *Population Reports*. Series J. No. 25. (January–February).

Chen Yiyun 1994. 'Out of the Traditional Halls of Academe: Exploring New Avenues for Research on Women'. In Christina K. Gilmartin, Gail Hershatter, Lisa Rofel and Tyrene White (eds). *Engendering China*. Cambridge, Mass.: Harvard University Press. Harvard Contemporary China Series, 10, 69–79.

Chen Zhongli 1979. 'Wei Ma Yinchu de 'Xin renkou lun' pingfan' [Rehabilitation of Ma Yinchu's New Population Theory]. *Renmin Ribao*. 13 June.

Chi Lung. [1973] 1980. 'China Explains Her View on the Population Question'. *Peking Review*. No. 17. (27 April 1973). In H. Yuan Tien (ed.). *Population Theory in China*. White Plains, New York: M.E. Sharpe, 90–93.

Choe, Minja Kim and Noriko O. Tsuya 1991. 'Why Chinese Women Practice Contraception? The Case of Rural Jilin Province'. *Studies in Family Planning*. Vol. 22. No. 1. (January/February), 39–51.

Choe, Minja Kim, Guo Fei, Wu Jianming and Zhang Ruyue 1992. 'Progression to Second and Third Births in China: Patterns and Covariates in Six Provinces'. *International Family Planning Perspectives*. Vol. 18. No. 4. (December), 130–136, 149.

Choe, Minja Kim, Wu Jianming, Zhang Ruyue and Guo Fei 1991. 'Timing of First Birth in Six Provinces of China: Findings from the In-Depth Fertility Survey Phase II'. In *Fertility in China*. International Statistical Institute Voorburg, The Netherlands, 187–204.

Chow, Rey 1993. 'Against the Lures of Diaspora: Minority Discourse, Chinese Women, and Intellectual Hegemony'. In Tonglin Lu (ed.). *Gender and Sexuality in Twentieth-Century Chinese Literature and Society*. New York: State University of New York Press, 47–66.

Coale, Ansley J 1981a. 'Population Trends, Population Policy and Population Studies in China'. *Population and Development Review*. Vol. 7. No. 1. (March), 85–97.

—— 1981b. 'A Further Note on Chinese Population Statistics'. *Population and Development Review*. Vol. 7. No. 3. (September), 512–518.

—— 1991. 'Excess Female Mortality and the Balance of the Sexes in the Population: an Estimate of the No. of "Missing Females". *Population and Development Review*. Vol. 17. No. 3. (September), 517–523.

Cohen, Jerome Alan 1968. *The Criminal Process in The People's Republic of China 1949–1963*. Cambridge, Mass.: Harvard University Press.

Cohen, Roberta 1987. 'People's Republic of China: the Human Rights Exception'. *Human Rights Quarterly*. Vol. 9, 447–549.

Cohen, Susan A. 1993. 'The Road from Rio to Cairo: Toward a Common Agenda'. *International Family Planning Perspectives*. Vol. 19. No. 2. (June), 61–66.

Commoner, Barry 1975. 'How Poverty Breeds Overpopulation (and Not the Other Way Round)'. *RAMPARTS*. Vol. 13. No. 10. (August–September), 21–25, 58–59.

Convention on the Elimination of All Forms of Discrimination against Women 18 December 1979. Reprinted by the United Nations Department of Public Information 1990.

Correa, Sonia 1993. *Dawn Research Effort: 1992/94, Population and Reproductive Rights Component*. Platform Document/Preliminary Ideas.

Croll, Elisabeth 1983. *Chinese Women since Mao*. London: Zed Books.

—— 1985a. 'Introduction: Fertility Norms and Family Size in China'. In Elisabeth Croll, Delia Davin and Penny Kane (eds). *China's One-Child Family Policy*. London: Macmillan, 1–37.

—— 1985b. 'The Single-Child Family in Beijing: a First-hand Report'. In Elisabeth Croll, Delia Davin and Penny Kane (eds). *China's One-Child Family Policy*. London: Macmillan, 190–232.

—— 1987. 'Short-term Field Investigation in China: a Personal View'. *China Information*. Vol. 1. No. 2, 17–26.

Croll, Elisabeth, Delia Davin and Penny Kane (eds) 1985. *China's One-Child Family Policy*. London: Macmillan.

Dai Kejing 1990. 'The Social Significance of Marriage and Family in China'. In Stella R. Quah (ed.). *The Family as an Asset*. Singapore: Times Academic Press, 174–212.

—— 1992. 'Tradition, Social Policy and Change in Marriage and Family in China'. In *Proceedings of Asia-Pacific Regional Conference on Future of the Family*. Beijing: China Social Science Documentation Publishing House, 4–12.

Davin, Delia 1985. 'The Single-Child Family Policy in the Countryside'. In Elisabeth Croll, Delia Davin and Penny Kane (eds). *China's One-Child Family Policy*. London: Macmillan, 37–82.

—— 1987. 'Gender and Population in the People's Republic of China'. In Haleh Afshar (ed.). *Women, State and Ideology*. London: Macmillan Press, 111–129.

—— 1990. 'Never mind if it's a girl, you can have another try'. In Jørgen Delman, Clemens Stubbe Østergaard and Flemming Christiansen (eds). *Remaking Peasant China*. Aarhus: Aarhus University Press, 81–91.

—— 1992. 'Population Policy and Reform. The Soviet Union, Eastern Europe and China'. In Shirin Rai, Hilary Pilkington and Annie Phizacklea (eds). *Women in the Face of Change*. London: Routledge, 79–104.

Davis, Deborah and Stevan Harrell 1993. 'Introduction: the Impact of Post-Mao Reforms on Family Life'. In Deborah Davis and Stevan Harrell (eds). *Chinese Families in the Post-Mao Era*. Berkeley, Los Angeles, London: University of California Press, 1–22.

Delman, Jørgen 1989. Fieldnotes 6 May 1989, interview with Sichuan Province, Cihang Township local government leaders.

Dixon-Mueller, Ruth 1993. *Population Policy and Women's Rights: Transforming Reproductive Choice*. Westport, Connecticut. London: Praeger.

Dongchengqu jihua shengyu bangongshi, Dongchengqu jihua shengyu xiehui [East District Birth Planning Office and East District Birth

Planning Association] 1990. *Zhi weihun qingnian yifeng xin* [Letter to Young Unmarrieds].

Dongchengqu jihua shengyu bangongshi, jihua shengyu xiehui [East District Birth Planning Office and Birth Planning Association]. Undated. *Xuexi 'Beijingshi jihua shengyu tiaoli' xuanchuan cailiao zhi wu* [Educational Materials No. 5 for studying 'The Beijing Municipality Birth Planning Regulations'].

DuBois, Marc 1991. 'The Governance of the Third World: a Foucauldian Perspective on Power Relations in Development'. *Alternatives*. 16, 1–30.

Egerö, Bertil 1980. 'People and Underdevelopment – the Example of Tanzania'. In Lars Bondestam and S. Bergström (eds). *Poverty and Population Control*. London: Academic Press, 197–211

—— 1992. 'A Discussion of Dr King's Version of the "Demographic Trap"'. In M. Hammarskjöld, B. Egerö and S. Lindberg (eds). *Population and the Development Crisis in the South*. Proceedings from a conference in Båstad, 17–18 April 1991. Lund: PROP Publications Series No. 2, 48–55.

Ehrlich, Paul R. and Anne H. Ehrlich 1991. *The Population Explosion*. London: Arrow Books. (First published by Hutchinson 1990).

Ely, Margot with Margaret Anzul, Teri Friedman, Diane Garner and Ann McCormack (eds) 1991. *Doing Qualitative Research: Circles within Circles*. London: The Falmer Press.

Epstein, T. Scarlett 1977. 'From "Accommodation" to "Intervention": Socio-economic Heterogeneity and Demographic Patterns'. In T. Scarlett Epstein and D. Jackson (eds). *The Feasibility of Fertility Planning*. Oxford: Pergamon Press, 219–236.

Estrada-Claudio, Sylvia 1991. 'Population Control and Reproductive Health Issues in the Philippines'. In *Women Creating Reproductive Freedom. Challenges and Dilemmas: a Critique of Population Control*. Introductory Presentations Made at a Workshop Organized by Women's Health Interaction and INTER PARES. Ottawa, 8 June, 4–9.

——1993. *Strengthening Women's Voices in Southeast, East and North Asia*. Keynote Address to the First Organizational Meeting for a Woman and Health Network in the Southeast, East and North Asian Region. December 1–5. Los Banos, Philippines.

Evans, Harriet 1992. 'Monogamy and Female Sexuality in the People's Republic of China'. In Shirin Rai, Hilary Pilkington and Annie Phizacklea (eds). *Women in the Face of Change*. London: Routledge, 147–163.

Family Planning in the 1980s: Challenges and Opportunities, Report on the International Conference on Family Planning in the 1980s, Jakarta, Indonesia, 26–30 April 1981. Co-sponsored by the United Nations

Fund for Population Activities, the International Planned Parenthood Federation and the Population Council, 1981.

Feeney, Griffith and Wang Feng 1993. 'Parity Progression and Birth Intervals in China: the Influence of Policy in Hastening Fertility Decline'. *Population and Development Review.* Vol. 19. No. 1. (March) 61–101.

Feng Xiaotian 1990. 'Zhongguo de dusheng zinü tamen de jiating, jiaoyu he weilai' [The Only Child in China: Family, Education and Future]. Unpublished Ph.D. dissertation, Peking University.

——1991. 'Dusheng zinü fumu de shengyu yiyuan' [Fertility Desires of the Parents of Only Children]. *Renkou Yanjiu.* No. 5, 30–33.

——1992. 'Lun chengshi dusheng zinü jiating de shehui tezheng' [A Discussion of Social Characteristics of Urban One-Child Families]. *Shehuixue yanjiu* [Sociological Research]. No. 1, 108–116.

Flax, Jane 1989. 'Postmodernism and Gender Relations in Feminist Theory'. In Micheline R. Malson, Jean F. O'Barr, Sarah Westphal-Wihl and Mary Wyer (eds). *Feminist Theory in Practice and Process.* Chicago: The University of Chicago Press, 51–73.

Fog, Jette 1985. 'Om den følsomme fornuft og den fornuftige følsomhed' [On the Sensitive Rationality and the Rational Sensitivity]. *Psyke og Logos.* No. 6, 59–84.

Fort, Alfredo L. 1989. 'Investigating the Social Context of Fertility and Family Planning: a Qualitative Study in Peru'. *International Family Planning Perspectives.* Vol. 15. No. 3. (September), 88–95.

Freeberne, Michael 1965. 'Birth Control in China'. *Population Studies.* Vol. XVIII, 1964–65, London, 5–16.

Freedmann, Ronald and Guo Shenyang 1988. 'Response of a Traditional Fishing Community to China's Family Planning Programme: a Case Study'. *International Family Planning Perspectives.* Vol. 14. No. 4. (December), 131–137.

Gao Ling 1993. 'Zhongguo renkou chusheng xingbiebi de fenxi' [The Sex Ratio at Birth of the Chinese Population]. *Renkou Yanjiu.* No. 1, 1–6.

Gates, Hill 1993. 'Cultural Support for Birth Limitation among Urban Capital-Owning Women'. In Deborah Davis and Stevan Harrell (eds). *Chinese Families in the Post-Mao Era.* Berkeley, Los Angeles: University of California Press, 251–274.

Gibbon, Peter 1992. 'Population and Poverty in the Changing Ideology of the World Bank'. In M. Hammarskjöld, B. Egerö and S. Lindberg (eds). *Population and the Development Crisis in the South.* Lund: The Programme on Population and Development in Poor Countries, PROP Publications Series. No. 2, 133–145

Gimenez, Martha 1973. 'Befolkningsproblemet. Marx kontra Malthus' [The Population Problem. Marx versus Malthus]. *Den Ny Verden.* No. 3, 74–88.

Giorgi, Amedeo 1975. 'An Application of Phenomenological Method in Psychology'. In A. Giorgi, C. Fisher and E. Murrey (eds). *Duquesne Studies in Phenomenological Psychology, II*. Pittsburg: Duquesne University, 82–103.

Glaser, Barney G. and Anselm L. Strauss 1967. *The Discovery of Grounded Theory*. New York: Aldine de Gruyter.

Gold, Thomas B. 1989. 'Guerrilla Interviewing among the Getihu'. In Perry Link, Richard Madsen and Paul G. Pickowicz (eds). *Unofficial China*. Boulder, San Francisco: Westview Press, 175–192.

Goldstein, Sidney 1990. 'Urbanization in China, 1982–87: Effects of Migration and Reclassification'. *Population and Development Review*. Vol. 16. No. 4. (June) 673–702.

Goodstadt, Leo F. 1978. 'Official Targets, Data, and Policies for China's Population Growth: an Assessment'. *Population and Development Review*. Vol. 2. No. 4. (June), 255–275.

Greenhalgh, Susan 1988. *Population Research in China: An Introduction and Guide to Institutes*. Center for Policy Studies. Working Papers. No. 137. (March), the Population Council, New York.

—— 1989. *The Evolution of the One-Child Policy in Shaanxi Province, 1979–88*. Working Papers, No. 5, Research Division, The Population Council, New York.

—— 1990a. 'The Evolution of the One-Child Policy in Shaanxi, 1979–88'. *The China Quarterly*. No. 122, 191–229.

—— 1990b. 'Population Studies in China: Privileged Past, Anxious Future'. *The Australian Journal of Chinese Affairs*. No. 24. (July), 357–384.

—— 1993. 'The Peasantization of the One-Child Policy in Shaanxi'. In Deborah Davis and Stevan Harrell (eds). *Chinese Families in the Post-Mao Era*. Berkeley, Los Angeles: University of California Press, 219–250.

Greenhalgh, Susan and John Bongaarts 1987. 'Fertility Policy in China: Future Options'. *Science*. Vol. 235. No. 4793. (6 March), 1167–1172.

Greer, Germaine 1984. *Sex and Destiny – the Politics of Human Fertility*. London: Secker & Warburg.

Guizhou sheng. Weihu funü ertong hefa quanyi de ruogan guiding [Guizhou Province. Regulations on the Protection of the Legal Rights of Women and Children] 1984-3-28. In: Quanguo renda neiwusifa weiyuanhui. Funü ertong zhuanmen xiaozu and Qingshaonian zhuanmen xiaozu (eds). *Funü he weichengnianren falü baohu quangshu* [Collection of Laws on Protection of Women and Youth] 1991. Beijing: Zhongguo jiancha chubanshe, 512–514.

Guo Fei and Minja Kim Choe 1991. 'The Trends of Marital Fertility, Second and Third Birth in Six Provinces of China, 1966–1987, –

Findings from the In-Depth Fertility Survey, (Phase II)'. In *Fertility in China*. International Statistical Institute, Voorburg, The Netherlands, 205–233.

Guofang kegongwei wuyisi yiyuan yiwusuo (National Defense Scientific Working Committee No 514 Clinic) 1992. *Guofang kegongwei can zhan xiangmu jianjie* [A Brief Introduction to the National Defence Scientific Working Committee Projects Included in the Exhibition]. Guofang kegongwei jihua shengyu lingdao xiaozu bangongshi banli. June 1992, Beijing.

Guojia jihua shengyu weiyuanhui guihua tongjisi [National Birth Planning Committee Statistical Planning Department] 1991. *Renkou he jihua shengyu canyue shuju* [Comparative Figures on Population and Birth Planning]. 7 April.

Han Changsen 1990. 'Guanyu jihuawai shengyu wenti de tansuo' [An Exploration of the Issue of Births Outside the Plan]. *Renkou Yunjiu*. No. 5, 51–54.

Han Xiangyan and Lang Jinghe (eds) 1986. *Xinhun weisheng* [Health for Newly Weds]. Compiled by the State Family Planning Commission and the Ideological Education Department. Beijing: Renmin weisheng chubanshe.

Hanying cidian [Chinese–English Dictionary] 1981. Beijing: Beijing waiguoyu xueyuan yingyu xi.

Hao Hongsheng, Gao Ling and Shen Qing 1991. 'Beijingshi butong shehui jingji tezheng funü shengyulü de bizhong fenxi' [A Comparative Analysis of the Fertility of Women with Various Socio-Economic Characteristics in Beijing]. *Renkou Yanjiu*. No. 6, 15–23.

Harevan, Tamara K. 1987. 'Reflections on Family Research in the People's Republic of China'. *Social Research*. Vol. 54. No. 4. (Winter), 663–689.

Hardee-Cleaveland, Karen and Judith Banister 1988. 'Fertility Policy and Implementation in China 1986–88'. *Population and Development Review*. Vol. 14. No. 2. (June), 245–286.

Harding, Sandra 1989. 'The Instability of the Analytical Categories of Feminist Theory'. In Micheline R. Malson, Jean F. O'Barr, Sarah Westphal-Wihl and Mary Wyer (eds). *Feminist Theory in Practice and Process*. Chicago: The University of Chicago Press, 15–34.

Hartmann, Betsy 1987. *Reproductive Rights and Wrongs: the Global Politics of Population Control and Contraceptive Choice*. New York: Harper & Row.

—— 1994. 'Consensus and Contradiction on the Road to Cairo'. Paper presented at the K.U.L.U. – Women and Development Seminar 'Population and Reproductive Rights – Strategizing for the UN Conference on Population and Development in Cairo in September 1994 – and beyond'. 27th May 1994. Copenhagen.

Hastrup, Kirsten 1992. Det Antropologiske Projekt – om Forbløffelse [The Anthropological Project – on Amazement]. Copenhagen: Nordisk Forlag.

Hawkesworth, Mary 1989. 'Knowers, Knowing, Known: Feminist Theory and Claims of Truth'. In Micheline R. Malson, Jean F. O'Barr, Sarah Westphal-Wihl and Mary Wyer (eds). *Feminist Theory in Practice and Process*. Chicago: The University of Chicago Press, 327–352.

Helgesen, Geir 1994. *Democracy in Korea*. NIAS Reports. No. 18. (July).

Hermalin, Albert I. and Xian Liu 1990. 'Gauging the Validity of Responses to Questions on Family Size Preferences in China'. *Population and Development Review*. Vol. 16. No. 2. (June), 337–54.

Ho, Ping-ti 1959. *Studies on the Population of China, 1368–1953*. Cambridge, Mass.: Harvard University Press.

Hofsten, Erland 1980. 'Bucharest and After'. In Lars Bondestam and Staffan Bergström (eds). *Poverty and Population Control*. London: Academic Press.

Honig, Emily and Gail Hershatter 1988. *Personal Voices. Chinese Women in the 1980's*. Stanford, California: Stanford University Press.

Hou Wenruo 1981. 'Population Policy'. In Liu Zheng, Song Jian *et al. China's Population: Problems and Prospects*. Beijing: New World Press, 55–76.

Hsu, Francis L.K. 1949. *Under the Ancestors' Shadow. Chinese Culture and Personality*. London: Routledge & Kegan Paul Limited.

Hua Guofeng 1979. 'Report on the Work of Government'. *Beijing Review* No. 27, 6 July, 5–31.

Hull, Terence H. 1990. 'Recent Trends in Sex Ratios at Birth in China'. *Population and Development Review*. Vol. 16. No. 1. (March), 63–83.

Human Rights in China 1991. Information Office of the State Council of The People's Republic of China.

Humphrey, Caroline 1992. 'Women and Ideology in East Asia'. In Shirley Ardener (ed.). *Persons and Powers of Women in Diverse Cultures*. New York/Oxford: Berg, 173–192.

Ikels, Charlotte 1993. 'Settling Accounts: The Intergenerational Contract in an Age of Reform'. In Deborah Davis and Stevan Harrell (eds). *Chinese Families in the Post-Mao Era*. Berkeley: University of California Press, 307–333.

Jacka, Tamara 1990. 'Back to the Wok: Women and Employment in Chinese Industry in the 1980s'. *The Australian Journal of Chinese Affairs*. Issue 24. (July), 1–23.

Jackson, Darrell 1977. 'Paradigms and Perspectives: a Cross-Cultural Approach to Population Growth and Rural Poverty'. In T. Scarlett Epstein and Darrell Jackson (eds). *The Feasibility of Fertility Planning*. Oxford: Pergamon Press, 3–20.

Jacobson, Jodi L. 1989. 'Baby Budget'. *World Watch*. Vol. 2. No. 25. (September–October), 21–31.

Jejeebhoy, Shireen 1990. 'FamPlan: The Great Debate Abates'. *International Family Planning Perspectives*. Vol. 16. No. 4. (December), 139–142.

Johansson, Annika 1993. *Strengthening Women's Voices*. Report from the first organizational meeting for a Women's Health Network in the East and South-East Asian Region, December 1–5, 1993, Los Banos, Philippines. Stockholm: Karolinska Institutet.

Johansson, Sten 1993. 'Kinas befolkningspolitik – barnbegränsningstvång i världens intress?' [The Population Policy of China – Coercive Childlimitation in the Interest of the World?]. In Bertil Egerö, Mikael Hammarskjöld and Ditte Mårtenson (eds). 'Befolkningsspørgsmål – et tema uden grænser' [Population – an Issue without Limits]. *Den Ny Verden*. Vol. 26. No. 3, 71–81.

Johansson, Sten and Ola Nygren 1991. 'The Missing Girls of China: a New Demographic Account'. *Population and Development Review*. Vol. 17. No. 1. (March), 35–51.

Johnson, Kay Ann 1983. *Women, the Family and Peasant Revolution in China*. Chicago: University of Chicago Press.

Johnson, Stanley P. 1987. *World Population and the United Nations: Challenge and Response*. Cambridge: Cambridge University Press.

Jowett, John A. 1989a. 'Mainland China: a National One-Child Program Does Not Exist (Part One)'. *Issues and Studies*. Vol. 25. No. 9. (September), 48–71.

——1989b. 'Mainland China: a National One-Child Program Does Not Exist (Part Two)'. *Issues and Studies*. Vol. 25. No. 10. (October), 71–98.

Kallgren, Joyce K. 1985. 'Politics, Welfare, and Change: the Single-Child Family in China'. In Elizabeth J. Perry and Christine Wong (eds). *The Political Economy of Reform in Post-Mao China*. Cambridge, Mass.: Harvard University Press, 131–156.

Kane, Penny 1977. 'Population Planning in China: the Individual and the State'. In T. Scarlett Epstein and Darrell Jackson (eds). *The Feasibility of Fertility Planning*. Oxford: Pergamon Press, 207–217.

—— 1987. *The Second Billion, Population and Family Planning in China*. Ringwood, Australia: Penguin Books.

Kaufmann, Joan, Zhang Zhirong, Qiao Xinjian and Zhang Yang 1992. 'The Creation of Family Planning Service Stations in China'. *International Family Planning Perspectives*. Vol. 18. No. 1, 18–23.

Kelley, Allan C. 1990. 'DevDev: a Balanced, Moderate and Eclectic Perspective'. *International Family Planning Perspectives*. Vol. 16. No. 4. (December), 143–145.

Keyfitz, Nathan 1984. 'The Population of China'. *Scientific American*. Vol. 250. No. 2. (February), 22–31.

King, Maurice 1990. 'Health is a Sustainable State'. *The Lancet*. Vol. 336, reprinted in M. Hammarskjöld, Bertil Egerö and Staffan Lindberg (eds). *Population and the Development Crisis in the South*. Lund: The Programme on Population and Development in Poor Countries, PROP Publications Series. No. 2, 1992: 165–173.

—— 1992. 'Escaping the Demographic Trap'. In M. Hammarskjöld, Bertil Egerö and Staffan Lindberg (eds). *Population and the Development Crisis in the South*. Lund: The Programme on Population and Development in Poor Countries, PROP Publications Series. No. 2, 38–44.

Kvale, Steinar 1979. 'Det kvalitative forskningsinterview – ansatser til en fænomenologisk-hermeneutisk forståelsesform' [The Qualitative Research Interview]. In Tom Broch, Karl Krarup, Per K. Larsen and Olaf Rieper (eds). *Kvalitative Metoder i Samfundsforskningen* [Qualitative Methods in Social Science]. Copenhagen: Nyt fra Samfundsvidenskaberne, 160–185.

—— 1983. 'The Qualitative Research Interview'. *Journal of Phenomenological Psychology*. Vol. 14. No. 2, 171–196.

—— 1989. 'To Validate Is to Question'. In Steinar Kvale (ed.). *Issues of Validity in Qualitative Research*. Lund: Studentlitteratur, 73–92.

Landman, Lynn C. 1981. 'China's One-Child Drive: Another Long March'. *International Family Planning Perspectives*. Vol. 7. No. 3. (September), 102–107.

Lappé, Frances Moore and Rachel Schurman. [1988] 1990. *Taking Population Seriously*. San Francisco: The Institute for Food and Development Policy.

Lee, Hong Yung 1991. *From Revolutionary Cadres to Party Technocrats in Socialist China*. Berkeley, California: University of California Press.

Li Jieping 1987. 'Shanghai jiaoxian qunzhong shengyu yiyuan de diaocha yu shengyu yuce' [Investigation of Fertility Preferences and Fertility Projection for Suburban Shanghai]. *Renkou Yanjiu*. No. 6, 44–45.

Li Lulu, Yang Xiao and Wang Fenyu 1991. 'The Structure of Social Stratification and the Modernization Process in Contemporary China'. *International Sociology*. Vol. 6. No. 1, 25–36.

Li Muzhen 1980. 'Dangqian jihua shengyu gongzuo de xingshi he renwu' [The Pattern and Tasks of Current Birth Planning Work]. *Renkou Yanjiu*. No. 1, 3–5, 47.

—— 1987. *Zhongguo renkou – Beijing fence* [China Population Series – Beijing Volume]. Beijing: Zhongguo caizheng jingji chubanshe.

—— 1990. *China Population Series – Beijing Volume*. Beijing: China Financial and Economic Publishing House. (Translated and abridged version of Li Muzhen 1987).

Li Shunjiang and Liu Xiaozhang (eds) 1990. *Nanxing biyun jieyu* [Male Contraception]. Beijing: Zhongguo renkou chubanshe.

Li Xiaojiang 1989. *Nüren de chulu* [A Solution for Women]. Shenyang: Liaoning renmin chubanshe.

—— 1991. 'Funü yanjiu zai Zhongguo de fazhan ji qi qianjing zhanwang' [The Development and Prospects of Women's Studies in China]. In Li Xiaojiang and Tan Shen (eds). *Funü yanjiu zai Zhongguo* [Women's Studies in China]. Henan: Henan renmin chubanshe, 3–22.

—— 1993. 'The Development of Women's Studies in China. A Comparison of Perspectives on the Women's Movement in China and in the West'. *Copenhagen Discussion Papers*. No. 20. (April).

Li Xiaojiang and Tan Shen (eds) 1991a. *Funü yanjiu zai Zhongguo* [Women's Studies in China]. Henan: Henan renmin chubanshe 1991.

—— 1991b. *Zhongguo funü fenceng yanjiu* [Stratified Study of Chinese Women]. Henan: Henan renmin chubanshe.

Li Yiping (ed.) 1991. *Renkou lilun jianming jiaocai* [Concise Teaching Materials in Population Theory]. Shanghai: Tongji daxue chubanshe.

Liang Jun 1989. 'Mantan dangdai funü yao zou de lu' [A Discussion of the Paths of Contemporary Women]. In Zhongyang renmin guangbo diantai 'Wujian banxiaoshi' (ed.). *Nüxing – Huntin – Fuqin* [Women – Marriage – Fathers]. Beijing: Zhongguo guoji guangbo chubanshe, 1–39

—— 1991. '80 niandai funü jiaoyu yu jiaoxue huodong zongshu' [Summary of Women's Education and Training Activities in the 1980s]. In Li Xiaojiang and Tan Shen (eds). *Funü yanjiu zai Zhongguo* [Women's Studies in China]. Henan: Henan renmin chubanshe, 150–182.

Liaoning jingji tongji nianjian (1989) [Liaoning Economic Statistical Yearbook 1989] 1989. Shenyang: Zhongguo tongji chubanshe.

Liaoning jingji tongji nianjian (1990) [Liaoning Economic Statistical Yearbook 1990] 1990. Shenyang: Zhongguo tongji chubanshe.

Liaoning renkou tongji nianjian (1985) [Population Statistical Yearbook of Liaoning Province 1985] 1986. Liaoning: Liaoningsheng tongjiju and Liaoningsheng renkou pucha bangongshi.

Liaoning renkou tongji nianjian (1988) [Population Statistical Yearbook of Liaoning Province 1988] 1989. Liaoning: Liaoningsheng tongjiju, Liaoningsheng gonganting and Liaoningsheng jihua shengyu weiyuanhui.

Lin Chuanjia (ed.) [1965] 1981. *Yuer changshi* [General Knowledge on Bringing up Children]. Beijing: Renmin weisheng chubanshe.

Liu Bingfu 1993. 'The Family and Economic Life of the Aged in Chinese Cities'. In Greg Guldin and Aidan Southall (eds). *Urban Anthropology in China*. Leiden, New York, Köln: E.J. Brill, 387–395.

Liu Chen and Wu Ts'ang-P'ing 1979. 'The Economic Rationale for Population Control in China'. *Population and Development Review*. Vol. 5. No. 3. (September), 559–563.

Liu Shuang 1986. 'A Brief Discussion on the Differences in the Sex Ratio at Birth of China's Population'. *Population Research*. Vol. 3. No. 3. (July), 45–47.

Liu Xiuhua 1991. 'Beijingshi yuling funü shengyu zhuangkuang fenxi' [An Analysis of Fertility of Women in Beijing]. *Renkou Yanjiu*. No. 6, 24–27.

Liu Zelun (ed.) 1991. *Taijiao de shiyong yu keyan* [Prenatal Education – Practice and Scientific Research]. Beijing: Jiaoyu kexue chubanshe.

Liu Zheng 1981. 'Correspondence between the Production of Human Beings and the Production of Material Goods'. *Social Sciences in China*. No. 1, 30–48.

Liu Zheng, Song Jian *et al.* 1981. *China's Population: Problems and Prospects*. Beijing: New World Press.

Lockett, Martin 1988. 'The Urban Collective Economy'. In S. Feuchtwang, A. Hussain and T. Pairault (eds). *Transforming China's Economy in the Eighties*. Vol. 2. London: Zed Books, 119–137.

Lu, Tonglin 1993. 'Introduction'. In Tonglin Lu (ed.). *Gender and Sexuality in Twentieth-Century Chinese Literature and Society*. New York: State University of New York Press, 1–21.

Lunddahl, Axel 1988. 'Field Research in China: the Yantai Project'. *China Information*. Vol. 2. No. 3. (Winter), 41–47.

Lyle, Katherine Ch'iu 1980. 'Report from China. Planned Birth in Tianjin'. *The China Quarterly*. No. 83. (September), 551–567.

Ma Yinchu 1957. 'Xin Renkoulun' [A New Theory of Population]. *Renmin Ribao* 5 July.

Mao Zedong. [1953] 1969. 'Weixin lishiguan de pochan'. 16 September 1949. In *Mao Zedong xuanji* [Selected Works of Mao Zedong]. Beijing: Renmin chubanshe. Vol. 4, 1398–1406. Translated as The Bankruptcy of the Idealist Conception of History. In *Selected Works of Mao Tse-tung*. Peking: Foreign Languages Press. Vol. IV, 451–459.

Matthiessen, Poul Christian 1984. *Befolkningens vækst* [Population Increase]. Copenhagen: Munksgaard.

McNicoll, Geoffrey 1990. 'AcCrit: an Argument Yet to Have Its Say'. *International Family Planning Perspectives*. Vol. 16. No. 4. (December), 146–148, 150.

Meizhong xueshu jiaoliu weiyuanhui [US–China Academic Exchange Committee] 1991. *China Exchange News.* Vol. 19. No. 2. (Summer), 2.

Milwertz, Cecilia 1994. 'Forskningsprocessen til debat: Kinesiske by-kvinders perspektiv på ét-barns politikken' [Debating the Research Process: the Perspective of Chinese Women on the One-Child Policy]. *SAMKVIND Skriftserie.* No. 17, 33–48.

—— 1995a. 'Når tvang opleves som omsorg accepteres befolknings-kontrol' [When Coercion Is Perceived as Care Population Control Is Accepted]. In *Kvinder, Køn og Forskning* [Women, Gender and Research]. No. 2, 8–29.

—— 1995b. 'Reproduktiv selvbestemmelse og befolkningsproblemet – Et barn pr. kvinde i Kina' [Reproductive Self-Determination and the Population Problem – One Child per Woman in China]. In Bente Rosenbeck og Robin Schott (eds). *Forplantning, Køn og Teknologi* [Reproduction, Gender and Technology]. Copenhagen, Museum Tusculanum, 57–73.

Moon, Okpyo 1992. 'Confucianism and Gender Segregation in Japan and Korea'. In Roger Goodman and Kirsten Refsing. *Ideology and Practice in Modern Japan.* London: Routledge, 196–210.

Munro, Donald J. 1969. *The Concept of Man in Early China.* Stanford: Stanford University Press.

Ningxia huizu zizhiqu. Baohu funü ertong hefa quanyi de ruogan guiding [Ningxia Hui Nationality Autonomous Region Regulations on the Protection of the Rights and Interests of Women and Children] 1985-11-23. In Quanguo renda neiwusifa weiyuanhui. Funü ertong zhuanmen xiaozu and Qingshaonian zhuanmen xiaozu (eds). *Funü he weichengnianren falii baohu quangshu* [Collection of Laws on Protection of Women and Youth] 1991. Beijing: Zhongguo jiancha chubanshe, 552–54.

Ng, Pedro Pak-tao 1979. 'Planned Fertility and Fertility Socialization in Kwangtung Province'. *The China Quarterly.* No. 78. (June), 351–59.

Odgaard, Ole.1991. 'Data Collection and the Use of Local Statistics – Some Experiences from Field Studies in Sichuan'. In Ole Bruun, Søren Poulsen and Hatla Thelle (eds). *Modern China Research: Danish Experiences. Copenhagen Discussion Papers Special Issue.* Centre for East and Southeast Asian Studies, University of Copenhagen. (September), 18–29.

Orleans, Leo A. 1960. 'Birth Control: Reversal or Postponement?' *The China Quarterly.* No. 3. (July–September), 59–70.

—— 1962. 'A New Birth Control Campaign?' *The China Quarterly.* No. 12. (October–December), 207–211.

—— 1969. 'Evidence from Chinese Medical Journals on Current Population Policy'. *The China Quarterly.* No. 40. (October–December), 137–47.

—— (ed.) 1979. *Chinese Approaches to Family Planning*. London: Macmillan.

Peng Peiyun 1991. *Zai zhonggong zhongyang, guowuyuan zhaokai de jihua shengyu gongzuo zuotanhui shang de fayan* [Speech at the Central Committee of the Communist Party and the State Council Symposium on Birth Planning Work]. April 7, 1991.

Peng Xizhi 1991. *Demographic Transition in China*. Oxford: Clarendon Press.

Pieke, Frank N. 1986–87. 'Social Science Fieldwork in the PRC: Implications of the Mosher Affair'. *China Information*. Vol. 1. No. 3. (Winter), 32–55.

—— 1991. 'Anthropological Field Work in Urban China: Methodological Considerations and Practical Constraints.' Paper presented at the International Conference on Sociological Research in China, Beijing. 23–27 July 1991.

Poston, Dudley L. Jr. and Baochang Gu 1987. 'Socioeconomic Development, Family Planning, and Fertility in China'. *Demography*. Vol. 24. No. 4. (November), 531–551.

Poston, Dudley L. Jr. and Toni Falbo 1990. 'Scholastic and Personality Characteristics of Only Chidren and Children with Siblings in China'. *International Family Planning Perspectives*. Vol. 16. No. 2. (June), 45–48.

Potter, Sulamith Heins and Jack M. Potter 1990. *China's Peasants*. Cambridge: Cambridge University Press.

Pradervand, Pierre 1980. 'People Are Precious – a Critical Look at the Population Movement'. In Lars Bondestam and Staffan Bergström (eds). *Poverty and Population Control*. London: Academic Press.

Proclamation of Teheran on Human Rights 1968. New York: United Nations Office of Public Information.

Pye, Lucian with Mary Pye 1985. *Asian Power and Politics*. Cambridge, Mass.: The Belknap Press of Harvard University Press.

—— 1991. 'The State and the Individual: an Overview Interpretation'. *The China Quarterly*. No. 127. (September), 443–466.

Refsing, Kirsten 1992. 'Japanese Educational Expansion: Quality or Equality'. In Roger Goodman and Kirsten Refsing (eds). *Ideology and Practice in Modern Japan*. London: Routledge, 116–129.

Renmin jiaoyu chubanshe renkou jiaoyu shi [Office on Population Education of the People's Education Publishers] (ed.) 1986. *Renkou jiaoyu*. (Population Education). Beijing: Renmin jiaoyu chubanshe.

Robinson, Jean C. 1985. 'Of Women and Washing Machines: Employment, Housework, and the Reproduction of Motherhood in Socialist China'. *The China Quarterly*. No. 101. (March), 32–57.

Rowley, John (ed.) 1989. 'A Policy in Transition'. *People*. Vol. 16. No. 1, 20–22.

Ruan Fangfu (ed.) 1981. *Yousheng xinzhi* [New Knowledge on Eugenics]. Beijing: Renmin weisheng chubanshe.

Sai, Fred T. and Janet Nassim 1989. 'The Need for a Reproductive Health Approach'. *International Journal of Gynecology and Obstetrics*. Supplement 3, 103–113.

Saith, Ashwani 1981. 'Economic Incentives for the One-child Family in Rural China'. *The China Quarterly.* No. 87. (September), 493–500.

—— 1984. 'China's New Population Policies'. In Keith Griffin (ed.). *Institutional Reform and Economic Development in the Chinese Countryside.* Armonk, New York: M.E. Sharpe, 176–209.

Salaff, Janet 1973. 'Institutionalized Motivation for Fertility Limitation'. In Marilyn B. Young (ed.). *Women in China.* Michigan Papers in Chinese Studies, No. 15, University of Michigan, 93–144.

Schoenhals, Martin 1993. *The Paradox of Power in a People's Republic of China Middle School.* Armonk, New York: M.E. Sharpe.

Schurmann, Franz. [1966] 1968. *Ideology and Organization in Communist China.* Berkeley, Los Angeles, London: University of California Press.

Sen, Gita and Caren Grown 1987. *Development, Crises, and Alternative Visions: Third World Women's Perspectives.* New York: Monthly Review Press.

Sen, Gita, Adrienne Germain and Lincoln C. Chen (eds) 1994. *Population Policies Reconsidered.* Harvard: Harvard University Press.

Shanghaishi ertong yiyuan, Shanghaishi diyi fuying baojianyuan, Shanghai jihua shengyu xuanchuan jiaoyu zhongxin [Shanghai Children's Hospital, Shanghai No. 1 Mother and Child Clinic, Shanghai Birth Planning Ideological Education Centre] (eds). No date. *Muru weiyang wenda* [Questions and Answers on Breast-feeding]. No publisher.

Shen Chonglin 1992. 'The Impact of Population Factors on the Family Structure in Urban China'. In *Proceedings of Asia-Pacific Regional Conference on Future of the Family.* Beijing: China Social Science Documentation Publishing House, 60–78.

Shen Guoxiang 1990. 'Jinyibu fahui xuanchuan jiaoyu zai jihua shengyu gongzuo zhong de zhongyao zuoyong' [Further Promote the Important Role of Ideological Education within Birth Planning Work]. In Zhang Pei and Chen Manping (eds). *Zhongguo jihua shengyu de weida shijian* [The Outstanding Practice of Chinese Birth Planning]. Beijing: Zhongguo renkou chubanshe.

Shen Yimin and Jia Tongjin 1991. 'China's In-Depth Fertility Survey – Organization and Survey Method'. In *Fertility in China.* International Statistical Institute Voorburg, The Netherlands, 1–7.

Shenyangshi jihua jingji weiyuanhui and 'Shenyang guotu ziliao' weiyuanhui (eds) 1989. *Shenyang guotu ziliao* [Shenyang Regional Data]. Shenyang: Shenyang chubanshi.

Sheridan, Mary and Salaff, Janet W. (eds) 1984. *Lives. Chinese Working Women*. Bloomington: Indiana University Press.

Shi Li (ed.) 1988. *Juese – kunhuo – zhuiqiu*. (Roles, Problems, Objectives). Beijing: Zhongguo funü chubanshe.

Shiva, Mira 1992. 'Environmental Degradation and Subversion of Health'. *Development Dialogue*. 1–2, 71–90.

Shiva, Vandana 1992. 'Women, Ecology and Health: an Introduction'. *Development Dialogue*. No. 1–2, 3–12.

Sichuan sheng. Baohu funü ertong hefa quanyi de ruogan guiding [Sichuan Province Regulations on the Protection of the Rights and Interests of Women and Children] 1983-12-27. In Quanguo renda neiwusifa weiyuanhui. Funü ertong zhuanmen xiaozu and Qingshaonian zhuanmen xiaozu (eds). *Funü he weichengnianren falü baohu quangshu* [Collection of Laws on Protection of Women and Youth] 1991. Beijing: Zhongguo jiancha chubanshe, 503–507.

Sievers, Sharon L. 1983. *Flowers in Salt. The Beginnings of Feminist Consciousness in Modern Japan*. Stanford: Stanford University Press.

Simmons, Ozzie G. 1988. *Perspectives on Development and Population Growth in the Third World*. New York: Plenum Press.

Smith, Dorothy E. 1988. *The Everyday World as Problematic*. Stony Stratford: Open University Press/Milton Keynes.

Song Jian 1981. 'Population Development – Goals and Plans'. In Liu Zheng, Song Jian *et al. China's Population: Problems and Prospects*. Beijing: New World Press, 25–31.

Song Jian and Yu Jingyuan 1991. 'Double-edged Limit of Total Fertility Rates'. *Population Research*. Vol. 8. No. 1. (March), 7–13.

Song Zexing (ed.) 1987. *Zhongguo renkou. Liaoning fence* [China Population Series – Liaoning Volume]. Beijing: Zhongguo caizheng jingji chubanshe.

Song Zicheng (ed.) 1981. *Dusheng zinü jiaoyu zhinan* [Guide To Education of Only Children]. Beijing: Zhishi chubanshe.

Spradley, James 1979. *The Ethnographic Interview*. New York: Holt, Rinehart & Winston.

Stacey, Judith 1983. *Patriarchy and Socialist Revolution in China*. Berkeley, Los Angeles: University of California Press.

Stepputat, Finn (ed.) 1987. 'Hverdagslivsstudier i den tredje verden' [Studies of Everyday Life in the Third World]. *Repro-serie*. No. 4. Department of Cultural Sociology, University of Copenhagen.

Strauss, Anselm L. [1987] 1991. *Qualitative Analysis for Social Scientists*. Cambridge: Cambridge University Press.

Strauss, Anselm and Juliet Corbin 1990. *Basics of Qualitative Research*. California, London, New Delhi: Sage Publications.

Sun, Lung-kee 1991. 'Contemporary Chinese Culture: Structure and Emotionality'. *Australian Journal of Chinese Affairs*. Issue 26. (July), 1–41.

Sun Rong 1993. 'Xingbie pianhao yu jiating guanxi' [Sex Preference and the New Pattern in Family Relations]. *Funü yanjiu luncong* [Collection of Women's Studies]. No. 2, 20–24.

Sun Shaoxian 1993. 'Reflections on Female Employment in China', *Copenhagen Discussion Papers*. Centre for East and Southeast Asian Studies, University of Copenhagen, No. 21. (October).

Svensson, Marina 1993. 'Kina och mänskliga rättigheter' [China and Human Rights]. *Svensk-Kinesisk Förenings Årbok om Kina* [The Sweden–China Association Yearbook on China], 106–125.

Tan Shen. No date. The Process and Achievements of the Study on Marriage and Family in China'. Unpublished paper.

——1991a. 'Dui jinnian funü yanjiu xianxiang de shehuixue kaocha' [A Sociologicl Study of the Phenomena of Women's Studies During Recent Years]. In Li Xiaojiang and Tan Shen (eds). *Funü yanjiu zai Zhongguo* [Women's Studies in China]. Henan: Henan renmin chubanshe, 23–42.

——1991b. 'Bufen funü yanjiu lunwen mulu suoyin' [References to a Selection of Reports on Women's Studies]. In Li Xiaojiang and Tan Shen (eds). *Funü yanjiu zai Zhongguo* [Women's Studies in China]. Henan: Henan renmin chubanshe, 315–327.

—— 1993. 'Women's Studies in China: a General Survey'. *Copenhagen Discussion Papers*. Centre for East and Southeast Asian Studies, University of Copenhagen. No. 19. (April).

The Constitution of the People's Republic of China 1983. Adopted on 4 December, 1982 by the Fifth National People's Congress of the People's Republic of China at its Fifth Session. Beijing: Foreign Languages Press.

The Marriage Law of the People's Republic of China 1982. Adopted by the Fifth National People's Congress at Its Third Session on 10 September, 1980, and put into effect from 1 January, 1981. Beijing: Foreign Languages Press.

The 1982 Population Census of China (Major Figures). The Population Census Office under the State Council. The Department of Population Statistics of the State Statistical Bureau. Hong Kong 1982.

Thøgersen, Stig 1991. 'Official Interviewing in China – Notes from Four Trips'. In Ole Bruun, Søren Poulsen and Hatla Thelle (eds). *Modern*

China Research: Danish Experiences. Copenhagen Discussion Papers Special Issue. Centre for East and Southeast Asian Studies, University of Copenhagen. (September), 30–44.

Tian Xueyuan 1981. 'A Survey of Population Growth Since 1949'. In Liu Zheng, Song Jian *et al.* 1981. *China's Population: Problems and Prospects.* Beijing: New World Press, 32–54.

Tien, H. Yuan 1980a. 'Wan Xi Shao: How China Meets Its Population Problem'. *International Family Planning Perspectives.* Vol. 6. No. 2. (June), 65–73.

—— (ed.) 1980b. *Population Theory in China.* White Plains, New York: M.E. Sharpe.

—— 1973. *China's Population Struggle: Demographic Decisions of the People's Republic, 1949–1969.* Columbus: Ohio State University Press.

—— 1983. China: 'Demographic Billionaire.' *Population Bulletin.* Vol. 38. No. 2. (April).

—— 1991. *China's Strategic Demographic Initiative.* New York: Praeger.

Tomaševski, Katarina 1994. *Human Rights in Population Policies.* Lund: The Swedish International Development Authority (SIDA).

Tsuya, Noriko O. and Minja Kim Choe 1988. 'Achievement of One-Child Fertility in Rural Areas of Jilin Province, China'. *International Family Planning Perspectives.* Vol. 14. No. 4. (December), 122–131.

Tu, Edward Jow-ching and Tin-yu Ting 1988. 'Consequences of Alternative Population Policies on Aging in Mainland China'. *Issues and Studies.* Vol. 24. No. 1. (January), 33–49.

Tu Ping 1993. 'Wo guo chusheng yinger xingbiebi wenti tansuo' [An Exploration of the Sex Ratio at Birth in China]. *Renkou Yanjiu.* No. 1, 6–13.

Tuan, Chi-hsien 1989. 'Women in China Today'. In K. Mahadevan (ed.). *Women and Population Dynamics.* London: Sage, 19–63.

UNFPA 1991. *The State of World Population.* New York: United Nations Population Fund.

Unger, Jonathan 1993. 'Urban Families in the Eighties: An Analysis of Chinese Surveys'. In Deborah Davis and Stevan Harrell (eds). *Chinese Families in the Post-Mao Era.* Berkeley: University of California Press, 25–49.

Van Manen, Max 1990. *Researching Lived Experience.* Ontario: The Althouse Press.

Walder, Andrew G. 1986. *Communist Neo-Traditionalism.* Berkeley: University of California Press.

—— 1991. 'Workers, Managers and the State: The Reform Era and the Political Crisis of 1989'. *The China Quarterly.* No. 127. (September), 467–492.

Wang Hong 1991. 'The Population Policy of China'. In Wang Jiye and Terence H. Hull (eds). *Population and Development Planning in China*. North Sydney: Allen & Unwin, 68–87.

Wang, Jichuan 1990. 'Women's Preferences for Children in Shifang County, Sichuan, China'. *Asian and Pacific Population Forum*. Vol. 4. No. 3. (Fall), 1–12, 27–28.

Wang Jiye and Terence H. Hull (eds) 1991. *Population and Development Planning in China*. North Sydney: Allen and Unwin.

Wang Li, Wu Shichang and Zhao Zongyu 1980. 'Jihua shengyu buyi lifa' [Birth Planning Legislation Is Inappropriate]. Zhengxie weiyuan zai xiaozu taolunhuishang fayan zhaideng [Selected Speeches of Members of the Chinese People's Political Consultative Conference at Small Group Meeting]. *Renmin Ribao*. 13 September, 5.

Wang Nairong 1981. 'Wo guo kongzhi renkou zengzhang zhengce de jige wenti' [Some Questions Related to the Policy of Controlling Population Increase]. *Renkou Yanjiu*. No. 2, 51–55.

Wang Qi 1991. 'Institutes and Issues: Women's Studies in Present China'. Paper presented at the European Conference 'Women in Changing Europe'. 18–22 August. Aalborg: Aalborg University Centre.

Wang Xingfa 1985. 'Woguo renkou xingbie goucheng fenxi'. *Renkou Yanjiu*. No. 5, 9–13. Translated as Wang Xingfa 1986. 'Analysis on Sex Structure of China's Population'. *Population Research*. Vol. 3. No. 2. (April), 28–34.

Wang Yalin 1992. 'City Women, Families and the Vicissitudes of Their Dual Roles'. In *Proceedings of Asia-Pacific Regional Conference on Future of the Family*. Beijing: China Social Science Documentation Publishing House, 85–90.

Wei Zhanglin 1990. 'The Family and Family Research in Contemporary China'. *International Social Science Journal*. No. 126, 493–509.

White, Tyrene 1990. 'Post-revolutionary Mobilization in China – the One-Child Policy Reconsidered'. *World Politics*. Vol. 43. No. 1. (October), 53–76.

—— 1992. 'Family Planning in China'. *Chinese Sociology and Anthropology*. Spring 1992.

—— 'The Origins of China's Birth Planning Policy'. In Christina K. Gilmartin, Gail Hershatter, Lisa Rofel and Tyrene White (eds). *Engendering China*. Cambridge, Mass.: Harvard University Press. Harvard Contemporary China Series, 10, 250–278.

Whyte, Martin King 1979. 'Family Change in China'. *Issues and Studies*. Vol. 15. No. 7, 48–63.

—— 1992a. *From Arranged Marriages to Love Matches in Urban China*. USC Seminar Series No. 5. Hong Kong: Hong Kong Institute of Asia-Pacific Studies. The Chinese University of Hong Kong.

—— 1992b. 'A Symposium on Rural Family Change. Introduction: Rural Economic Reforms and Chinese Family Patterns'. *The China Quarterly.* No. 130. (June), 317–322.

Whyte, Martin King and S.Z. Gu 1987. 'Popular Response to China's Fertility Transition'. *Population and Development Review.* Vol. 13. No. 3, 471–93.

Whyte, Martin King and William L. Parish 1984. *Urban Life in Contemporary China.* Chicago: The University of Chicago Press.

Wilson, Amy Auerbach, Sydney L. Greenblatt and R.W. Wilson 1983. *Methodological Issues in Chinese Studies.* New York: Praeger.

Wolf, Margery 1972. *Women and the Family in Rural Taiwan.* Stanford, California: Stanford University Press.

—— 1985. *Revolution Postponed.* Stanford, California: Stanford University Press.

—— 1992. *A Tale Thrice Told.* Stanford, California: Stanford University Press.

Wong Siu-lun 1984. 'The Consequences of China's New Population Policy'. *The China Quarterly.* No. 98. (June), 220–241.

Wu Cangping (ed.) 1990. *Gaige kaifang yu renkou fazhan* [Reforms and Population Development]. Shenyang: Liaoning daxue chubanshi.

Wu, Z.C., E.S. Gao, X.Y. Ku, S.Y. Lu, M.J. Wang, W.C. Hong and L.P. Chow 1992. 'Induced Abortion among Unmarried Women in Shanghai, China'. *International Family Planning Perspectives,* Vol. 18. No. 2. (June), 51–53, 65.

Xiaochu dui funü yiqie xingshi qishi gongyue [Convention on the Elimination of All Forms of Discrimination Against Women] 1991. In *Funü he weichengnianren falü baohu quanshu* [Collection of Protective Laws for Women and Adolescents]. Beijing: Zhongguo jiancha chubanshe, 1161–1169.

Xu Anqi 1992. 'The Changes of Women's Role and Status and Transformation of Family'. In *Proceedings of Asia-Pacific Regional Conference on Future of the Family.* Beijing: China Social Science Documentation Publishing House, 101–107.

Xu Dixin 1981. 'Guanyu renkou kexue de jige wenti' [Some Questions on Population Science]. In Beijing jingji xueyuan renkou jingji yanjiusuo (ed.). *Zhongguo renkou kexue lunji* [Symposium of Chinese Population Science]. Beijing: Zhongguo xueshu chubanshe.

Xu Gang and Yu Jingwei 1991. 'An Analysis on Fertility Preferences of Chinese Women'. In *Fertility in China.* International Statistical Institute Voorburg, The Netherlands, 177–186.

Xu Jinsheng 1991. 'The Quality of Population and Economic Development in China'. *Population Research.* Vol. 8. No. 3, 37–48.

Xue Suzhen 1992. 'Changes of Women's Status and Role and Trends of Family Development in China'. In *Proceedings of Asia-Pacific Regional Conference on Future of the Family.* Beijing: China Social Science Documentation Publishing House, 108–118.

Yang Deqing 1982. *Renkouxue gailun* [An Introduction to Demography]. Hebei: Hebei renmin chubanshe.

Yin, Robert K. 1989. *Case Study Research.* Newbury Park, London, New Delhi: Sage Publications.

Yu Wang [1973] 1980. 'Chinese Observer on the Population Question'. (Originally *Peking Review.* No. 49. 1973). Excerpts in Tien (ed.). *Population Theory in China.* New York: M.E. Sharpe, 94–96.

Zeng Yi 1986. 'Changes in Family Structure in China: A Simulation Study'. *Population and Development Review.* Vol. 12. No. 4. (December), 675–703.

Zhang Hongshang (ed.) 1989. *Tianmi de mingtian* [Happy Future]. Zhongguo jihua shengyu xiehui (Chinese Family Planning Association) and Zhongguo renkou fuli jijinhui [China Population Welfare Fund]. Jiangsu: Jiangsu renmin chubanshe.

Zhang Ju 1992. 'Chinese Perspective on Eugenics'. In Wu Jieping and Yan Renying (eds). *Proceedings of the International Conference on Improving Birth Quality and Child Upbringing, 24–27 May 1992, Beijing, China.* Beijing: International Academic Publishers, 33–34.

Zhang Lianzhen (ed.) 1988. *Gaige zhong de funü wenti* [Women's Issues During the Reform Period]. Jiangsu: Jiangsu chubanshe.

Zhang Pei and Chen Manping (eds). [1989] 1990. *Zhongguo jihua shengyu de weida shijian* [The Great Practice of Chinese Birth Planning]. Beijing: Zhongguo renkou chubanshe.

Zhao Zixiang and Huang Mei. *Research on People's Living Ideology and Working Attitudes in the Seven Cities in China.* Undated paper. Institute of Sociology, Liaoning Academy of Social Sciences, Shenyang.

Zhonggong zhongyang guanyu kongzhi wo guo renkou zengzhang wenti zhi quanti gongchandangyuan, gongqingtuanyuan de gongkaixin [Open Letter of the Central Committee of the Communist Party of China to the General Membership of the Communist Party and of the Communist Youth League on Controlling Population Growth in China]. *Renmin ribao* [People's Daily]. 25 September 1980.

Zhonggong zhongyang, guowuyuan guanyu jiaqiang jihua shengyu gongzuo yange kongzhi renkou zengzhang de guiding [Central Committee of the Communist Party and State Council Decision on Strictly Controlling Population Growth] *1991-5-12.*

Zhonggong zhongyang, guowuyuan guanyu jinyibu zuo hao jihua shengyu gongzuo de zhibiao (1982-2-9) [Directive of the Central Committee of the Communist Party of China and the State Council of the PRC on Doing a Better Job with Birth Planning Work] 1986. In Zhongguo shehui kexueyuan renkou yanjiu zhongxin (ed.). *Zhongguo renkou nianjian 1985* [Almanac of China's Population 1985]. Beijing: Zhongguo shehui kexue chubanshe, 45–48. Translated in White 1992.

Zhongguo dierqi shenru de shengyuli diaocha guojia baogao [China In-Depth Fertility Survey (Phase II), Principal Report] October 1989. Beijing: Guojia tongjiju renkou tongjisi [State Statistical Bureau Department of Population Statistics]. Vol. 1–3.

Zhongguo disici renkou pucha de zhuyao shuju [Major Figures of the Fourth National Population Census of China] 1991. Guowuyuan renkou pucha bangongshi [The National Population Census Office under the State Council]. Beijing: Zhongguo tongji chubanshe.

'*Zhongguo funü shehui diwei diaocha*' ketizu 1992. 'Zhongguo funü diwei diaocha chubu fenxi baogao' [Preliminary Report on the Investigation on the Status of Chinese Women]. *Funü yanjiu luncong* [Collection of Women's Studies]. No. 1. (March), 22–25.

Zhongguo funü tongji ziliao (1949–1989) [Statistics on Chinese Women (1949–1989)] 1991. Zhonghua quanguo funü lianhehui funü yanjiusuo and Shaanxisheng funü lianhehui yanjiushi [Research Institute of the All-China Women's Federation and Research Office of Shaanxi Provincial Women's Federation] (eds). Beijing: Zhongguo tongji chubanshe.

Zhongguo renkou ziliao shouce (1990) [China Population Information Handbook] 1991. Zhongguo renkou qingbao yanjiu zhongxin [China Population Information Research Centre]. Beijing: Beijing jingji xueyuan chubanshe.

Zhongguo renkou nianjian (1992) [Almanac of China's Population (1992)] 1992. Zhongguo shehui kexueyuan renkou yanjiusuo [Population Research Institute, the Chinese Academy of Social Sciences]. Beijing: Jingji guanli chubanshe.

Zhongguo 1990 nian renkou pucha ziliao [Tabulation of the 1990 Population Census of the People's Republic of China] 1993. Guowuyuan renkou pucha bangongshi, Guojia tongjiju renkou tongjisi. Beijing: Zhongguo tongji chubanshe. Vol. 1–4.

Zhongguo tongji nianjian (1991) [Statistical Yearbook of China] 1991. Guojia tongjiju. Beijing: Zhongguo tongji chubanshe.

Zhonghua quanguo funü lianhehui [All-China Women's Federation] (ed.) 1982. *Hunyin jiating yu ertong gongzuo* [On the Work Concerning Marriage, Family and Children]. Beijing: Renmin chubanshe.

Zhonghua renmin gongheguo funü quanyi baozhangfa [Law of the People's Republic of China on the Protection of Rights and Interests of Women]. Adopted at the Fifth Session of the Seventh National People's Congress on 3 April, 1992.

Zhou Boping 1990. 'Jihua shengyu xiehui' [The Family Planning Association]. In Zhang Pei and Chen Manping (eds). *Zhongguo jihua shengyu de weida shijian* [The Great Practice of Chinese Birth Planning]. Beijing: Zhongguo renkou chubanshe, 26–36.

Zhou Xiaozheng, Guo Daping, Shen Ding and Shi Xilai 1990. 'Neighbouring Elastic Family'. In Zeng Yi, Zhang Chunyuan and Peng Songjian (eds). *Changing Family Structure and Population Aging in China – A Comparative Approach*. Peking: Peking University Press, 258–268.

Zhu Chuzhu 1990. 'Gaige beijing xia de Zhongguo nüxing renkou' [China's Female Population During the Reforms]. In Wu Cangping (ed.). *Gaige kaifang yu renkou fazhan* [Reforms and Population Development]. Shenyang: Liaoning daxue chubanshi, 272–283.

—— 1992. 'Guanyu "Zhongguo funü jiuye yu shengyulü guanxi" de yanjiu' [On the Reseach Project 'Relations Between Employment and Fertility of Chinese Women']. *Funü yanjiu luncong* [Collection of Women's Studies]. No. 1. (March), 26–32.

Zhu Chuzhu and Jiang Zhenghua 1991. *Zhongguo nüxing renkou* [China's Female Population]. Funü yanjiu congshu [Women's Studies Series], Zhengzhou: Henan renmin chubanshi.

Zhu Qingfang 1991. 'Guanyu funü diwei de zhibiao tixi' [An Index for the Position of Women]. In Li Xiaojiang and Tan Shen (eds). *Funü yanjiu zai Zhongguo* [Women's Studies in China]. Henan: Henan renmin chubanshe, 304–311.

Index

The Nordic Institute of Asian Studies (NIAS) is funded by the governments of Denmark, Finland, Iceland, Norway and Sweden via the Nordic Council of Ministers, and works to encourage and support Asian studies in the Nordic countries. In so doing, NIAS has published well in excess of one hundred books in the last twenty-five years, most of them in co-operation with Curzon Press.

Nordic Council of Ministers